THE INVENTION OF MIDDLE ENGLISH

An Anthology of Primary Sources

THE INVENTION OF MIDDLE ENGLISH

An Anthology of Primary Sources

David Matthews

THE PENNSYLVANIA STATE UNIVERSITY PRESS
UNIVERSITY PARK, PENNSYLVANIA

Copyright © 2000 Brepols Publishers

Published in 2000 in paperback by The Pennsylvania State University Press, University Park, PA 16802-1003

First published in 2000 in a clothbound edition by Brepols Publishers in the Making the Middle Ages series.

ISBN 0-271-02082-2 (paper)

Library of Congress Cataloging-in-Publication Data

The invention of Middle English : an anthology of primary sources / [edited by] David Matthews.
  "First published in 2000 in a clothbound edition by Brepols Publishers in the 'Making of the Middle Ages' series"—T.p. verso.
  Includes bibliographical references (p.) and index.
  ISBN 0-271-02082-2 (pbk : alk. paper)
  1. English philology—Middle English, 1100–1500—History—Sources. 2. English philology—Middle English, 1100–1500—Study and teaching—History—Sources. 3. English literature—Middle English, 1100–1500—History and criticism—Theory, etc. 4. Great Britain—History—Medieval period, 1066–1485—Historiography. 5. Medievalism—Great Britain—History—Sources. I. Matthews, David, 1963– II. Making the Middle Ages ; 2.

  PE515 .I58 2000
  427'.02—dc21

00-028411

Printed in the European Union

Printed on acid-free paper.

To my father, Brian Matthews

Contents

Part I: Language

Part II: Literary criticism and commentary

Abbreviations

Add MS	Additional manuscript
AEMR	Joseph Ritson, ed. *Ancient Engleish Metrical Romanceës*, 3 vols (London, 1802)
AN	Anglo-Norman
ANTS	Anglo-Norman Text Society
BL	British Library
Bodl	Bodleian Library
CT	*The Canterbury Tales*
CTC	Thomas Tyrwhitt, ed. *The Canterbury Tales of Chaucer*, 5 vols (London, 1775-78)
DNB	Sir Leslie Stephen and Sir Sidney Lee, eds., *The Dictionary of National Biography*, 66 vols. (London, 1885-1901)
EG	Arthur Johnston, *Enchanted Ground: The Study of Medieval Romance in the Eighteenth Century* (London: Athlone, 1964)
EETS	Early English Text Society
FSA	Fellow of the Society of Antiquaries
Harl MS	Harleian manuscript
HEP	Thomas Warton, *The History of English Poetry, from the Close of the Eleventh to the Commencement of the Eighteenth Century*, 3 vols. (London, 1774-81)

MEL   J. A. W. Bennett, *Middle English Literature*, ed. and completed
           by Douglas Gray (Oxford: Clarendon Press, 1986)

MME   David Matthews, *The Making of Middle English, 1765-1910*
           (Minneapolis: University of Minnesota Press, 1999)

MRTS   Medieval and Renaissance Texts and Studies

MSBS2   Helen Damico, ed. with Donald Fennema and Karmen Lenz,
           *Medieval Scholarship: Biographical Studies on the Formation
           of a Discipline*: Vol. 2. *Literature and Philology*. Garland
           Reference Library of the Humanities 2071. (New York:
           Garland, 1998)

MWME   Albert E. Hartung, gen. ed. *A Manual of the Writings in
           Middle English, 1050-1500*, 9 vols. (New Haven: Connecticut
           Academy of Arts and Sciences, 1967-1993)

RAEP   Thomas Percy, *Reliques of Ancient English Poetry*, 3 vols.
           (London: Dodsley, 1765)

RS   Rolls Series

STC   A. W. Pollard and G. R. Redgrave, *A Short-Title Catalogue of
           Books Printed in England, Scotland and Ireland and of
           English Books Printed Abroad, 1475-1640* (London:
           Bibliographical Society, 1926)

STS   Scottish Text Society

Thesaurus George Hickes, *Linguarum Vett. Septentrionalium Thesaurus
           Grammatico-Criticus et Archæologicus*, 2 vols. (Oxford:
           Sheldonian Theatre, 1703-05)

References to the works of Chaucer, unless otherwise noted, are to Larry D.
Benson, gen. ed. *The Riverside Chaucer*, 3rd edn. (Oxford: Clarendon Press,
1988)

Acknowledgements

This book is a kind of sequel to my *The Making of Middle English* and I feel that everyone thanked there deserves thanks again. The current book was begun with the encouragement of Geraldine Barnes and later took shape under the sympathetic and expert guidance of Margaret Clunies Ross. My grateful thanks go to them both. Thanks too to Simon Forde at Brepols and James Simpson, who wrote a sympathetic and helpful reader's report on the original proposal. I am grateful for a period of leave from the University of Newcastle which enabled me to complete the work. At all stages Simon French of the Centre for Medieval Studies at the University of Sydney adeptly handled the voluminous electronic traffic between London and Sydney that the book's final stages produced; I would like to thank him also for the design and final appearance of the work. The staff of the Rare Books room at the British Library made the research possible (in often trying conditions). Bernhard Klein gave up his time to go over my German translations, doing so with equal measures of expertise and forbearance at what I made of his native language; Juanita Ruys and Margaret Clunies Ross did the translation from Hickes and Margaret supplied the notes (responsibility for the final form of the translations rests with me). The bulk of the work was done in London and, as ever, Patricia Erasmus, Ruth Evans, John Potts and Sally Thomson, Andy Gordon, Eliane Glaser and Sue Wiseman made my stays in Britain a pleasure. For their various contributions to smoothing the way of a scholar far from home I would like to record my special thanks to Caterina Albano, Philip and Psiche Hughes, and Bernhard Klein and Ina Habermann in Europe, and, in Australia, to Clare Forster.

Introduction

What is Middle English?

Imagine a medieval England in which Harold Godwinsson had kept the vow of loyalty that the Bayeux tapestry tells us he made to William of Normandy; in which William succeeds peacefully to the English throne promised him by Edward the Confessor, and his Norman cavalry help Anglo-Saxon spearmen to obliterate the Scandinavian forces at Stamford Bridge. In the years that follow, Anglo-Saxon earls find themselves increasingly marginalized as French becomes the language of court and William, naturally, rewards his own followers with land. There are uprisings against the Normans, quickly put down and used as excuses to replace native earls with Norman-born men. Harold and his brothers are among the first to be forced out; others leave voluntarily, seeking sanctuary in Scotland. English becomes the language of the common people, large in numbers but small in influence, while the barons listen to literary works composed in what will much later be dubbed Anglo-Norman. The English kings continue to hold lands across the Channel, provoking tensions with the French crown which will one day result in a protracted war...

What then would be Middle English?

To come to the point of this question, we need to look first at what Middle English is now, at the literature that pertains to it, and why it is we read what we do in Middle English.

Most modern writings on Middle English language suggest that it belongs roughly to the period 1100-1500, or between the immediate post-Conquest period and the establishment of the Tudor dynasty, a generally accepted date for the end of the Middle Ages in England. Most such writings also feature ritual disclaimers of the possibility that such clear dates can be imposed on a language. In practice, however, these dates can exercise a powerful effect. It is well known that the linguistic changes which brought about the shift from Old to Middle English were taking place before the Norman Conquest and were not the result of it, but it is difficult not to let the Conquest loom large as a decisive juncture. The Tudor accession is less cataclysmic but tradition has made it similarly significant.

Middle English literature, it would seem, must therefore be the literature of this period: a straightforward proposition. This apparent stability and consensus, however, is belied by the actual history of the development of Middle English. I aim to show, through the documents in this anthology, just how ambiguously constructed Middle English has been. This is partly the result of semantic ambivalence. The 'Middle' of Middle English is a technical linguistic term indicating a stage of a language but its more literal sense also has some force in suggesting that 'Middle' English must be the middle between two other things. And Middle English has frequently been constructed in this way, as serving to keep apart modernity on one side and the culture of Anglo-Saxon England — regarded as quite alien — on the other. A 'middle', in this respect, lacks definition without recourse to the two things it comes between and this lack of a positive definition, as I have argued elsewhere, has been a constant feature of the study of Middle English in the modern period.[1] Middle English literature has tended to be defined as not-modern, and even those who were concerned to revive it usually saw it as irretrievably on the wrong side of a great cultural divide. At the other end of its history there was the problem of how to separate it from what was usually called 'Saxon'; the question of when Saxon became English dominated philological inquiry, as many of the documents here will show.

What we study as Middle English literature today has, for better or for worse, a relatively stable canon of core texts. As in most literary study of the European Middle Ages, verse is privileged while many prose writings have a liminal status. Malory's works are obviously 'literature', but what of the Middle English homilies? Many of them clearly use the narrative techniques we associate with literary fiction, but they are not much written about, edited, or read. Conversely, verse, alone, does not guarantee canonical status; the verse chronicles of Robert Mannyng of Brunne and Robert of Gloucester were much read (relatively) in the nineteenth century but are not popular today; the latter has not been edited for more than a century.

The core of most teaching of Middle English, and a great deal of the critical writing on it, is the literature of just a few decades in the whole four-hundred year period — the time of Chaucer, Langland, Gower, and the Gawain-poet. We can add to the corpus these writers provide most of the

---

[1] In *MME*, esp. introduction and conclusion.

much-studied romances and it is still no more than a long fourteenth century which is the focus of the bulk of the study of Middle English. Writings outside this period are usually on the margins where criticism, editing, and readership are concerned. John Lydgate, the most prolific poet in the English language, is a minor figure; Laȝamon, author of the second-longest poem in the language, is in theory important yet, as Lesley Johnson notes, he 'occupies, at best, a marginal place in the fair field of Middle English studies over which the figure of Chaucer towers [...]'.[2]

Anyone studying Middle English in the past fifty years has inherited this broad consensus about what the subject is. But this consensus and relative certainty are actually of very recent origin. For much of the history of the study of Middle English texts — certainly well into the twentieth century — the field was a very poorly mapped one indeed, to the point that the use of the unifying term, 'Middle English', was in fact extremely rare until the 1870s, and not uniform after then.

If we step back from the long fourteenth century, it is not difficult to begin to see why. In the case of Anglo-Saxon literature, we can see both neat dates for the actual period, and apparently neat periodising of the study.[3] Middle English, by contrast, is a more sprawlingly plural subject, spreading diachronically across centuries of considerable change and synchronically across widely varying dialect areas. In this respect, of course, the contrasting neatness of Anglo-Saxon is artificial because of the survival of texts principally in a single dialect. The diversity of Middle English texts caused the scholars who began unearthing them in the eighteenth and nineteenth centuries to see more plurality in the literature than uniformity. If we imagine someone coming for the first time to the *Brut* of Laȝamon or the *Ormulum* — someone whose expectations of Middle English were formed on the basis of the *Canterbury Tales* — this should not surprise. The early scholars saw too much diversity to be able to discern a coherent period between 1100 and 1500.

In any case, the early scholars were not likely to see a coherence where they were not looking for one. What most of them wanted to find was the beginning of English, real English. This could involve quite different paradigms. For many, the trick was to distinguish when it was that 'Saxon' mutated into 'English'. This opposed Saxon to English, seeing the transition

---

[2] Lesley Johnson, 'Tracking Laȝamon's *Brut*', *Leeds Studies in English* 22 (1991), p. 139.

[3] On the institutional history of Anglo-Saxon studies see Carl T. Berkhout and Milton McC. Gatch, eds, *Anglo-Saxon Scholarship: The First Three Centuries* (Boston: Hall, 1982); Allen J. Frantzen, *Desire for Origins: New Language, Old English, and Teaching the Tradition* (New Brunswick, N.J.: Rutgers University Press, 1990).

away from Saxon as welcome; it can be seen in several of the extracts (see in particular **Warton** and **Ritson**).[4] It is associated with the pervasive idea that such a change is brought about by skilful poets who renovate a barbarous language, purging it of its Germanisms.

Other writers, however, making much of the fact that some form of the term 'English' was used as far back as the ninth century, wanted to construct a greater continuity for English stretching back to Anglo-Saxon times. The Anglo-Saxon Professor **John Earle** is one who shows an obvious sympathy for the lost purity of the Anglo-Saxon tongue, destroyed by the Norman yoke. Earle simply ignored the arguments that existed even then against the Conquest as having caused a decline in the inflexional system. The philologist **R. G. Latham** had argued the inevitability of this alteration in his *The English Language* thirty years before and, even in the mid-eighteenth century, some scholars knew that the Conquest could not be blamed for the changes in Anglo-Saxon: it was the 'changes of its own forms and terminations', Samuel Johnson recognized, that were crucial in the alteration of Saxon, even if at that time the precise nature of the change was a mystery.[5]

These two opposed ideological agendas, the pro- and anti-Germanic, caused widely varying constructions of medieval English in the eighteenth and nineteenth centuries. As the extracts in part I show, we owe the term 'Middle English' to **Jacob Grimm**, who pioneered the notion of the 'Old', 'Middle', and 'New' or 'Modern' phases of Germanic languages in *Deutsche Grammatik* (1819). However, because the term 'Anglo-Saxon' was already widely used at the time, Grimm retained it and emplaced 'Old English' not as a synonym for it but as the term for the immediately succeeding linguistic phase — what we now think of as Early Middle English. 'Mittelenglisch', applied to the phase that followed that, was therefore a narrow term referring only to a subsection of what is now called Middle English.

This would have been confusing enough even if it had been uniformly adopted. But it was not. Before Grimm, the term 'Semi-Saxon' had been used to describe what some scholars thought of as a liminal form of English between Anglo-Saxon and later Middle English. It was common for both British and German scholars to regard such works as the *Ormulum*, Laʒamon's *Brut*, and the *Ancrene Wisse* as 'Semi-Saxon' works, with the consequence that these texts were more typically attached to Anglo-Saxon Studies than to a nascent study of Middle English. In 1831 the Society of Antiquaries established a committee designed to further the printing of 'Saxon' works and under its aegis the *Brut* appeared in 1847 (described as a Semi-Saxon work) and as late as 1852 the *Ormulum* was edited by the then

---

[4] Names in bold are those represented in the extracts.

[5] Samuel Johnson, *A Dictionary of the English Language*, 2 vols (London, 1755), I, Eii[r], col. 2.

Rawlinson Professor of Anglo-Saxon, and prefaced with a discussion which places it entirely in the context of Anglo-Saxon Studies. Extracts from both also appeared in Benjamin Thorpe's *Analecta Anglo-Saxonica* (1834), described there as 'Semi-Saxon' in a book that, as its title implies, was concerned principally with Anglo-Saxon literature.[6]

As the extracts show, successive grammars in the nineteenth century blurred rather than clarified the picture. As late as the 1860s **Friedrich Koch** reconfigured Semi-Saxon as 'New Anglo-Saxon', opposed to an 'Old Anglo-Saxon'. Many writers, attempting to pinpoint the beginnings of a 'true' English, located the origins of English with remarkable precision. One English scholar, **T. L. Kington Oliphant**, sees the beginning of 'new' English in 1303 (when Robert Mannyng began *Handlyng Synne*) while for the German grammarian **Eduard Mätzner**, new English appears as late as 1558 and the reign of Elizabeth. **George Craik** sees Middle English as persisting up to 1550, and represents it as the youth of the language while Modern English is its 'Manhood'.

Mätzner makes clear what is implicit in these writings. He calls medieval English 'old English', a term in simple opposition to the 'new English' that obtains from the beginning of Elizabeth's reign. Explicitly, for Mätzner the line of demarcation between the two is simply the line at the beginning of modern culture. 'New' English coincides with modern culture, so by definition medieval English is whatever is alien, other, to modern culture. What defines Middle English here is simply that it is not-modern, and in this respect it is not so much a *middle*, as a *before*. Julius Zupitza wanted 'old English' in both senses. In his *Altenglisches Übungsbuch*, invoking the fact that the English had always called their language English, he wrote that in its narrow sense Old English should refer to what is also called Anglo-Saxon or Old Anglo-Saxon, But he also intended a wider sense: 'In the title I use Old English in contrast to modern English, as one calls that which is not modern German, Old German [...]'.[7]

The 1870s were a dynamic time in the study of English (partly impelled by the Early English Text Society and the *Oxford English Dictionary* project), from which, under the influence of such scholars as **Henry Sweet** and **Walter**

---

[6] Benjamin Thorpe, Analecta Anglo-Saxonica. *A Selection, in Prose and Verse, from Anglo-Saxon Authors of Various Ages; with a Glossary. Designed Chiefly as a first book for students* (London: Arch, 1834).

[7] 'Auf dem titel brauche ich altenglisch im gegensatz zu modernem englisch, wie man altdeutsch nennt, was nicht modernes deutsch ist [...]'. Julius Zupitza, *Altenglisches Übungsbuch* (Vienna: Braumüller, 1874), p. iii. In the light of this statement it is interesting that the work's later editions were titled *Alt- und Mittelenglisches Übungsbuch* (from 1882) though it contained Middle English material from the beginning.

Skeat, 'Middle English' was extended to refer to everything between the Conquest and the English Renaissance. The scheme we recognize today was gradually adopted. However, as the extracts show (**Richard Morris**; **James Murray** in the *Encyclopaedia Britannica*, 9th edition), competing schemes were still possible. Some English and German scholars persisted with more complicated linguistic maps restricting Middle English principally to the fourteenth century. R. P. Wülcker's *Altenglisches Lesebuch* (1874) contained Middle English and as late as 1878, the use of 'old English' in the broad sense is still seen in K. Böddeker's *Altenglische Dichtungen* — an edition of verse from the fourteenth-century manuscript Harl 2253.

The progress of dictionaries of Middle English exhibits a similar history of ambiguity. By the early nineteenth century, Anglo-Saxonists could go to the dictionaries of William Somner (1659), Franciscus Junius (ed. Lye 1743), Edward Lye and Owen Manning (1772), while that of Joseph Bosworth would appear in 1838. Middle English scholars had no equivalent, something which **Frederic Madden** and **Henry Weber** deplore in almost identical terms. Scholars were forced to use glossaries of such existing works as Tyrwhitt's *Canterbury Tales*, and the dictionaries that did appear covered only part of the period. James Orchard Halliwell published his *A Dictionary of Archaic and Provincial Words, Obsolete Phrases, Proverbs, and Ancient Customs, from the Fourteenth Century* in 1846; in this title, 'from' meant 'from the fourteenth century onwards', so, although it was useful to scholars of Middle English, it by no means met their needs entirely. Herbert Coleridge, the original editor of the *Oxford English Dictionary*, published *A Glossarial Index to the Printed English Literature of the Thirteenth Century* in 1859, while Franz Heinrich Stratmann's dictionary first appeared (in Germany but in English) in 1864-7, covering only the thirteenth, fourteenth, and fifteenth centuries. A second edition (1871-3) added the twelfth century, but in both the subject matter was referred to as 'Old English'. It was not until the Clarendon Press edition, revised and enlarged by Henry Bradley (1891), that Stratmann's work was retitled as a dictionary of 'Middle English', and in this role it succeeded the 1888 *Concise Dictionary of Middle English* by A. L. Mayhew and W. W. Skeat.

These varied constructions of Middle English reflect what appears to have been a continuing unwillingness or inability to see the entire Middle English period as a coherency. Some writers still found it necessary to separate the earlier from the later part of the period; German scholars seemed to want to subdivide English literature and language into its more and less Germanic phases by moving the crucial divide up from the Conquest to the period around 1200, and were followed in this by such British scholars as Morris. In these circumstances it was impossible for either the linguistic specialist or the educated general reader to understand the period between 1100 and 1500 as a linguistic and cultural coherence. As the textbooks, both specialist and popular, disagreed with one another, there was still no strong category of Middle English literature. It appeared to come into being in the 1870s, but even then competing ways of dividing up the period survived as late as the 1911 *Encyclopaedia Britannica*, in which James Murray's 1878 article was reprinted with only slight alterations. But with the establishment of English departments, a process not completed in the ancient English universities until after the First World War, the orthodoxy that had begun to emerge in the 1870s asserted itself.

Had it not been for the convenient decisiveness of the Conquest as a political and cultural event, Anglo-Saxonists would probably today be scholars who studied the literature between 600 and 1200 (teaching survey courses like 'Caedmon to Laʒamon'). Middle English scholars would see their subject as lying between the deaths of Richard I and Richard III, or between Magna Carta and the accession of Henry VII, or other dates of equally illusory convenience. This is probably what would have happened if the Conquest had been less of an event (in the manner I suggested at the outset) and had not exerted a kind of historical gravitational pull on philology in excess of its actual effect on the language.

If the Conquest had not happened would this have made any difference to the current shape of the disciplines? Would Anglo-Saxon Studies be less embattled today if it had secured Laʒamon and Orm for its own? Unlikely. Middle English Studies would be dominated by the long fourteenth century. It would be a subject that rushed along the slow upslope of the rising prestige of English to reach the peak of the late fourteenth century, with less attention paid to the trough immediately following. In other words, it would be exactly the same as it is today, only with more reason to be that way. Some of its exclusions (Laʒamon, the *Ormulum*, the earlier saints' lives) would have been made for it by history rather than by neglect. Perhaps also a reduced Middle English could not have afforded to have neglected Lydgate and Hoccleve.

Instead, Middle English is an oddly unbalanced subject. In publishing and pedagogical terms it is driven by Ricardian poetry (regardless of whether that label is accepted or not) and in particular by a Chaucer industry which rivals that of Shakespeare. In other words, Middle English study is built around the writers who look the least Middle English, the most modern. 'Not coincidentally', Tim William Machan observes, 'those writers whose aesthetics are the most responsive to modern critical methods or whose sense of authorial identity seems the strongest — Langland, Chaucer, and Gower in particular — are the writers on whose works the greatest textual-critical effort has been expended'. Others, like Minot and Lydgate, whose works are 'more typical of medieval aesthetics and literary attitudes [...] appear in very old, essentially diplomatic editions'.[8] So Middle English literature, on the basis of a handful of texts, is represented to the world as having an attractive *identity* with the modern aesthetic, a manoeuvre which sees the bulk of that literature,

---

[8] Tim William Machan, *Textual Criticism and Middle English Texts* (Charlottesville: University Press of Virginia, 1994), p. 134.

characterized by its difference from that aesthetic, left in an uneasy relation to modernity.

The Rise of Middle English

The purpose of this anthology is to show through a representative collection of primary sources how the modern study of Middle English became the way it is. As the remarks above suggest, it is not a progressivist history leading from error to transcendent clarity; it is rather designed to show the peculiar turns Middle English studies has taken. I try to trace a line of organized study of Middle English, beginning with George Hickes and running through to Walter Skeat. Most of the excerpts consist of critical or literary-historical material; I have also included Walter Scott's *jeu d'esprit* inspired by *Sir Tristrem* and to conclude, a more direct glimpse at pedagogy in Skeat's examination questions. But organized study, of course, does not tell the whole story. Middle English has been 'studied' almost from the beginning, before the period itself even came to an end. In this respect, once again, it is unlike its companion study of Old English, which has such clearcut beginnings in the wake of the dissolution of the monasteries. In Middle English, Chaucer was edited and made the subject of study before the end of the fifteenth century, if we include the writings of Caxton and the editorial interventions of unknown scribes.[9] The 'Ricardians' (except for the Gawain-poet) were all edited in the sixteenth century, showing a continuity that suggests that unlike Anglo-Saxon, which had to be revived, Middle English never went away.[10]

But interest in Middle English then did decline, rapidly, in the later sixteenth and in the seventeenth centuries. The ideological motives that, it is generally agreed, impelled the Reformation renewal of interest in Anglo-Saxon texts did not have a parallel effect on Middle English, as Anne Hudson and Machan have noted.[11] The mid-sixteenth-century peak saw editions of

---

[9] On Chaucer editions, see Paul G. Ruggiers, ed. *Editing Chaucer: The Great Tradition* (Norman, Okla.: Pilgrim Books, 1984); on scribal interventions, see Seth Lerer, *Chaucer and His Readers: Imagining the Author in Late-Medieval England* (Princeton, N.J.: Princeton University Press, 1993).

[10] It should be noted however that there is an argument that there was some continuity of Old English throughout the Middle English period; some later medieval scribes could read, and some even write, Old English. See Angus F. Cameron, 'Middle English in Old English Manuscripts', in Beryl Rowland, ed. *Chaucer and Middle English Studies in Honour of Rossell Hope Robbins* (London: Allen & Unwin, 1974), pp. 218-29, and Fred C. Robinson, *The Tomb of Beowulf and other Essays on Old English* (Oxford: Blackwell, 1993), pp. 278-79.

[11] On Anglo-Saxon in the Reformation see Frantzen, *Desire for Origins*, pp. 23-24, 37-

Chaucer's complete works by William Thynne (1532, re-edited 1542) and John Stow (1561), Thomas Berthelette's *Confessio Amantis* (1532, reprinted 1554), and Robert Crowley's three impressions of *Piers Plowman* (1550) followed by Owen Rogers's re-edition along with *Pierce the Plowman's Crede* (1561). But thereafter there was little publishing except of Chaucer — and even he experienced lean times between the reissue of Thomas Speght's 1598 edition in 1602 and John Urry's edition of 1721. Malory was published by William Stansby in 1634 and not again till the early nineteenth century. Metrical romances and ballads attracted interest in the seventeenth and eighteenth centuries but, as Machan says, 'interest in even these works was qualified' (p. 49). There remain such peculiarities as the apparently immense popularity of Mandeville's *Travels*, to judge by its frequent re-publishings in the seventeenth and early eighteenth centuries.

The history or non-history of Middle English texts in this period is still to be written. Why, given that Chaucer was so easily re-appropriated by the Reformation, was other Middle English not deemed worth enlisting? Why was the anti-clerical appeal of *Piers Plowman* not sufficient to keep the poem in view? The answer is probably that despite the ideological appeal that could have been generated from these texts their actual medieval form was increasingly unacceptable to canons of taste driven by classical learning. In this respect Anglo-Saxon texts had the advantage that they were in a language so comprehensively alien that it did not suffer from being perceived as simply a particularly poor kind of English. Even so, the study of Anglo-Saxon had also declined, in England at least, by the end of the eighteenth century. Middle English texts were simply barbarous, and even their enthusiastic supporters in the late eighteenth century did not hesitate to apply this term to them.

The beginnings of a revival in Middle English (or in what would later be seen as Middle English) occur in the early eighteenth century, at first as a branch of antiquarianism driven by historical curiosity for its own sake, but later as a more comprehensive reaction against the canons of neo-classical taste. Middle English was not George Hickes's principal topic when he compiled the *Thesaurus*, but chapter twenty-four of his Anglo-Saxon grammar forms an Early Middle English reader. Thomas Hearne's edition of the *Chronicle* of Robert of Gloucester is justly regarded as an early landmark of Middle English editing; Edmund Gibson included in his *Chronicon Saxonicum* (1692) the Early Middle English continuation at Peterborough of

---

45, but see also the riposte of Carl Berkhout in his biography of Laurence Nowell in Damico, ed., *MSBS2*, 14. Anne Hudson, 'Middle English', in A. G. Rigg, ed. *Editing Medieval Texts: English, French and Latin Written in England* (New York and London: Garland Publishing, 1977), p. 34-57 (p. 35); Machan, p. 48.

the Anglo-Saxon Chronicle.

Hickes's and Gibson's works obviously attached what they could imagine as Early Middle English to Anglo-Saxon. As far as publishing went, Hearne and Gibson did not produce emulators and work in medieval literature once again languished before a new interest was sparked later in the century, this time under the impetus of the romantic revival and the work of Thomas Percy, Richard Hurd, Thomas Warton, Joseph Ritson, and later Walter Scott, Henry Weber, and George Ellis. These scholars were responsible for a rapid rise of interest and publishing activity in Middle English. Just as Hearne and Gibson saw themselves as working with Saxon texts, though, these new editors did not see what they were working in as Middle English. Romance was overwhelmingly the genre of choice in this period, with some attention given to ballads. Much of what these antiquarians published and wrote about was governed by generic rather than chronological considerations, so there was not a strong sense of the medieval in their work so much as a rather vague 'early' or 'ancient' English past, which often comprised the early modern period as well as the later Middle Ages.

The work of Thomas Tyrwhitt, the editor whose *Canterbury Tales* (1774-78) is usually said to be the first modern Chaucer edition, does not really belong in the same paradigm as the work of the romantics. Tyrwhitt was more a classicist who made one significant venture into medieval literature. Likewise, Thomas Dunham Whitaker was a writer of local histories who became interested in Langland. His 1813 edition of *Piers Plowman* — the first since the mid-sixteenth-century — was a free-standing volume rather than something associated with a 'school' or way of thought and, apart from a simple reprint of *Pierce the Plowman's Crede* (1514), Whitaker did nothing more in medieval studies. Robert Southey's Malory edition (1817) was more what readers wanted. Walter Scott, who was to have been the Malory editor, had earlier edited *Sir Tristrem* (1804), privileging a single romance in one volume in a way that broke with the earlier practice of printing anthologies, common from Percy's *Reliques of Ancient English Poetry* (1765) through to Scott's own *Minstrelsy of the Scottish Border* (1802-3) and beyond.

Alexander Chalmers published *Confessio Amantis* (for the first time since the sixteenth century) in 1810 in volume two of his twenty-one volume collection of *The Works of the English Poets*. This was unusual; such collections usually opened with Chaucer and left the Middle Ages at that. Apart from Chaucer, romance remained by far the most popular and best known genre of later medieval writing by the time the Roxburghe Club was founded in 1812. Though it was not exclusively or even principally concerned with medieval literature, the club is significant because its model of a gentlemanly-cum-scholarly society, with a system of annual subscriptions, pointed the way for the great nineteenth-century publishing clubs and societies: the Bannatyne Club (established 1823), the Maitland Club (1828), the Abbotsford Club (1833), the Camden Society (1838), the Percy Society (1840), the Philological Society (1842), and eventually the Early English Text Society (1864) and the Chaucer Society (1868), both established by the dynamic figure of late nineteenth-century medieval studies, Frederick

Furnivall. The Roxburghe Club included amongst its publications some Middle English verse and drama, usually in attractive but very unscholarly editions. Following this model, the Bannatyne Club was established in Edinburgh, printing some Middle English material, while the Abbotsford and Maitland Clubs, also Scottish, published romances.

Working initially through the book clubs, Frederic Madden became the towering figure of mid-nineteenth-century Middle English editing, producing *Havelok the Dane* (Roxburghe, 1828), *William of Palerne* (Roxburghe, 1832), *Sir Gawain and the Green Knight* (Bannatyne, 1839), the two texts of Laȝamon's *Brut* (Society of Antiquaries, 1847), and the Wycliffite Bible (1850). For his unparalleled palaeographical skills and new emphasis on accuracy in editing, Madden is the choice of many as founding figure for Middle English editing, especially because of the *Gawayne* edition.[12]

The club model of publication, which tended to be restricted to an aristocratic and upper-middle-class membership, shifted in the late 1830s to a model of more democratic societies, best seen in the Camden Society. Unlike the clubs, the societies were more dedicated to the wide availability of the texts they printed. Their subscription model was not designed to exclude outsiders but to make available material of historical interest which the general public would have been unwilling to subsidize, and for which a specialist audience in universities did not yet exist. Apart from the obviously author-centred Chaucer Society, not one of these societies, including the EETS, was exclusively devoted to medieval literature. But they all contributed to the publication of Middle English literature in the middle of the nineteenth century.

The clubs also broadened the generic focus. The original emphasis on romance was somewhat diminished (though the central place of romance is still evident in Middle English studies today). The interest in historical documents shown by Hearne and Gibson had a revival in the work of James Halliwell (later Halliwell-Phillipps) and Thomas Wright in the mid-nineteenth century. Either jointly or alone, these two were responsible for many diverse publications, some, such as Wright's *Piers Plowman* (1842), his *Canterbury Tales* (1847-51), and Halliwell's alliterative *Morte Arthure* (1847) in the mainstream, others, such as their *Reliquiae Antiquae: Scraps from Ancient Manuscripts* (1841-43), of a decidedly non-canonical character. Later a

---

[12] See for example Hans Aarsleff, *The Study of Language in England, 1780-1860* (London: Athlone; Minneapolis: University of Minnesota Press, 1983), p. 202; Robert W. Ackerman and Gretchen Ackerman, *Sir Frederic Madden: A Biographical Sketch and Bibliography* (New York: Garland, 1979), p. ix; A. S. G. Edwards, 'Observations on the History of Middle English Editing', in *Manuscripts and Texts: Editorial Problems in Later Middle English Literature*, ed. by Derek Pearsall (Cambridge: Brewer, 1987), p. 44.

government initiative, the Rolls Series, would see the editing of historical material, including the chronicles of Robert Mannyng and Robert of Gloucester (both 1887).

The EETS sparked enough interest to attract the attention of the ancient universities, particularly Oxford. The university press there established its own medieval text series in the 1880s, which was notable for more careful scholarship than that of the EETS. In this program, the superb edition of the York plays by Lucy Toulmin Smith provided a rare entry into a hitherto male world by a female scholar. By this time German scholars were producing editions of Middle English texts, often in journals of English studies such as *Anglia* and *Englische Studien* that did not then have equivalents in England; other eminent German scholars, such as Julius Zupitza, did work for the EETS, and Reinhold Pauli's *Confessio Amantis* (1857) was also published in London by Bell and Daldy, who later produced a complete Chaucer under the editorship of Richard Morris. The Bell and Daldy editions were superseded when Oxford University Press published Walter Skeat's Chaucer, the standard edition of its day, in 1894, and G. C. Macaulay's complete Gower edition in 1899-1902.

So in the last quarter of the nineteenth century, more and more texts were becoming available, and men such as Skeat and Furnivall were proselytising inside and outside the universities. Others who have become less visible today, such as Thomas Wright and Richard Morris, must also have had a great impact through the sheer volume of their productions. As English literary study began to entrench itself in universities, Middle English became part of the curriculum. In 1896, the first lectureship in English at Cambridge was taken up by a medievalist, Israel Gollancz, who later became an influential figure when he took the Chair of English Language and Literature at King's College London in 1903. All of these moves signal the way in which the publishing and teaching of Middle English literature had become entrenched as a secure subject, apparently confident of its disciplinary boundaries. I hope the extracts in this volume remind us of a slightly different history.

Selection and arrangement

The bulk of the documents reproduced here come from the period between the 1760s and the 1870s, which I regard as the formative period for Middle English studies. Hickes and Hearne provide something of a false start for Middle English study, but it is a start nevertheless, so the anthology goes back to the early eighteenth century. There seemed little point in going later than the 1870s as the most important works tend to be available in old editions in the bigger libraries, and sometimes in reprints. I have in general avoided material that is easily available in facsimile reprint, which is why Lucy Toulmin Smith's York plays edition is not here (reprinted, New York: Russell & Russell, 1963). Likewise, Tyrwhitt's 'An Essay on the Language and Versification of Chaucer' and 'An Introductory Discourse to the Canterbury Tales' are not found here. Chaucer is in any case relatively de-emphasized in this anthology, partly to redress an imbalance, partly because there is no point in reproducing material already in Caroline Spurgeon, *Five Hundred Years of Chaucer Criticism and Allusion* (8 vols, London: Chaucer Society, 1914-25). So, with some reluctance, I have omitted writings by Frederick Furnivall and Bernhard ten Brink. Much of the latter's writings are easy to find in English translation, and I recommend Furnivall's *Trial-Forewords to my 'Parallel-Text Edition of Chaucer's Minor Poems'* (London: Chaucer Society, 1871; also in Spurgeon) which gives the unique flavour of Furnivall's idiosyncratic style. Exceptions to the reprint rule are Warton's *History of English Poetry* (*History of English Poetry In Four Volumes*, intro. by Rene Wellek [New York: Johnson Reprint Corporation, 1968]), and Hickes: both are too important to be left out, and it seemed worth gleaning from these two massive works the material on Middle English.

Within the extracts themselves I have not hesitated to cut the lengthy sections which do no more than summarize plots or list texts. Idiosyncrasies of spelling and punctuation are reproduced and I have tried to keep the notation '*sic*' to a minimum. I have cut quotations from Middle English literature except where they are central to the argument. My practice with quotations has been to supply a reference to a modern edition, risking anachronism for the sake of the reader's convenience; I have of course left quotations as they appear in the original rather than updating them to conform with the modern edition. There are, however, places where it seemed important to try to track down the actual edition used by the antiquarian.

I have discarded a large number of the original notes in these texts, many of which can be highly discursive and serve as an excuse for the incorporation of tracts of primary material. I have retained notes which are still bibliographically useful, or which make an interesting point. Such notes are distinguished by the addition of the original author's initial; they have been silently edited where necessary to provide fuller bibliographical information in accord with modern practice and house style, and very occasionally to correct slight errors such as incorrect page numbers. All other footnotes are editorial. I have added footnotes supplying bibliographical information where an original quotation did not do so; in addition some references given by authors in the body of their texts have been expanded, using square brackets. Square brackets in notes and text are editorial unless indicated otherwise.

I considered organising the material thematically but have settled for ordering by author within the two parts, with the date of publication of the author's first excerpted work determining the chronology. There are some recurrent themes however, and for the benefit of those seeking to trace particular topics, romance and the vexed topic of the role of the minstrels can be followed in Percy, Warton, Ritson, Ellis, Scott, Weber, Utterson, Laing, Madden, Michel, and Robson; the evolution of an understanding of Anglo-Norman writing is seen in Ritson, Scott, Madden, Hallam, Michel, and Wright. Langland, *Piers Plowman* and the understanding of alliterative poetry can be traced in Percy, Warton, Ritson, Ellis, Whitaker, and Hallam.

Finally, a great deal of what the antiquarians write will seem, obviously, wrong. In this respect the anthology is to a large extent a history of error. While I do not set out actually to mislead, and try in the notes to point out errors, the perception of error rests to some extent on our own conviction of our rightness. We see the ideologies of past scholarship with a clarity we do not always apply to our own work. Retrieving these ideologies is what I think makes the task of this anthology worthwhile and perhaps bringing them into view might encourage fresh scrutiny of what it is Middle English does now.

Part I: Language

1. George Hickes (1642-1715)

George Hickes is described by his most recent biographer as a 'theological and political controversialist and eminent philologist of medieval Germanic studies [...]' (Harris 1998, p. 19). He is today best remembered for his *Thesaurus*, a massive compendium of philological learning which grew out of his earlier publication, *Institutiones Grammaticae Anglo-Saxonicae et Moeso-Gothicae* (1689). The revised *Institutiones* formed part 1 of volume 1 of the *Thesaurus* and chapters 19-24, according to Richard L. Harris, 'constitute the first history of the English language' (1998, p. 26). Hickes was Dean of Worcester when he began this work in the mid-1680s but did not operate from a comfortable sinecure. Preferred by Charles II, Hickes was publicly opposed to Roman Catholicism and so did not prosper under James II. On the accession of William and Mary he became one of the Nonjurors (who felt they were still bound by their oaths of allegiance to James) and so fell foul of the new monarchs after their coronation in 1689. He was outlawed in 1691 and consequently conducted the bulk of his famous work a fugitive in his own country before his situation was eased in 1699. Principally concerned with 'septentrional' studies (the philology and literature of the old Germanic languages), Hickes's work also provided what was effectively the first Middle English reader in chapter twenty-four of the first part of the *Thesaurus*.

For biography and critical assessment of Hickes's work see Richard L. Harris, 'George Hickes', in Damico, ed., *MSBS2*, 19-32 and, for more detail, the same author's *A Chorus of Grammars: The Correspondence of George Hickes and his Collaborators on the 'Thesaurus linguarum septentrionalium'* (Toronto: Pontifical Institute of Mediaeval Studies, 1992). See also David C. Douglas, *English Scholars 1660-1730* , 2nd rev. edn (London: Eyre &

Spottiswoode, 1951), ch. 4. See also Shaun F. D. Hughes, 'The Anglo-Saxon Grammars of George Hickes and Elizabeth Elstob', in *Anglo-Saxon Scholarship: The First Three Centuries*, ed. by Carl T. Berkhout and Milton McC. Gatch (Boston: Hall, 1982), pp. 119-147.

George Hickes, *Linguarum Vett. Septentrionalium Thesaurus Grammatico-Criticus et Archæologicus*, 2 vols. (Oxford: Sheldonian Theatre, 1703-5).

From: Caput Vigesimumsecundum, 'De Dialecto Normanno-Saxonica' (I, chapter 22, 134, 156-58).

De dialecto **Normanno-Saxonica** *sive* **Anglo-Normannica;** & *de dialecto* **Semi-Saxonicâ.**

I. Hactenus de dialecto *Dano-Saxonica*, quâ, tam solutâ, quàm vinctâ oratione qui scripserunt, usi sunt *Boreales Angli* imperio *Danorum* subjecti; quibuscum diuturna consuetudine & mutuis conjugiis sociati, tandem in unum quasi populum, ut *Sabini & Romani*, coierunt. Ordo igitur postulat, ut de dialecto *Normanno-Saxonicâ* tractemus. Verum ut quæ ei elucidandæ serviunt clarius & distinctius tradamus, de dialecto *Semi-Saxonica*, ut vocatur, dicendum est; in quam australis illa *Saxonica* (sub qua semper & occidentalem comprehendo,) quam puriorem *Anglo-Saxonicam* supra vocavimus, tandem, pariter ac purior ille sermo antiquorum *Anglorum* qui *Northymbriam* veterem incoluerunt, in *Dano-Saxonicam* mutata & corrupta erat. *Semi-Saxonicam* autem eam docti nominant, quòd medius quasi sermo, vel pene medius esset, inter puriorem Anglo-Saxonicum, & *Anglicanum* illum, qui majoribus nostris ante centum & quinquaginta annos vernaculus erat. Quemadmodum enim *vinum acescens*, nondum tamen in acetum conversum, *semivinum* & *semiacetum* dici, usu adprobante, possit; sic australium nostrorum *Saxonum* medium illum, vel ad medium accedentem sermonem *Semi-Saxonicum*, & si usus vellet, *Semi-Anglicum* haud absurde nuncupandum esse judicamus.

[...]

XXV. In superioribus, ut australium *Saxonum* sermo primo *Danorum*, dein *Normannorum* linguis, moribus & institutis, quoad scripturam, voces & phrases mutatus, & innovatus est; atque tandem in dialectos *Semi-Saxonicam*, & dein *Normanno-Saxonicam*, quam *Anglo-Normannicam* etiam voco, conversus est, ostendi. Jam igitur demonstrandum restat, quantum ab indole sua iis etiam immutatus est quoad syntaxin, cujus omnia præcepta, quæ purus servavit, adeo corruptus neglexit & contemsit, ut quum trium, quas vocant Grammatici, concordantiarum regulas, tum regimen præpositionum, tum denique duorum substantivorum diversæ significationis concurrentium, & verborum transitivorum accusativum exigentium, constructionem barbarus factus amandavit.

Regulam etiam de verbis acquisitivis, quæ in omnibus linguis dativum adsciscunt, adspernit jam in *Semi-Saxonicum*, & *Normanno-Saxonicum* conversus *Anglo-Saxonicus* sermo.

[...]

XXVI. Traditis tandem, deo adjuvante, iis, quæ opus essent ad monstrandum quibus quasi gradibus australium *Saxonum* sermo, indies in deterius ruens, primo in *Semi-Saxonicam* ut vocant, dein in *Normanno-Saxonicam*, sive *Anglo-Saxonicam* linguam mutatus est; jam nescio quo impellente genio percitus urgeor, ut è vetustis utriusque dialecti monumentis nonnulla expromam, in quibus se exerceat studiosus lector, & quæ per regulas à nobis in superioribus datas examinet, & exploret. Incipiam igitur à charta *Eadvardi Confessoris* dicti, quam extracta forte capsula ductile in bibliotheca *Cottoniana*, cum altera *Gullhialmi*, quam supra exhibui, *conquæstoris*, inter alias repperi, & quæ præmisso signo crucis sic scripta legitur. [...]

On the Norman-Saxon or Anglo-Norman dialect; and on the Semi-Saxon dialect.

I. Hitherto [we have discussed] the *Dano-Saxon* dialect, which was used by the *Northern Angles*, who wrote both prose and poetry. They were subject to the rule of the *Danes*, and, linked together with them by daily custom and intermarriage, they finally came together as one people, just as the *Sabines and Romans* did. Order of succession therefore demands that we speak of the *Norman-Saxon* dialect.

However, so that we may relate those things that serve to elucidate it more clearly and distinctly, it is to be spoken of as the *Semi-Saxon* dialect, into which that South *Saxon* dialect (under which I always subsume the Western [dialect]), which we have above called the purer *Anglo-Saxon*, [and] really, equally and more purely that language of the ancient *Angles* who inhabited old Northumbria, was changed and corrupted into *Dano-Saxon*. Scholars, however, call this *Semi-Saxon*, because it was, so to speak, an intermediate language, or almost intermediate, between the purer Anglo-Saxon and that English [*Anglicanus*] which, for our ancestors, had been the vernacular for one hundred and fifty years. For, just as wine, having soured, but not yet turned to vinegar, may be called semi-wine and semi-vinegar in acceptable usage, so that intermediate or almost intermediate language of our southern *Saxons* may be called *Semi-Saxon* and, if custom allows, we consider that it would not be inappropriate to call it *Semi-English*.

[...]

XXV. I have shown above that the speech of the southern *Saxons* was changed and altered by the languages, customs and practices first of the *Danes* and then of the *Normans* with regard to writing, speech, and diction, and was finally transformed into the *Semi-Saxon* dialects, and then into the *Norman-Saxon*, which I also call the *Anglo-Norman*. Now, therefore, it remains to demonstrate the extent to which it was also changed from its natural state by these causes with respect to syntax, all of whose rules, which the pure [language] preserved, the corrupted language disregarded and scorned to the point when, having become barbaric, it banished the rules of the three concords, as grammarians call them, then the government of prepositions, and then finally the construction of two nouns of different meaning being in apposition, and of transitive verbs governing the accusative.

The *Anglo-Saxon* language, now transformed into *Semi-Saxon* and *Norman-Saxon*, even rejects the rule concerning verbs of acquisition, which in all languages take the dative.

[...]

XXVI. Having finally, with God's help, communicated those things which were necessary to demonstrating the stages, as it were, by which the language of the southern *Saxons*, daily falling into a worse condition, was changed first into the *Semi-Saxon* language, as they called it, and then into *Norman-Saxon* or *Anglo-Saxon*, I am now urged on by some compelling genius or other to set forth some of the ancient records of each dialect, with which the studious reader may busy himself, and which he may consider and investigate by using the rules that we have given above. I shall therefore begin with a charter of Edward, called the Confessor, which I discovered among others taken by chance from a small malleable book box[1] in the Cotton library, together with a second one of William the Conqueror, which I presented above, and which, written thus with the sign of the cross preceding it, reads as follows [...]

---

[1] The meaning of the adjective *ductilis* (*-e*) is not clear; it may refer to the fact that the *capsula* was made of malleable metal, or it may possibly mean that it was portable, if *ductile* is interpreted in another sense.

2. Thomas Warton (1728-90)

Thomas Warton was a Fellow of Trinity College, Oxford, from 1751, Professor of Poetry (1757-67), and Professor of History and Poet Laureate from 1785. The sprawling *History of English Poetry* is his best known work. It was deplored by many for its dilatoriness and often slipshod scholarship almost from the moment it was published; as Lawrence Lipking writes, 'it obeys contradictory impulses and irrational motivations'.[2] But it is a key document in many areas of the study of English literature, especially in the linked fields of romanticism and medieval literature and it was in its time the most comprehensive English literary history available.

The extract provides Warton's most explicit statement on the nature of linguistic change in the English language, and in doing so demonstrates the typical concern of writers of this period not so much with characterizing the whole Middle English period as a single linguistic coherency, as with the point at which 'true' English could be said to have emerged from Saxon. Warton has no technical term for the vernacular language of the later fourteenth century; he simply calls it English. Worth noting also is Warton's version of the 'Norman yoke' thesis. (For further references and information see the introductory note to Warton in Part II.)

Thomas Warton, *The History of English Poetry* (London, 1774-81).

From: Section 1, 1774 (pp. 1-7).

The Saxon language spoken in England, is distinguished by three several epochs, and may therefore be divided into three dialects. The first of these is that which the Saxons used, from their entrance into this island, till the irruption of the Danes, for the space of three hundred and thirty years. This has been called the British Saxon: and no monument of it remains, except a small metrical fragment of the genuine Caedmon, inserted in Alfred's version of the Venerable Bede's ecclesiastical history.[3] The second is the Danish Saxon, which prevailed from the Danish to the Norman invasion; and of which many considerable specimens, both in verse and prose, are still preserved: particularly, two literal versions of the four gospels, and the spurious Caedmon's beautiful poetical paraphrase of the Book of Genesis,

---

[2] Lawrence Lipking, *The Ordering of the Arts in Eighteenth-Century England* (Princeton, N.J.: Princeton University Press, 1970), p. 355.

[3] 'Caedmon's Hymn', the famous poem in the Anglo-Saxon version of Bede's *Historia Ecclesiastica* (book IV, chapter 24). Warton probably read this in the 1722 edition of the *Historia* by John Smith, which contained both the Latin and Anglo-Saxon texts.

and the prophet Daniel. The third may be properly styled the Norman Saxon; which began about the time of the Norman accession, and continued beyond the reign of Henry the second.

The last of these three dialects, with which these Annals of English Poetry commence, formed a language extremely barbarous, irregular, and intractable; and consequently promises no very striking specimens in any species of composition. Its substance was the Danish Saxon, adulterated with French. The Saxon indeed, a language subsisting on uniform principles, and polished by poets and theologists, however corrupted by the Danes, had much perspicuity, strength, and harmony: but the French imported by the Conqueror and his people, was a confused jargon of Teutonic, Gaulish, and vitiated Latin. In this fluctuating state of our national speech, the French predominated. Even before the conquest the Saxon language began to fall into contempt, and the French, or Frankish, to be substituted in its stead: a circumstance, which at once facilitated and foretold the Norman accession. In the year 652, it was the common practice of the Anglo-Saxons, to send their youth to the monasteries of France for education: and not only the language, but the manners of the French, were esteemed the most polite accomplishments. In the reign of Edward the Confessor, the resort of Normans to the English court was so frequent, that the affectation of imitating the Frankish customs became almost universal: and even the lower class of people were ambitious of catching the Frankish idiom. It was no difficult task for the Norman lords to banish that language, of which the natives began to be absurdly ashamed. The new invaders commanded the laws to be administered in French. Many charters of monasteries were forged in Latin by the Saxon monks, for the present security of their possessions, in consequence of that aversion which the Normans professed to the Saxon tongue. Even children at school were forbidden to read in the native language, and instructed in a knowledge of the Norman only. In the mean time we should have some regard to the general and political state of the nation. The natives were so universally reduced to the lowest condition of neglect and indigence, that the English name became a term of reproach: and several generations elapsed, before one family of Saxon pedigree was raised to any distinguished honours, or could so much as attain the rank of baronage. Among other instances of that absolute and voluntary submission, with which our Saxon ancestors received a foreign yoke, it appears that they suffered their hand-writing to fall into discredit and disuse; which by degrees became so difficult and obsolete, that few beside the oldest men could understand the characters. [...] The Saxon was probably spoken in the country, yet not without various adulterations from the French: the courtly language was French, yet perhaps with some vestiges of the vernacular Saxon. But the nobles, in the reign of Henry the second, constantly sent their children into France, lest they should contract habits of barbarism in their speech, which could not have been avoided in an English education. [...] About the same time [1385], or rather before, the students of our universities, were ordered to converse in French or Latin. The latter was much affected by the Normans. All the Norman accompts were in Latin. The plan of the great royal revenue-rolls, now called the pipe-rolls, were of their construction, and in that language. But from the declension of the barons, and prevalence of the commons, most of whom were of English ancestry, the native language of England gradually gained ground: till at length the interest of the commons so far succeeded with Edward the third, that an act of parliament was passed, appointing all pleas and proceedings of law to be carried on in English: although the same statute decrees, in the true Norman spirit, that all such pleas and proceedings should be enrolled in Latin. Yet this change did not restore either the Saxon alphabet or language. It abolished a token of subjection and disgrace: and in some degree, contributed to prevent further French innovations in the language then used, which yet remained in a compound state, and retained a considerable mixture of foreign phraseology. In the mean time, it must be remembered, that this corruption of the Saxon was not only owing to the admission of new words, occasioned by the new alliance, but to changes of its own forms and terminations, arising from reasons which we cannot investigate or explain.[4]

---

[4] Warton notes at this point that he will examine these changes in the following section. What he then gives is not a description of morphological change in Middle English but, through copious quotation, an account of how the better writers improved the native tongue.

3. Jacob Grimm (1785-1863)

The work of Jacob Grimm is fundamental to comparative philology. In the first edition of *Deutsche Grammatik* in 1819, Grimm used throughout his terminology of 'Old', 'Middle', and 'New' or 'Modern' to describe the phases of Germanic languages, so it is in this work that the term 'Middle English' first appears. However (as is discussed at greater length in the introduction), it did not have the same broad sense it was later to gain.

For a biography and critical assessment see Maria Dobozy, 'Jacob and Wilhelm Grimm', in Damico, ed., *MSBS2*, 93-108.

Jacob Grimm, *Deutsche Grammatik*, 2nd edn, 4 vols (Göttingen: Dieterichsche Buchhandlung, 1822-37).

From: I p. 506.

Mittelenglische buchstaben.

Ich gebe aus mangel an raum und zureichendem studium oberflächliche übersichten. Die quellen sind nicht unbedeutend und zu genauerer bearbeitung einladend; außer Tristrem und Chaucers werken steht das wichtigste bei Ritson und Weber gesammelt, der zeit nach fallen sie wiederum dem 13. und 14. jahrh. zu. Schon die niederländische sprache zeigte größere zumischung romanischer wörter als die hochdeutsche, doch eine unvergleichbar geringere, als sie im englischen eingetreten ist. Offenbar haben die materiell immer noch überwiegenden deutschen bestandtheile in der gesellschaft so vieler fremder wörter und laute von dem organischen verhältnis sowohl der buchstaben als der flexionen manches verlieren müßen.

Middle English letters.

Owing to lack of space and adequate study I give a superficial overview. The sources are not insignificant and invite more detailed treatment; apart from *Tristrem*, and Chaucer's works, the most important have been collected by Ritson and Weber; they belong, again, to the thirteenth and fourteenth centuries. Already the Dutch language showed a greater admixture of romance words than the High German, but a much more insignificant admixture than in English. In a material sense, the Germanic components were still predominant and, in the company of so many foreign words and sounds, they apparently had to lose something of the organic relationship as much of the letters as of the inflections.

4. Robert Gordon Latham (1812-88)

Robert Gordon Latham was Professor of English Language and Literature at University College London when he produced his textbook on language, which would remain, over several editions, a popular text through the middle decades of the century. Latham became a fellow of King's College Cambridge in 1832, and moved to the Continent for a year to study philology. Time spent in Germany and Denmark left a clear mark on his work, which incorporates Germanic philology more than most English works on language of this era. In *The English Language*, Latham acknowledged his debt to Grimm, and also to Rasmus Rask, the Danish philologist whose *Undersøgelse om det gamle Nordiske eller Islandske Sprogs Oprindelse* (*Investigation on the Origin of the Old Norse or Icelandic Language*) appeared in 1818 and furthered the understanding of Germanic languages which Grimm would later extend.

See further Hans Aarsleff, *The Study of Language in England, 1780-1860*, 2nd edn (Minneapolis: University of Minnesota Press, 1983), ch. 6.

R. G. Latham, *The English Language* (London: Taylor and Walton, 1841).

From: Chapter 4, 'The Relation of the English to the Anglo-Saxon and the Stages of the English Language' (pp. 55-68).

[Latham first establishes that languages alter at different rates, and argues against the common idea that the Norman Conquest was responsible for the decline in the inflectional system of Old English, noting that other inflected languages underwent similar alterations.]

At a given period, then, the Anglo-Saxon of the standard, and (if the expression may be used) classical authors, such as Cædmon, Alfred, Ælfric, &c. &c. had undergone such a change as to induce the scholars of the present age to denominate it, not Saxon, but *Semi*-Saxon. It had ceased to be genuine Saxon, but had not yet become English. In certain parts of the kingdom where the mode of speech changed more rapidly than elsewhere, the Semi-Saxon stage of our language came earlier. It was, as it were precipitated.

The History of King Leir and his Daughters is found in two forms. Between these there is a difference either of dialect or of date, and possibly of both. Each, however, is Semi-Saxon.[5] [...]

The Grave, a poetical fragment, the latter part of the Saxon Chronicle, a

---

[5] Latham is referring to the story found in the two versions of Laȝamon's *Brut*. He quotes at this point the Lear story as found in both manuscripts, printed in Benjamin Thorpe's *Analecta Anglo-Saxonica* (London: Arch, 1834), pp. 143-70.

Homily for St. Edmund's Day [...] and above all the printed extracts of the poem of Layamon, are the more accessible specimens of the Semi-Saxon.[6] The Ormulum, although in many points English rather than Saxon, retains the Dual Number of the Anglo-Saxon Pronouns. However, lest too much stress be laid upon this circumstance, the epistolary character of the Ormulum must be borne in mind.

It is very evident that if, even in the present day, there were spoken in some remote district the language of Alfred and Ælfric, such a mode of speech would be called, not Modern English, but Anglo-Saxon. This teaches us that the stage of language is to be measured, not by its date, but by its structure. Hence, Saxon ends and Semi-Saxon begins, not at a given year A.D., but at that time (whenever it be) when certain grammatical Inflections disappear, and certain characters of a more advanced stage are introduced.
[Latham then gives the details of some of these inflectional changes, and adds:]

The preponderance (not the occasional occurrence) of forms like those above constitute [sic] Semi-Saxon in contradistinction to Standard Saxon, Classical Saxon, or Anglo-Saxon Proper.

[...] Further changes convert Semi-Saxon into Old English.
[Latham details the changes, which principally involve the loss of the dative plural in -um and the extension of -es generally as a genitive and as a plural, and notes:]

The preponderance of the forms above (and not their occasional occurrence) constitutes Old English in contradistinction to Semi-Saxon.

The following extract from Henry's History (Vol. viii. Append. iv.) is the proclamation of Henry III. to the people of Huntingdonshire, A.D. 1258. It currently passes for the earliest specimen of English.[7]

---

[6] They were accessible because they had been printed by Thorpe in his *Analecta*. The chronicle to which Latham refers is of course the *Peterborough Chronicle*. The homily was printed by Thorpe from Bodl 343 (2406), a manuscript of the second half of the twelfth century; he thought it to be 'in barbarous Semi-Saxon, apparently in the East-Anglian dialect [...].' (*Analecta*, p. v). See the edition of 'St Edmund, King and Martyr' (based on the version in the early eleventh century Cotton MS Julius E VII) by G. I. Needham, *Aelfric: Lives of Three English Saints* (London: Methuen, 1966), pp. 43-59. 'The Grave' is also found in the Bodleian manuscript as an addition, according to Ker, of the late twelfth/early thirteenth century (see the edition by Arnold Schröer, *Anglia* 5 [1882], 289-90). Neither Thorpe nor Latham allows for the post-Conquest copying of Anglo-Saxon prose, assuming rather that writing in a manuscript must have represented a living language, which artificially heightens the sense of a 'Semi-Saxon' phase of English. See N. R. Ker, *Catalogue of Manuscripts Containing Anglo-Saxon* (Oxford: Clarendon Press, 1957), pp. 368, 370, 374.

[7] For the proclamation of Henry III to the people of Huntingdonshire, see the discussion and edition in Bruce Dickins and R. M. Wilson, eds., *Early Middle English Texts* (London:

[...]

The Songs amongst the Political Verses printed by the Camden Society, the Romance of Havelok the Dane, William and the Werwolf, the Gestes of Alisaundre, King Horn, Ipomedon, and the King of Tars; and, amongst the longer works, Robert of Gloucester's Chronicle, and the Poems of Robert of Bourn (Brunne), are (amongst others) Old English.[8] Broadly speaking, the *Old* English may be said to begin with the reign of Henry III, and to end with that of Edward III.

[...]

In Chaucer and Mandeville, and perhaps in all the writers of the reign of Edward III, we have a transition from the Old to the Middle English. The last characteristic of a Grammar different from that of the present English, is the Plural form in -*en*; *We tellen, Ye tellen, They tellen.* As this disappears, which it does in the reign of Queen Elizabeth, (Spenser has it continually,)[9] the Middle English may be said to pass into the New or Modern English.

Bowes & Bowes, 1951), pp. 7-9. Latham's reference is to Robert Henry's popular and much reprinted *History of Great Britain*, first published in six volumes in 1771-93.

[8] The songs to which Latham refers were in *The Political Songs of England, From the Reign of John to that of Edward II*, ed. and trans. by Thomas Wright (London: Camden Society, 1839). They were principally taken from MS Harl. 2253, c.1340-50. *William and the Werwolf* is the romance now known as *William of Palerne*.

[9] Latham here apparently fails to recognise Spenser's conscious archaising.

5. George Lillie Craik (1798-1866)

George Lillie Craik was Professor of English Literature and History at Queen's College, Belfast, from 1849 and the author of several historical works aimed at schools. He also wrote *The Pursuit of Knowledge Under Difficulties, Illustrated by Anecdotes* (1830-31) and a supplement to the same, 'illustrated by female examples' (1847). His text on language was designed for use in schools and colleges and passed through many editions. It presented the abstracts of a lecture series given at Queen's.

George L. Craik, *Outlines of the History of the English Language* (London: Chapman and Hall, 1851).

From: pp. 65-119.

XV. In reference to the progress of the language, the space from about the middle of the Eleventh to the middle of the Thirteenth century, or the first two centuries after the Conquest, may be designated the *Period of Semi-Saxon*. In the popular dialect of this period we have a work of considerable length in verse, the *Chronicle of Layamon*.

[...]

It is impossible to compare the extracts that have been given from *Layamon* and the *Ormulum* without being led to entertain the strongest doubts as to the correctness of the common assumption that they are works of the same age. They do not exhibit the language in the same stage, or, at least, in the same state.[10] The grammar of *Layamon* is half Saxon, or more than half Saxon; it may be questioned if that of the *Ormulum* have retained a vestige of what is distinctively Saxon. If it were certain that the two works were of the same age, we should be compelled to conclude that the language had in one part of the country advanced a complete stage beyond the point to which it had attained in another,—that the people of the west were still speaking Saxon while those of the eastern counties were speaking English. But, in truth, there is no evidence whatever that the two works are of the same age. The *Ormulum*, like many other pieces which have been assigned to the twelfth century, is much more probably of the latter part of the thirteenth. In that case, *Layamon* and it will belong, according to the arrangement here adopted, to different periods in the history of the language. [...]

XVI. After the middle of the Thirteenth century, the language assumes the general shape and physiognomy of the English which we now write and speak. It may be called English rough-hewn. The space from about the

---

[10] In fact, although there are difficulties in dating these texts, the current consensus is that both are likely to date from the end of the twelfth century.

middle of the Thirteenth to the middle of the Fourteenth century may be designated the *Period of Old or* (better) *Early English.*

This division would accord sufficiently with the common statement which gives as our earliest specimen of English (as distinguished from Saxon or semi-Saxon) a proclamation of King Henry the Third to the people of Huntingdonshire in 1258. It may be found, with a literal translation interlined, in the 4th. vol. of Henry's *History of Great Britain* (*Append.* IV.). This historian does not say where he got it. It is printed, from the original preserved among the Patent Rolls in the Tower of London, in the new edition of *Rymer's Fœdera.*[11]

But this legal paper can scarcely be safely quoted as exhibiting the current language of the time. Like all such documents, it is made up in great part of established phrases of form, many of which had probably become obsolete in ordinary speech and writing. The English of the proclamation of 1258 is much less modern than that of the *Ormulum*, and fully as Saxon, both in the words and in the grammar, as any part of *Layamon's Chronicle*, if not rather more so.

The two principal literary works belonging to this period (that of *Early English*) are the metrical Chronicles of *Robert of Gloucester* and of *Robert of Brunne.*

The Chronicle of Robert of Gloucester was edited by Thomas Hearne in 1724.[12] The writer may be considered as belonging to the first half of the present period: it has been shown by Sir Frederic Madden that he must have survived the year 1297.[13] [...]

XVII. Meanwhile, in the literature of the country, and also in the oral intercourse of the most influential classes of the population, the native language may be said to have been for the First century after the Norman Conquest completely overborne by the French; for the Second, to have been in a state of revolt against that foreign tongue; during the Third, to have been rapidly making head against it and regaining its old supremacy.

Or the three stages may be thus distinguished:— The first, comprehending the reigns of the Conqueror, his two sons, and Stephen, a space of 88 years;

---

[11] On the proclamation, see note 7. The *Fœdera* of the critic and poet Thomas Rymer (1641-1713) was a vast compendium of treaties, conventions and other forms of agreement made between Britain and other powers. It originally appeared in seventeen volumes in 1704-1717; by the new edition, Craik must mean the third edition commenced by the Record Commission in 1816, but far from complete when work on it was suspended in 1830.

[12] Thomas Hearne, ed. *Robert of Gloucester's Chronicle*, 2 vols (Oxford: Sheldonian Theatre, 1724); see extract in Part II.

[13] Frederic Madden, ed. *The Ancient English Romance of Havelok the Dane* (London: Roxburghe Club, 1828), p. lii.

the second, the reigns of Henry II., his two sons, and Henry III., a space of 118 years; the third, the reigns of Edward I., II., and III., a space of 105 years. In a loose or general sense the first and second of these spaces will correspond to what has been designated the Period of Semi-Saxon, and the third to the Period of Early English. [...]

XX. The space from about the middle of the Fourteenth to the middle of the Sixteenth Century may be styled the *Period of Middle English*; and that designation may be understood to express not only the position of the Period, but the transition of the language, in respect both of its vocabulary and of its grammar, from its earliest and rudest form to that in which it now exists. To the commencement of this Period belong the writings of Chaucer, the Homer of our Poetry and the true Father of English Literature. [...]

[...]

The English of the age of Chaucer, being the earlier part of the Middle or Transitional Period of the language, though reduced or restored to considerable regularity, has evidently not yet attained its final form and structure, but is still in a state of growth or movement under two tendencies which had been for some time previous at work in it, and had brought it to its actual condition:—the first, a tendency to drop more of the Anglo-Saxon; the second, a tendency to assume more from the French. [...]

XXI. We may call the First Century after the Norman Conquest the Infancy of the English Language (as distinct from Saxon); the Second its Childhood; the Third its Boyhood; the Fourth and Fifth its Youth, or Adolescence; and the time that has since elapsed its Manhood. Its Infancy and Childhood will thus correspond with what has before been designated the Period of Saxon and Semi-Saxon; its Boyhood with that of Early English; its Youth with that of Middle English; its Manhood with that of Modern English.

The entire history that has been gone over may be exhibited in a tabular form as follows:—

Periods	Reigns	Dates	Position in Relation to the French	Ages
I. Semi-Saxon	William I. William II. Henry I. Stephen	A.D. 1066-1154	Suppressed and superseded.	Infancy: 88 years.
	Henry II. Richard I. John. Henry III	1154-1272	In revolt	Childhood: 118 years
II. Early English	Edward I. Edward II. Edward III.	1272-1377	In ascendancy	Boyhood: 105 years.
III. Middle English	Richard II. Henry IV. Henry V. Henry VI. Edward IV. Edward V. Richard III. Henry VII. Henry VIII. Edward VI. Mary	1377-1558	In supremacy	Youth: 181 years
IV. Modern English.	Elizabeth, &c.	1558	In sole dominion	Manhood

6. Eduard Mätzner (1804-92)

Eduard Mätzner studied philology and theology at Greifswald and Heidelberg, leaning increasingly to philology, and taught in several gymnasiums, later becoming a headmaster in Berlin. He published editions of classical writings and a grammar of French, and became an honorary member of London's Philological Society in 1869. He published *Englische Grammatik*, 3 vols. (Berlin: Weidmannsche Buchhandlung, 1860-65), which appeared in a second edition in 1873-5 and a third in 1880-5. It is here presented in the translation of Clair James Grece as *An English Grammar: Methodical, Analytical, and Historical*, 3 vols. (London, 1874). Grece, an agitator for electoral and legislative reform, was a Fellow of the Philological Society.

From: 'Introduction: The English Language' (I, 6-8).

The language which now [in the later fourteenth century] began to take the place of the French is to be regarded as a full grown language, the English. Its formation is preceded by a period of transition, that of the Half-Saxon (in the 12th century) which is expressed in literature by the extensive writings of Layamon and Orme (whence the name Ormulum). The language is already called English (Ice þatt þis Ennglissh hafe sett (compare Ormulum in Thorpe Annal. Angl. sax. p. 174).[14] It has already taken up and assimilated many French words, perceptibly altered the former spelling and treated the alliteration with neglect. The declination exhibits the mixture of the single form with the strong and weak Anglosaxon form. The plural begins, with the abandonment of the distinctions of gender and declination, to adopt the plural in *s*. The forms of the pronoun still resist the complete obliteration of their terminations. In the adjective we often perceive the confounding of the strong and the weak form, but frequently also the strong and the weak form stunted. In the verb, along with the termination of the plural of the present indicative *ad, ed*, the termination *en* already shews itself; the prefix *ge* in the perfect participle of the strong verbs appears commonly in the form *y, i*, and the *n* of the infinitive, and the participle of the strong verbs is frequently dropped. The weakening of the unaccented and especially of the final vowels of all parts of speech and, generally, the shortening of words is observable even in the Halfsaxon.

The English language, in the stricter sense, begins in the thirteenth century. Its further and more constant development is nowhere abruptly broken, but in long spaces of time wide differences become manifest;

---

[14] i.e., Benjamin Thorpe, *Analecta Anglo-Saxonica* (London: Arch, 1834).

wherefore we have to divide the period of the Old English and that of the New English from each other, the boundary being generally coincident with the commencement of modern culture.

Under the name Old English we comprehend the linguistic period from the thirteenth century to the age of Elizabeth (1558). If, within this space of time we would distinguish an Old-English period (1250-1350) and a Middle English (1350-1558), we must consider on the other hand that, in point of fact, no epoch of change in the forms of the English language occurred in the middle of the fourteenth century, although the age of Edward the Third gave a new impulse to English literature. Those who wish to specify sharp distinctions in the forms of the language of these periods are justly in perplexity. No new principle of formation enters into the language, no one dialect is raised decidedly into a literary standard, it being currently said of the language, even by Chaucer: Ther is so great diversite in English and in writing of our tong p. 332 Tyrwh., with which Trevisa also agrees in his translation of Higden's Polychronicon (1387). And, if the formation and renovation of the English tongue is still ascribed, as it was by Skelton, to the poets Gower, and to Chaucer, the unsurpassed during two centuries, (compare Skelton I. 75 and 377), this refers to the syntactic and stylistic aspect of the tongue more than to its forms and their mutations. Moreover we shall, in the exposition of the Old-english forms, have the authors of the thirteenth and fourteenth centuries especially in our eye, who, in regard to the Anglo-saxon vocabulary and to the strong verbal forms still preserved, are, of course, richer than subsequent ones; in which respect Skelton might say that Gower's English was in his age obsolete; as also generally that, at the end of the Old English period, the linguistic revolution was so accelerated that Caxton could say, in 1490, that the language was then very different from that in use at the time of his birth in 1412.

The Modern English language, further developed under the influences of the art of printing, of newly reviving science and of the Reformation, and, from the sixteenth century, methodically cultivated, is, however, separated from the Old English by no sharp line of demarcation. Spencer and Shakespeare, who, in part consciously, affect archaisms, stand on the confines and at the same time reach back beyond them. Yet the language now gradually gains more and more in orthographical and grammatical consistency, although the golden age of Elizabeth is not at the same time the age of classical correctness of the language, chiefly because the study of the ancient languages operated immediately more upon the form than upon the substance of the literature. Nevertheless this study soon contributed to fix also the English prosody, which, in Old English, was fluctuating. Although the spelling has continued in certain particulars uncertain and complicated even to the present day, the settlement of the orthography, prosody and grammar since the beginning of the seventeenth century is an essential mark of distinction between the Old English and the Modern English. Herewith is associated the securing of a literary idiom, to which contributed not so much the translations from the classical languages and from the Italian, as the translation of the Bible, composed by order of James the First, (1607-11) still the authorized one, and not only an excellent work for its own age, but, even for the present, a model of classical language. The home of the present literary dialect is moreover universally shifted to the ancient confines of the Angles and West Saxons. Some place it in the dialect of Northamptonshire (Thom. Sternberg); others, in that of Leicestershire (Guest); yet the same freedom from provincialisms is also attributed to the dialects of Bedfordshire and Herefordshire. The language of the educated is at present every where under the influence of the literary language, and it is a matter of course that the living speech of the inhabitants of the capital is regarded as the standard for cultivated intercourse, even in regard to pronunciation.

7. George Perkins Marsh (1801-82)

George Perkins Marsh had a varied career as, amongst other things, lawyer, politician, editor, and farmer. As a scholar his best known publications were in philology. He was the American secretary for the *New English Dictionary* (later the *Oxford English Dictionary*) in its earliest phase. He taught a course on English language at Columbia University in 1858-9, and published the lectures to acclaim; in 1860-1 he delivered a set of lectures at the Lowell Institute, Boston, and compiled this influential book from them.

See further David Lowenthal, *George Perkins Marsh: Versatile Vermonter* (New York: Columbia University Press, 1958).

George P. Marsh, *The Origin and History of the English Language and of the Early Literature it Embodies* (London: Sampson Low, 1862).

From: 'Lecture IV. Semi-Saxon Literature' (pp. 138-50).

That which is sown is not quickened except it die. The decay of an old literature is a necessary condition precedent for the origination of a new mode of intellectual life, in any people which has a prose and a poetry of its own. Had not the speech of the Anglo-Saxons perished, and with it the forms of literary effort which employed it as a medium, the broader-spreading and more generous vine, which now refreshes the whole earth, had never sprung from the regenerated root of that old stock.

The Norman Conquest gave the finishing stroke to the effete commonwealth of which I spoke in a former lecture, and through the intellectual winter and spring-time of three centuries, which followed that event, the germ of a new and nobler nationality lay buried in the soil, undergoing the slow and almost imperceptible changes that were gradually fitting it for a vigorous and prolific growth.

During this period, the Saxon, the Norman, the Danish settler and the few remains of the Celt were slowly melting and coalescing into a harmonized whole, if not into a homogeneous mass, and thus a new nation, a new character, and a new social and political influence in the world of letters, of art and of arms, were gradually developed.

The immediate moral and intellectual results of the Conquest were fully realized, and the character of the English intellect, taste and temper, so far at least as foreign action was concerned, was completely formed in the reign of Edward III.—the era of Langlande, and Chaucer, and Gower, and Wycliffe. The new ingredients had been introduced and incorporated, and a unity of feeling and spirit established, before those great writers commenced their labours. In short, English nationality had become full-grown, and all that it remained for the Continent to do, in its capacity of an informing influence, was to furnish new additions to the stock of words at the command of the English writer, and models of literary form to serve as leading-strings for the first essays of an incipient literature.

[...]

Philologists have found it impossible to fix, on linguistic grounds, a period when Anglo-Saxon can be said to have ceased and English to have begun; and this is one of the reasons why some are disposed to deny that any such metamorphosis ever took place, and to maintain the identity of the old speech and the new. The change from the one to the other was so gradual, that if we take any quarter or even half of a century, it is not easy to point out any marked characteristic difference between the general language of the beginning and the end of it, though particular manuscripts of the same work, differing not very much in date, sometimes exhibit dialects in very different states of resolution and reconstruction. The difficulty of discriminating the successive phases of the language by a chronological arrangement is much increased by the fact, that although there are numerous written monuments from every age of English history, yet there is, in the series of printed vernacular writings, almost a hiatus, which extends through a large part of the thirteenth century, or in other words through one of the most important eras of English philological revolution. Besides this, we are in many cases wholly unable to distinguish with certainty, or even with reasonable probability, dialectic or individual peculiarities from the landmarks of general change and progress; for notwithstanding the confidence with which critics assign particular writings to particular localities, upon internal evidence alone, we really know very little on the subject. In fact, in the present linguistic school, British as well as Continental, hastily generalized conclusions and positive assertion are so often substituted for sufficient documentary proof, that he, who studies the early philology of modern Europe only so far as it is exhibited in grammars and dictionaries, and speculative essays, is very frequent [*sic*] accumulating unsubstantial theories, instead of acquiring definite truths which can be shown to have ever had a real existence.

In ages, when a native literature has not yet been created, or the structural forms of language established by the authoritative example of great and generally circulated works of genius, there can be no standard of diction or of grammar. Most writers will be persons whose intellectual training has been acquired through older literatures and foreign tongues. Their first efforts will incline to be imitative, and they will follow alien models not only in theme and treatment, but even in grammatical composition. Every author will aim to be a philological reformer, and will adopt such system of orthography and of syntactical form and arrangement as accidental circumstances, or his own special tastes and habits of study, may have suggested to him. Hence no safe conclusions as to the common dialect of an age or country, at a period of linguistic transition, can be drawn from a single example, or from the consistent usage of a single writer. No historically probable theory of progress and change can explain the remarkable grammatical differences between the older and the not much later text of Layamon, or between either of these and the nearly contemporaneous work of Ormin, because the intervening period is entirely too short for such revolutions to have been accomplished. And in like manner, even after the language had assumed the general character which now marks it, we find between the two texts of the Wycliffite translations of the Bible, or rather between Hereford's and Wycliffe's translation and the first recension of it, grammatical differences, which it would be extravagant to ascribe to a general change in English syntax during the very few years that are supposed to have elapsed between the execution of the first version and the revision of it by Purvey.

Although the process of transformation from Anglo-Saxon to English was too gradual and too obscure to admit of precise chronological determination, yet subsequent epochs of change in our vernacular, after it had once dropped the formal, or, to speak more accurately, the inflectional peculiarities of Anglo-Saxon grammar, are somewhat more distinctly marked, and it is practicable to indicate its successive periods by tolerably well characterised and easily recognisable tokens, though, as in the history of other languages, the dates assumed as the beginning and the end of those epochs are somewhat arbitrary. It is not, however, that the later growth of English has actually been more *per saltum* than at earlier periods, but because, from the increasing uniformity of the written dialect — a natural result of the general circulation of the works of distinguished authors, and the consequent universal prevalence of the forms which they had consecrated — and also from the much greater number of literary monuments which are historically known to have been produced in different parts of the island, we can trace the history of the language, and follow all its movements with far greater facility than through periods when contemporaneous writers differed more widely and the philological memorials are fewer.

The London Philological Society, in its 'Proposal for the publication of a New English Dictionary', divides English, for philological purposes, into three periods: the first, from its rise, about 1250, to the Reformation, of which the first printed English translation of the New Testament, in 1526, may be taken as the earliest monument; the second, from the Reformation to and including the time of Milton, or from 1526 to 1674, the date of Milton's death; and the third, from Milton to our own day.[15]

---

[15] This was the original proposal for what was to become the *OED*; Herbert Coleridge, then the editor, made the division Marsh notes here. See K. M. Elisabeth Murray, *Caught in the Web of Words: James A. H. Murray and the 'Oxford English Dictionary'* (New Haven, Conn.: Yale University Press, 1977), p. 137.

These periods, I suppose, are fixed for lexicographical convenience in the collection of authorities, as I do not discover any other sufficient ground for the division. Neither is Craik's distribution altogether satisfactory.[16] The first, or Early English period of that author extends from 1250 to 1350; his second, or Middle English, from the latter date to 1530; and his third, or modern English, from the middle of the sixteenth century to the present day. This, however, seems an objectionable division as to the second period, because it embraces, in one group, writers so unlike in literary and philological character as Langlande and Wyatt, Wycliffe and Sir Thomas More; and as to the last, because it overlooks the philological revolution due to the introduction of printing, the more general diffusion of classical literature, and the first impulse of the Reformation, and classes together writers who have so little in common as Sir Philip Sidney and Walter Scott. I attach very little importance to these arbitrary divisions of the annals of our language and literature, but having on a former occasion adopted an arrangement not coinciding with either of these systems, I shall, both for the sake of uniformity, and because I have found it at once convenient and suited to my views of English philological history, substantially adhere to it in this course.[17] The first period I would, with Craik, consider as extending from about the middle of the thirteenth to the middle of the fourteenth century; the second would terminate with the third quarter of the sixteenth century; the third would embrace all subsequent phases of both the language and the literature down to the time of Milton, with whom the second period of the Philological Society concludes.

[...]

When then can England be said to have first possessed a native and peculiar literature? The mere existence of numerous manuscripts, in the popular dialect, belonging to any given period, does not prove the existence of a national literature at that epoch. A national literature commences only when the genius of the people expresses itself, through native authors, upon topics of permanent interest, in the grammatical and rhetorical forms best suited to the essential character of the vernacular, and of those who speak it. It is under such circumstances only that prose or poetry exerts a visible influence upon the speech, the tastes or the opinions of a nation, only by concurrent action and re-action that literature and associate life begin to stimulate and modify each other. In order that such effects may be produced in a mixed people, the races which enter into the composition of the nation, and the dialects of those races, must have, to a considerable extent, been

---

[16] See the table in the Craik extract above.

[17] George P. Marsh, *Lectures on English Language*, 4th edn, rev. and enl. (New York: Scribner, 1963), pp. 48-50.

harmonized and melted into one, and the people and the speech, though ethnologically and historically derived from different and unallied sources, must have become so far amalgamated as to excite a feeling of conscious individuality of nature and community of interest in the population, and of oneness of substance and structure in the tongue.

In a composite nation, such a union of races and of tongues strange to each other, such a neutralization and, finally, assimilation of antagonist elements, can only be the effect of a gradual interfusion and a long commingling, or of some *vis ab extra* which forces the reciprocally repellent particles into that near contiguity when, as in the case of magnetic bodies, repulsion ceases and attraction begins.

The English political and other occasional ballads and songs of the thirteenth, the beginning of the fourteenth and probably earlier centuries, do not constitute a literature, nor would they do so, were they ten times more numerous, because neither the public to which they were addressed, nor the speech in which they were penned, yet possessed any oneness of spirit or of dialectic form, and because they were founded on events too circumscribed in their action, and on interests too temporary in their nature, to appeal to the sympathies of more than a single class or province or generation.

These compositions were sometimes in Latin, sometimes in Norman-French, and sometimes in dialects of Saxon-English, which had lost all the power of poetic expression that characterized the ancient Anglican tongue, without having yet acquired anything of the graces of diction and adaptation to versified composition already developed in the neighbouring Romance languages; and lastly, they were sometimes macaronic. They cannot, therefore, be regarded as the expression of anything which deserves to be called the national mind, though, indeed, we trace in them, here and there, the germs which were soon to be quickened to a strong and genial growth.

The welding heat, which finally brought the constituents of English nationality into a consistent and coherent mass, was generated by the Continental wars of Edward III. The connection between those constituents had been hitherto a political aggregation, not a social union; they had formed a group of provinces and of races, not an entire and organized commonwealth. Up to this period, the Latin as the official language of the clergy, the Norman-French as that of the court, the nobility, and the multitude of associates, retainers, dependents, and tradesmen whom the Norman Conquest had brought over to the island, and the native English as the speech of the people of Saxon descent, had co-existed without much clashing interference, and without any powerfully active influence upon each other; and those who habitually spoke them, though apparently not violently hostile races, were, nevertheless, in their associations and their interests, almost as distinct and unrelated as the languages themselves.

There was, then, neither a national speech nor a national spirit, and of course there was and could be no national literature, until the latter half of the fourteenth century. True, the Ormulum, and the chronicles of Robert of Gloucester, and Robert of Brunne, voluminous works to be noticed hereafter, as well as many minor productions in the native language, existed earlier; but they were in no sense organic products of English genius, or stamped with any of the peculiarities which we now recognise as characteristic of the literature of England. We have no proof that any of these writings exerted much general influence in the formation of the English character or the English tongue, but they are important as evidences of the nature and amount of changes which political, social, and commercial causes, rather than higher intellectual impulses, had produced in the language and the people.

In one aspect, then, the general subject of our course properly begins with the age of Langlande and Wycliffe and Gower and Chaucer; but we propose to make a special study of the language, not merely as a passive medium of literary effort, but as an informing element in the character of that effort; and hence we must preface our more formal literary discussions with something more than a hasty glance at an era of blind and obscure influences—a stage of that organic, involuntary, and, so to speak, vegetal action by which the materials of our maternal tongue were assimilated, and its members fashioned, just as in animal physiology the powers of nature form the body and its organs before the breath of conscious life is breathed into them.

[...]

I shall have occasion to illustrate the Dark Age of English philological history, the thirteenth century, by more or less full references to many of its most important relics, but the attention of the student should be specially directed to the four most conspicuous monuments which serve to mark the progress of change from the Anglo-Saxon to the English. These are Layamon's Chronicle of Brutus, the Ancren Riwle, the Ormulum, and Robert of Gloucester's Chronicle. The dialect of the first three of these is generally called Semi-Saxon; that of the last Early-English, or simply, English. Excepting the Ancren Riwle, they are, unfortunately, all in verse. I say unfortunately, because in tracing the history of the fluctuations of language, prose writings are generally much more to be depended on than poetry. The dialect of poetry is, for rhetorical reasons, always more or less removed from the common speech, and the fetters of rhythm, metre, alliteration, and rhyme inevitably affect both the choice of words and the employment of inflected forms. [...]

8. Carl Friedrich Koch (1813-72)

The career trajectory of Carl Friedrich Koch was similar to that of Eduard Mätzner. He studied theology at Jena in the 1830s and later taught in schools. His work on German grammar and the production of an elementary grammar handbook led him to Anglo-Saxon, on which he wrote several articles. His English grammar was his major work, and was widely held to supersede Mätzner's. A second edition was produced by Julius Zupitza in 1882.

C. Friedrich Koch, *Historische Grammatik der englischen Sprache*, 3 vols. (Weimar: Böhlau, 1863-68).

From: I, 7-11.

Diese deutschen Dialecte, welche seit dem 5 Jahrh. in England erklangen von der südlichen Küste bis zum schottischen Gebirgslande, von der Ostküste bis zu den Bergen von Cornwallis, Wales und Cumberland, benennt man mit dem gemeinsamen Namen des Angelsächsischen — ein Name, der erst später eintritt und das einfachere Sächsisch, wie die Briten sagten, oder Anglisch, Englisch (on englisc, Aelfred) verdrängt. Es laßen sich zwei Perioden desselben unterscheiden, die am bezeichnendsten mit Altangelsächsisch und Neuangelsächsisch genannt werden. Englische Grammatiker nennen letztere Halbsächsisch (semi-saxon).

1) Das AAgs. (= Altangelsächsisch) liegt in einer reichen Literatur vor aus früher Zeit bis gegen 1100. Die schriftlichen Denkmale sind zum Theil frühe [*sic*] abgefaßt, wenn auch die Handschriften, die wir besitzen, wohl schwerlich über das 10. Jahrh. hinaufgehen. Ein Beowulf konnte z. B. nur niedergeschrieben werden, als das Interesse an der alten Heldensage noch nicht geschwächt war durch die schweren Kämpfe in Britannien und der alte Heidenglaube der neuen christlichen Bildung noch nicht als ein Greuel erschien. Auch die Sprache weist Abfaßung und Handschrift weit aus einander. Die kurzen, abgerißenen Sätze, die oft unverbunden sich folgen, der sparsame Gebrauch der Mittel, deren die Aelfred'sche Sprache sich zu logisch genauerem Ausdrucke bedient, wie Artikel, Pronomen, Präposition und Conjunction, weisen auf eine frühe Zeit hin, während die Wortformen denen des 9. Jahrh. fast gleich stehen. Eine so geringe lautliche Aenderung aber im Verlaufe einiger Jahrhunderte neben so großer syntactischer Verschiedenheit läßt sich nur durch die Annahme erklären, daß die frühern Satzformen geblieben, die Wortformen aber fortgeschrieben sind.

2) Die zweite Periode, das Neuangelsächsische, reicht etwa von 1100 bis gegen die Mitte des 13. Jahrh. Die Entwicklung der beiden Dialecte, des südlichen und des nördlichen, zeigen Laʒ. = Laʒamon's brut, or Chronicle of Britain; a poetical semi-saxon paraphrase of the Brut of Wace. By Sir Frederic Madden. 3 vols. London [Society of Antiquaries,] 1847 und Orm. = The

Ormulum. Now first edited from the original manuscript in the Bodleian with notes and a glossary by Robert Meadows White, 2 vols. Oxford [Oxford University Press,] 1852.

Laʒamon war Priester in Ernleʒe am Severn, südös[t]lich von Bewdley, Worcestershire. Der Schluß seines Werkes fällt in's Jahr 1205 (cf. Vers 31977). Der Herausgeber stellt zwei Handschriften neben einander, A und B; die geschwächten Formen der letzteren laßen diese jünger erscheinen. Laʒ. vertritt die Sprache des Südens und Westens im 12. Jahrh. — Orm soll im Anfang des 13. Jahrh. in Northumbrien gelebt haben. Man bringt die Abfaßung seiner Paraphrase in Verbindung mit dem 1229 auf dem Concil zu Toulouse erfolgten Verbote, daß die Laien die Bibel haben sollen. Allein entweder muß die Abschleifung der Bildungen und Flexionen im Norden rascher erfolgt sein oder die Abfaßung fällt in eine spätere Zeit. Orm zeichnet sich aus durch sichere und einfache Vocalisation und durch genaue Bezeichnung der Lautverhältnisse, besonders der der Quantität.

Der Sprachstoff ist fast durchgehends deutsch, Laʒamon hat etwa nur 90 französische Wörter, und Orm fügt nordische Elemente hinzu. Die Formen erfahren durchaus Schwächung, die vollen Vocale werden zu einförmigen e und auch diese fallen bei Laʒ. oft ab. Laʒ. bewahrt noch den Unterschied zwischen starker und schwacher Substantivflexion und die Unterscheidung des Genus; Orm giebt sie auf und die Flexionen mindern sich zum Genitiv Sing. und zum Plural. In der Pronominalflexion werden die Genitive und der Dual selten. Laʒ. hat die doppelte Adjectivflexion, aber ohne Unterscheidung; Orm beide zerrüttet. Die Ablaute beginnen in Laʒ. zu schwanken, während Orm sie in auffallender Reinheit bewahrt. — Das geringe französische Element scheint sich, bis auf die Eigennamen, deutscher Betonung zu fügen.

These Germanic dialects, which since the fifth century resounded in England from the southern coast up to the Scottish Highlands, from the east coast to the hills of Cornwall, Wales and Cumberland, are given the common name of 'Anglo-Saxon' — a name which appears at a later stage and which supplants the simpler 'Saxon', as the British called it, or 'Anglish', 'English' (*on englisc*, Aelfred). Two periods of this language can be distinguished, which are most appropriately named 'Old Anglo-Saxon' and 'New Anglo-Saxon'. English grammarians name the latter Half-Saxon (semi-Saxon).

1) Old Anglo-Saxon exists in the form of a rich literature from early times up to about 1100. Some of the written monuments are composed early, though the manuscripts we possess hardly go beyond the tenth century. A *Beowulf*, for example, could only be written down when the interest in the old heroic epic had not yet been weakened by the hard struggles in Britain, and the old paganism had not yet become a horror to the new Christian education. Also the language shows composition and manuscript to be widely separated. The short, disconnected sentences, which often follow on one another in an

unconnected manner; the sparing use of the means that the Alfredian language makes use of for a logically more exact expression — such as the article, pronoun, preposition and conjunction — suggest an early period, while the word-forms are almost the same as those of the ninth century. But such a minor phonetic change in the course of several centuries, beside so great a syntactic difference, can only be explained by the assumption that the early sentence-forms remained, while the word-forms were updated.

[Koch now discusses 'Old Anglo-Saxon', in which he includes *Beowulf, The Fight at Finnesburh, The Anglo-Saxon Chronicle*, and the poetry of the Exeter Book.]

2) The second period, the New Anglo-Saxon, lasts from about 1100 up to the middle of the thirteenth century. Laȝamon's *Brut* [Laȝamon's brut, or Chronicle of Britain; a poetical semi-saxon paraphrase of the Brut of Wace. By Sir Frederic Madden. 3 vols. London [Society of Antiquaries,] 1847] and the *Ormulum* [The Ormulum. Now first edited from the original manuscript in the Bodleian with notes and a glossary by Robert Meadows White, 2 vols. Oxford [Oxford University Press,] 1852] show the development of the two dialects, the southern and the northern.

Laȝamon was a priest in Erneley on the Severn, south-east of Bewdley, Worcestershire. He concluded his work in the year 1205 (cf. line 31977). The editor places the two manuscripts, A and B, side by side; the weakened forms of the latter make it appear to be the more recent. Laȝamon represents the language of the south and west in the twelfth century. Orm is said to have lived at the beginning of the thirteenth century in Northumbria. The composition of his paraphrase has been connected with the prohibition of the council of Toulouse in 1229 of laypeople owning the Bible. However, either the smoothing away of forms and inflections must have taken place more quickly in the North, or the composition must date from a later time. Orm is notable for an assured and simple vowel-system and precise indication of the phonetic system, especially as regards quantity.

The vocabulary is Germanic almost throughout; Laȝamon has only about ninety French words, and Orm adds Nordic elements besides. The forms definitely undergo weakening; the full vowels become uniform 'e' and even these are frequently dropped in Laȝamon. Laȝamon preserves the difference between strong and weak noun inflections and the differentiation of gender; Orm abandons them and the inflections are reduced to the genitive singular and the plural. In the pronominal declension the genitive and the dual have become infrequent. Laȝamon has the double adjective declension, but without differentiation; Orm has both in corrupted form. In Laȝamon the ablaut is beginning to falter, whereas Orm preserves it in striking clarity. The small French element, except for the proper names, appears to be brought into line with Germanic pronunciation.

9. John Earle (1824-1903)

John Earle was a Fellow of Oriel College from 1848 and twice Professor of Anglo-Saxon at the University of Oxford, first taking the Chair in 1849 when it was still a five-year post. He was reappointed to it in 1876 and held it the rest of his life. The present textbook was one of his more popular works; he also edited a parallel-text edition of the Parker and Peterborough versions of *The Anglo-Saxon Chronicle* for Macmillan in 1865. Earle was the first general editor of what became the complete works of Chaucer produced by Oxford University Press, but he was not a success in this position and resigned before the work was much advanced.

John Earle, *The Philology of the English Tongue* (Oxford: Clarendon Press, 1871).

From: 'Historic Sketch of the Rise and Formation of the English Language' (pp. 16-97).

[Earle opens with a lengthy description of the place of the Anglo-Saxon language in the Indo-European group and then of Anglo-Saxon itself. In the course of this he notes the following:]

The name of 'Saxon' has always adhered to our nation, though we have seemed almost as if we had been willing to divest ourselves of it. We have called our country *England*, and our language *English*: yet our neighbours west and north, the Welsh and the Gael, have still called us Saxons, and our language Saxonish. It has become the literary habit of recent times to use the term 'Saxon' as a distinction for the early period of our history and language and literature, and to reserve the term 'English' for the later period. There is some degree of literary impropriety in this, because the Saxons called their own language *Englisc*. On this ground some critics insist that we should let the word *English* stand for the whole extent of our insular history, which they would divide into Old English, Middle English, and New English. But on the whole, the terms already in use seem bolder, and more distinct. They enable us to distinguish between Saxon and Anglian; and they also comprise the united nation under the compound term Anglo-Saxon. As expressive of the dominant power, it is not very irregular to call the whole nation briefly SAXON. [The description of 'Saxon' continues:]

Such were some of the features of the Saxon speech, as well as we can illustrate them by reference to modern English. Speaking relatively to the times, it was not a rude language, but probably the most disciplined of all the vernaculars of western Europe, and certainly the most cultivated of all the dialects of the Gothic barbarians. [...]

Such was the state of our language when its insular security was disturbed by the Norman invasion. Great and speedy must have been the effect of the

Conquest in ruining the ancient grammar, which rested almost entirely on literary culture.[18] The leading men in the state having no interest in the vernacular, its cultivation fell immediately into neglect. The chief of the Saxon clergy deposed or removed, who should now keep up that supply of religious Saxon literature, of the copiousness of which we may judge even in our day by the considerable remains that have outlived hostility and neglect? Now that the Saxon landowners were dispossessed, who should patronise the Saxon bard, and welcome the man of song in the halls of mirth?

The shock of the Conquest gave a death-blow to Saxon literature. There is but one of the Chroniclers that goes on to any length after the Conquest; and one of them stops short exactly at A.D. 1066, as if that sad year had bereft his task of all further interest. We have Saxon poetry up to that date or very near to it, but we have none for some generations after it. The Englisc language continued to be spoken by the masses who could speak no other; and here and there a secluded student continued to write in it. But its honours and emoluments were gone, and a gloomy period of depression lay before the Saxon language as before the Saxon people. It is not too much to say that the Norman Conquest entailed the *dissolution* of the old cultivated language of the Saxons, the literary Englisc. The inflection-system could not live through this trying period. Just as we accumulate superfluities about us in prosperity, but in adversity we get rid of them as encumbrances, and we like to travel light when we have only our own legs to carry us — just so it happened to the Englisc language. For now all these sounding terminations that made so handsome a figure in Saxon courts — the -AN, the -UM, the -ERA and the -ANA, the -IGENNE and -IGENDUM, — all these, superfluous as bells on idle horses, were laid aside when the nation had lost its old political life and its pride of nationality, and had received leaders and teachers who spoke a strange tongue.

But this was not the only effect of the introduction of a new language into the country. The Normans had learnt by their sojourn in France to speak French, and this foreign language they brought with them to England. Sometimes this language is spoken of as the Norman-French. [...]

The Saxon had never ceased to be the speech of the body of the people. The Conquest could not alter this fact. What the Conquest did was to destroy the cultivated Englisc, which depended for its propagation upon literature and literary men. This once extinct, there was no central or standard language. The French language in some respects supplied the place of a standard

---

[18] This is one example of the way in which Earle's writing rests on popular ideas rather than extensive scholarship; the persistent notion that the Conquest was entirely responsible for the mutation of Anglo-Saxon had been refuted by R. G. Latham 30 years before (see the extract from his work).

language, as the medium of intercourse between persons in the best ranks of society. The native speech bereft of its central standard, fell abroad again. It fell back into that divided condition, in which each speaker and each writer is guided by the dialect of his own locality, undisciplined by any central standard of propriety. Our language became dialectic. And hence it comes to pass that of the authors whose books are preserved from the year A.D. 1100 to 1350, no two of them are uniform in dialect; each speaks a tongue of its own. It must be understood here, and wherever figures are given to distinguish periods in the history of language, that it is intended for the convenience of writer and reader, for distinctness of arrangement and as an aid to the memory, rather than as a rigid limit. For in such things the two bordering forms so shade off and blend into one another, that they are not to be rigidly outlined any more than the primary colours in the rainbow.

For convenience sake [*sic*], we may divide the 'transition' into two parts, and add a third era for the infancy of the national language:—

TRANSITION.

Broken Saxon (Latin documentary period) from 1100 to 1215
Early English (the French documentary period) 1215 to 1350
First national English 1350 to 1550.

Of the first division of this period, the grand landmarks are the two poems of Layamon's *Brut*, and the *Ormulum*; the *Brut* representing the dialect of the Upper Severn; and the *Ormulum* having been written (we will say by way of a definition) somewhere between London and Peterborough.

The *Brut* of Layamon, a work which embodies in a poetic form the legends of British history, and which exceeds 30,000 lines, has been splendidly edited, with an English translation, by Sir Frederic Madden, 1847. [...] There is no direct intimation of the date at which it was written, but the editor has fixed on 1205, for reasons which appear conclusive. But we have only to look at such a poem as this to perceive at once that it was not the work of any one year or even of a few years. It must be regarded as the literary hobby of the whole life of Layamon the priest, who lived at Areley Kings, on the west bank of the Severn, opposite Stourport, and who there served the church, being the chaplain and inmate of 'the good knight' of the parish. And hence it is that the language runs back and claims a near relationship to that of the close of the latest Saxon Chronicle: nearer than we might have expected from the space which separates them in geography. But we must remember that we know nothing of Layamon's birthplace and the scene of his education. We are only informed as to the scene of his life-long service. And though his diction bears marks of the western dialect, yet this cannot be affirmed exclusively. It would be tolerably safe to say that he wrote in Southern English, inclining to the western dialect. In other words, Layamon represents the old dialect of Wessex in the twelfth century. But it is easier to describe Layamon by his literary than by his local affinities. He is the last writer who retains an echo of the literary Englisc. Though he wrote for popular use, yet the scholar is apparent, and he had conned the old native literature enough to give a tinge to his diction, and to preserve a little of the ancient grammar.

[Earle goes on to discuss a few of the features of the text and then to mention the second text of the *Brut*, which he felt 'was plainly written in Northumbria, and which bears some distinct features of Northern English'. He then quotes some short passages.]

The *Ormulum* may be proximately dated at A.D. 1215.[19] As the date cannot be given with precision, the date of *Magna Carta* is here selected, for the sake of its bearing on the subject, as will be seen presently. The *Ormulum* is a versified narrative of the Gospels, addressed by Ormin or (curtly) Orm to his brother Walter, and after his own name called by the author 'Ormulum'; by which designation it is commonly known. [...] As the *Brut* represents the western type of English, so this does the eastern. In this poem we find for the first time 'English' in the mature form. Layamon has the forms *englisc*, *englis*, *ænglis*, *anglisce*, &c.; but Orm has *enngliss*, and still more frequently the fully developed form *ennglissh*.

The excess of consonants with which this word is written is a constant feature of the *Ormulum*. The author was one of Nature's philologists, and he displayed his talent by attempting a phonetic system of spelling. [...]

Before we pass on to the next group, to those which are more particularly known as *Early English*, a remark should be made on the significance of the date 1215, to which we are now arrived. It is a marked date as being that of Magna Carta; and it is the year in which French first appears in our public instruments. After the Conquest Latin was the documentary language up to this date, when French began and soon became general. [...]

The darkest time of depression for our language has now passed. We approach a kind of dawn. A new literature begins to rise, first in dissonant dialects, and then in a central and standard form. The language had admitted a variety of new material which had distinctly affected its complexion. One particular class of words shall be noticed in this place as the result of the French rule in England. This is a group of words which will serve to depict the times in which they were stamped on our speech. They are the utterance of the violent and selfish passions.

Almost all the sinister and ill-favoured words which were in the English language at the time of Shakspeare, owed their origin to this unhappy era.

---

[19] See above, note 10, on the dating of the *Ormulum*, and also the extract from Koch.

The malignant passions were let loose, as if without control of reason or of religion; men hotly pursued after the objects of their ambition, covetousness, or other passions, till they grew insensible to every feeling of tenderness and humanity; they regarded one another in no other light but as obstructives or auxiliaries in their own path. What wonder that such a state of society furnished little or nothing for expressing the delicate emotions, while it supplied the nascent English with such a mass of opprobrious epithets as to have lasted, with few occasional additions, till the present day. Of these words a few may be cited by way of example. And first I will instance the word *juggler*. This word has two senses. It is first a person who makes a livelihood by amusing tricks. Secondly, it has the moral sense of an impostor or deceiver. The latter is the prevalent modern use. Both these senses originated in the French period of our history.

[Earle gives many more examples of 'sinister and ill-favoured words', all derived from French.]

The same period is stigmatised by another bad characteristic, and that is, the facility with which it disparaged good and respectable words.

Villain [...] was simply a class-name, by which a humble order of men was designated; *ceorl* was a Saxon name of like import: both of these became disparaged at the time we speak of into the injurious sense of *villain* and *churl*.

[Further examples are given, to show how French words tend to pertain to low-life, or have had a pejorative effect on the English language.]

[...]

But the most remarkable of all the productions of the transition period is the poem entitled *The Owl and the Nightingale*. Its locality is established by internal evidence, as having been written at or near Portesham in Dorsetshire. It is a singular combination of archaic English with ripe and mature versification. The forms of words and even the terms of expression frequently recall Mr. Barnes's *Poems in the Dorset Dialect*.[20] A prominent feature is the frequent use of *v* where we write *f*, as *vo* for foe; *vlize* = flies; *vairer* = fairer; *vram* = from; *vor* = for; but *so for-vorþ* for 'so far forth'; *ware-vore* = wherefore; &c. In connection with which it ought to be remembered that we in modern English use the *v* in many places where the Saxon orthography had *f*. Instances:—heaven, Saxon *heofon*; love, Saxon *lufu*; but this alteration avoids initial *f*'s which remain with us as in Saxon times. The change may be well illustrated by the numeral *five*, Saxon *fife*; where the first *f* stands unaltered, but the second has been transformed to *v*. The fact is that the break

---

[20] William Barnes's *Poems of Rural Life, in the Dorset Dialect* first appeared in 1844 and thereafter in several editions; the explicit motivation for the work was Barnes's contention that the dialect was purer than standard modern English and closer to Anglo-Saxon.

in the continuity of our literary language opened the way for much of west-country style that never could have been admitted unless such an interruption had taken place. It has already been shewn above that the Saxon literary language was not really native to Wessex, that it was not originally Saxon at all, but Anglian. This poem may safely be pronounced the oldest extant specimen of the pure Wessex dialect. And when we add that it is one of the most lovely idylls of any age or of any language, we hope that some Englishmen will be induced to master the dialects of the thirteenth century, in order to be able to appreciate this exquisite pastoral. Its date may be somewhere about A.D. 1280.[21] So far from substituting *s* for *sc* (=*sh*) this poem spells *schaltu, schule, scholde, schonde, schame, schakeð, schende, schuniet, scharp*, &c. On the other hand it tends to soften the *ch* guttural.

In the *Romance of King Alexander* we first begin to hear a sound as of the coming English language. Most of the transition pieces are widely distinct from the diction of Gower and Chaucer, but this has the air of a preparation for those writers. This romance sometimes resembles not distantly the *Romaunt of the Rose*. The feature which most claims attention is the working in of French words with the English. This is a translation of the poem which was the grand and general favorite before the Romance of the Rose superseded it. It was a French work of the year A.D. 1200, consisting of 20,000 long twelve-syllable lines, a measure which thenceforward became famous in literature, and took the name of 'Alexandrine', after this romance. The English version was made some time in the thirteenth century, in a lax tetrameter. It was not till Spenser that the Alexandrine metre was systematically employed in our national poetry.

As the poem was originally French, this may partly account for the number of French words and phrases in the translation. Partly, but not altogether: *Havelok* is from a French original, but it is very free from French words. The fact seems to be that this translation carries us in to the atmosphere of the court; not only by the variety and pureness of the French words in it, but also by its metrical resemblance to that eminently courtly work, Chaucer's *Romaunt of the Rose*. Moreover, the language is in other respects so like the court-English of the fourteenth century, that we cannot but regard it as in a special manner one of the dawning lights of the standard language. In Chaucer and Gower the French words are often so Anglicised, that a reader might pass them for pure Saxon. Not so in the Romance of King Alexander. The two languages do not yet appear blended together, but only mixed bilingually. The following lines will illustrate this crude mixture of French with English:

---

[21] One of the two manuscripts of the poem (Jesus College Oxford 29) may well date from this time, but composition is usually dated to the late twelfth or early thirteenth century.

1.   That us telleth the *maistres saunz faile*.
2.   Hy ne ben no more *verreyment*.
3.   And to have horses *auenaunt*,
     To hem stalworth and *asperaunt*
4.   Of alle men hy ben *queintest*.
5.   Toppe and rugge, and croupe and *cors*
     Is *semblabel* to an hors.

[Earle goes on to discuss Robert of Gloucester, especially in relation to his statement on the bilingual nature of England around 1300.[22] The language, until well into the fourteenth century is diverse and without 'convergency to a common type' (66).]

In fact we have a phenomenon to account for. In the fourteenth century there suddenly appeared a standard English language. It appeared at once in full vigour, and was acknowledged on all hands without dispute. The study of the previous age does not make us acquainted with a general process of convergency towards this result, but rather indicates that each locality was getting confirmed in its own peculiar habits of speech, and that the divergence was growing wider. Now there appeared a mature form of English which was generally received.

The two writers of the fourteenth century who most powerfully display this language are Chaucer and Gower. Piers Plowman is in a dialect; Wiclif's Bible Version is in a dialect: but Chaucer and Gower write in a speech which is thenceforward recognised as THE ENGLISH LANGUAGE, and which before their time is hardly found. This seems to admit of but one explanation. It must have been simply the language that had formed itself in the court about the person of the monarch. Chaucer and Gower differ from the other chief writers of their time in this particular, which they have in common between themselves, that they were both conversant with court life, and moved in the highest regions of English society. They wrote in fact *King's English*. This advantage, joined to the excellence of the works themselves, procured for these two writers, but more especially for Chaucer, the preference over all that had written in English. We have not yet done indeed with provincial specimens, even among our most important examples of English; but we are from this date in possession of a standard, relatively to which all diverging forms of English are local and secondary. Having a standard, we are now in a position for the first time to designate all other English as 'provincial'.

[...]

---

[22] For this passage, which Earle quotes, see William Aldis Wright, ed. *The Metrical Chronicle of Robert of Gloucester*, 2 vols (London: HMSO, 1887), II, 541-44, ll. 7494-7547.

[Earle quotes various kinds of 'English', beginning with Henry III's proclamation of 1258, which he views as an artificial form of English composed by a French speaker struggling in the vernacular. A letter of Prince Henry to his father Henry IV in 1402 is seen as the 'King's English'; he also quotes from 'The Death of Edward I'.[23]]

But it is in the writings of Chaucer and Gower that we have for the first time the full display of King's English. These two names have been coupled together all through the whole course of English literature. Skelton, the poet laureate of Henry VII, joins the two names together. So does our literary king, James I. So have all writers who have had occasion to speak of the fourteenth century, down to the present day. [...] Thus these two names have grown together, and their connection is soldered by habit and tradition. One is apt to imagine, previous to a study of their works, that they were a *par nobile fratrum*, brothers and equals in poetry and genius, and that they had contributed equally, or nearly so, towards the making of English literature. But this is very far from being the case. That which united them at first, and which continues to be the sole ground of coupling their names together, is just this, — that they wrote in the same general strain and in the same language. By this is meant, first, that they were both versed in the learning then most prized, and both delivered what they had to say in the terms then most admired; and secondly, that both wrote the English of the court. If affinity of genius had been the basis of classification, the author of *Piers Plowman* had more right to rank with Chaucer than the prosaic Gower. But in this Chaucer and Gower are united in that they both wrote the particular form of English which was henceforward to be established as the standard form of the national language, and their books were the leading English classics of the best society down to the opening of a new era under Elizabeth.

And now the question naturally rises, What was this new language? what was it that distinguished the King's English from the various forms of provincial English of which examples have been given in the group of writers noticed above, or from Piers Plowman and other contemporaries of Chaucer? In answer to this it may be said, that it is no more possible to convey the idea of a language by description than of a piece of music. The writings must be looked into by all who desire to realise the distinctions here to be pointed out. A moderate course of reading, such as that laid out in Mr. Morris's *Specimens*

---

[23] On the proclamation, see above, note 7; the letter is in facsimile (with a transcript) in Colonel Sir Henry James, *Facsimiles of National Manuscripts From William the Conqueror to Queen Anne*, 4 vols (Southampton: Ordnance Survey Office, 1865-68), II (1865), 39; for 'The Death of Edward I', see R. T. Davies, *Medieval English Lyrics* (London: Faber, 1963), pp. 91-94.

of Early English would enable a student to follow our description.[24]
[A long discussion of the French influence on the 'King's English' ensues, in which Earle concludes that this influence was paramount in forming that version of English. Dialects of English are distinguished by the fact that they were not strongly influenced by French. He concludes:]

If we want to describe the transition from the Saxon state-language of the eleventh century to the Court-English of the fourteenth, and to reduce the description to its simplest terms, it comes in fact just to this: That a French family settled in England, and edited the English language.

---

[24] Richard Morris, *Specimens of Early English Selected from the Chief English Authors A.D. 1250-A.D. 1400* (Oxford: Clarendon Press, 1867). This was the chief textbook for Middle English of the time; a revised version appeared under the authorship of Morris and Walter Skeat in 1872.

10. Thomas Laurence Kington Oliphant (b. 1831)

Thomas Laurence Kington Oliphant was a FSA and took an MA at Balliol College, Oxford, before being called to the bar at the Inner Temple. In 1864 he succeeded to a Scottish estate, and thereafter devoted himself to historical and philological writings. *The Sources of Standard English* was republished in revised and greatly expanded form as *The Old and Middle English* (London: Macmillan, 1878) and as a separate work, *The New English* (1886). These works argue a similar view of the linguistic map of English to that which appears below.

T. L. Kington Oliphant, *The Sources of Standard English* (London: Macmillan, 1873).

From: Chapter 3, 'The Rise of the New English' (pp. 182-84).

[Oliphant's scheme is Old English, 680-1120 and Middle English, 1120-1300 (p. 35). The last date is explained as follows:]

It was in 1303 that Robert of Brunne (known also as Robert Manning) began to compile the Handlyng Synne, the work which, more clearly than any former one, foreshadowed the road that English literature was to tread from that time forward. Like many other lays of King Edward I's time, the new piece was a translation from a French poem; the Manuel des Pechés had been written about thirty years earlier by William of Waddington. The English poem differs from all the others that had gone before it in its diction; for it contains a most scanty proportion of those Teutonic words that were soon to drop out of speech, and a most copious proportion of French words. Indeed there are so many foreign words, that we should set the writer fifty years later than his true date, had he not himself *written* it down. In this book we catch our first glimpse of many a word and idiom, that were afterwards to live for ever in the English Bible and Prayer Book, works still in the womb of Time. Indeed the new Teutonic idioms that took root in our speech after this age were few in number, a mere drop in the bucket, if we compare them with the idioms imported between 1120 and 1300. This shows what we owe to Robert Manning; even as the highest praise of our Revolution of 1688 is, that it was our last. The Handlyng Synne is indeed a landmark worthy of the carefullest study. I shall give long extracts from it, and I shall further add specimens of the English spoken in many other shires between 1300 and 1340. We are lucky in having so many English manuscripts, drawn up at this particular time: the contrasts are strongly marked. Thus it will be easy to see that the Lincolnshire bard may be called the patriarch of the New English, much as Cadmon was of the Old English six hundred years earlier. [...]

The Handlyng Synne shows how the different tides of speech, flowing from Southern, Western, and Northern shires alike, met in the neighbourhood of Rutland, and all helped to shape the New English. [...]

11. Henry Sweet (1845-1912)

The Anglo-Saxonist and phonetician Henry Sweet was another English scholar formed under the influence of the work of Rask and Grimm. He spent time at the University of Heidelberg in 1864 before entering Balliol College, Oxford, in 1869 and becoming involved in London's Philological Society. But he was repeatedly denied the many university positions he applied for and published his many and influential works as an independent scholar. His widely used *Anglo-Saxon Reader* appeared in 1876 and he belatedly took up a Readership in phonetics at Oxford in 1901.

For biography and critical assessment see Michael K. C. MacMahon, 'Henry Sweet', in Damico, ed. *MSBS2*, 167-75.

Henry Sweet, *A History of English Sounds: From the Earliest Period, including an Investigation of the General Laws of Sound Change, and Full Word Lists* (London: English Dialect Society, 1874; republished from the *Transactions of the Philological Society* for 1873-74).

From: 'On the Periods of English' (pp. 157-61).

One of the most troublesome questions of English philology is that of the designation of its various stages. I have throughout this paper adopted the threefold division of Old, Middle, and Modern: it will, therefore, be necessary to say a few words in its justification.

The first question is, shall we retain the name 'Anglo-Saxon' for the earliest period of our language, or discard it entirely? The great majority of English scholars are decidedly hostile to the word. They argue that it is a barbarous half-Latin compound, which, although justifiable as applied to a political confederation of Angles and Saxons, is entirely misleading when applied to the *language* spoken by these tribes, implying, as it does, that the English language before the Conquest was an actual mixture of the Anglian and Saxon dialects. The reverse was of course the case, and we consequently have to distinguish between the Anglian dialect of Anglo-Saxon and the Saxon dialect of Anglo-Saxon.[25] The most serious objection, however, to the word Anglo-Saxon is that it conceals the unbroken development of our language, and thrusts the oldest period of our language outside the pale of our sympathies. Hence, to a great extent, the slowness with which the study of our language makes its way among the great mass of educated people in

---

[25] If any period of our language is to be called 'Anglo-Saxon', let it be the present one — as far, at least, as the literary language is concerned, which is really a mixture of Saxon and Anglian forms. – S.

England — if people can be called educated who are ignorant of the history of their own language.
[Sweet criticises an article on Old English by an American philologist.]

While differing from Professor March on these points, I fully agree with him in protesting against the loose way in which 'Old English' is made to designate any period from Alfred to Chaucer. It is quite clear that the inflectional stage of our language must have a distinctive name, and therefore that Old English must be reserved for it alone. The difficulty is with the later stages. The period I call Middle English is now often called 'Early English', while those who retain 'Anglo-Saxon' call the intermediate periods 'Semi-Saxon' or 'Old English', while others make various arbitrary distinctions between 'Early', 'Old', and 'Middle' English. It does not seem to be generally acknowledged that each of these terms really implies a definite correlative, that if we call one period 'Early', we are bound to have a 'Late' one, and that 'Middle' implies a beginning and an end — to talk therefore of one period as 'Early', as opposed to a 'Middle' one, is entirely arbitrary.

Such divisions err also in being too minute. When we consider how one period merges into another, and how the language changed with much greater rapidity in the North than in the South, we see that it is necessary to start with a few broad divisions, not with impracticably minute ones.

I propose, therefore, to start with the three main divisions of *Old*, *Middle*, and *Modern*, based mainly on the inflectional characteristics of each stage. Old English is the period of *full* inflections, (*nama*, *gifan*, *caru*), Middle English of *levelled* inflections (*naame*, *given*, *caare*), and Modern English of *lost* inflections (*naam*, *giv*, *caar*). We have besides two periods of *transition*, one in which *nama* and *name* exist side by side, and another in which final *e* is beginning to drop. The latter is of very little importance, the former, commonly called Semi-Saxon (a legitimate abbreviation of Semi-Anglo-Saxon), is characterized by many far-reaching changes. I propose, therefore to call the first the *Transition* period *par excellence*, distinguishing the two, when necessary, as first and second Transition, the more important one being generally called simply *Transition* or *Transition-English*.

Whenever minute divisions are wanted, *Early* and *Late* can be used — Early Old, Late Middle, Early Modern, etc. Still minuter distinctions can be made by employing *Earlier*, *Earliest*, etc., till we fall back on the century or decade.

These divisions could also be applied to the different dialect-names. Thus *Old Anglian* would be equivalent to 'Anglian dialect of Old English', *Modern Saxon* would designate the Dorsetshire dialect, etc.

As regards the Northern dialects of the Middle period, they ought strictly to be classed as Modern, as they soon lost the final *e* entirely. But as they have all the other characteristics of the Middle period, it seems most convenient to take the dominant speech of Chaucer and Gower as our criterion.

12. Richard Morris (1833-94)

A schoolmaster, Richard Morris was not a powerful personality like his colleagues Skeat and Furnivall, and his work has not had the continued impact of theirs. But he should be thought of as almost equal with them in influence on the construction of Middle English late in the nineteenth century in his role as a prolific editor for the Early English Text Society. He produced a complete Chaucer edition before Skeat and he wrote several textbooks standard in their time. *Specimens of Early English* (1867) was the first handbook in Middle English studies. When he produced *Elementary Lessons*, Morris was president of the Philological Society.

Richard Morris, *Elementary Lessons in Historical English Grammar* (London: Macmillan, 1874).

From: pp. 33-34.

Periods of the English Language.
    (1) Old English (A.D. 450-1100). [...]
    (2) Early English (A.D. 1100-1250).—The language in this period shows many changes both in orthography and grammar. In the first part of this period the modifications were chiefly orthographical, but they affected the endings of words, and thus led the way to the grammatical changes which took place in the latter part of the thirteenth century.
    To the earlier part of this period belong the following works: the *Brut*, written by *Layamon*; the *Ormulum*, by *Ormin*; the *Ancren Riwle*, &c. To the latter half belong the *Story of Genesis and Exodus*, the *Owl and Nightingale*, &c.
    (3) Middle English (A.D. 1250-1485).—Most of the older inflexions of nouns and adjectives have now disappeared. The verbal inflexions are much altered, and many strong verbs have been replaced by weak ones. To the first half of this period belong a *Metrical Chronicle*, and *Lives of Saints*, attributed to Robert of Gloucester; Langtoft's *Metrical Chronicle*, translated by *Robert of Brunne*, and the *Handlyng Synne*, by the same writer; the *Pricke of Conscience*, by Hampole; the *Ayenbite of Inwyt* by Dan Michel of Northgate, Kent. To the second half belong the works of *Wicliffe*, *William Langley* (or *Langland*), *Gower*, and *Chaucer*, &c.
    (4) Modern English, from A.D. 1485 to the present time. We might subdivide this period into two parts, calling the language in the earlier period from 1485 to 1600 Tudor English.

13. James A. H. Murray (1837-1915)

Largely self-taught, James Murray had made his mark in the Philological Society after joining in 1868, and with several publications on language, especially dialectology. At the time he wrote this encyclopedia entry he was deeply, if reluctantly, involved in negotiations over what would become the *Oxford English Dictionary*. He officially became editor in 1879 and worked on it the rest of his life.

See further K. M. Elisabeth Murray, *Caught in the Web of Words: James A. H. Murray and the 'Oxford English Dictionary'* (New Haven, Conn.: Yale University Press, 1977).

James Murray, 'English Language', in *Encyclopædia Britannica*, 9th edn, 24 vols (Edinburgh: Adam and Charles Black, 1875-89).

From: 'English Language' (VIII [1878], 390-398).

In its widest sense, the name is now conveniently used to comprehend the language of the English people from their settlement in Britain to the present day, the various stages through which it has passed being distinguished as Old, Middle, and New or Modern English. In works yet recent, and even in some still current, the name *English* is confined to the third, or at most extended to the second and third of these stages, since the language assumed in the main the vocabulary and grammatical forms which it now presents, the oldest or inflected stage being treated as a separate language, under the title of *Anglo-Saxon*, while the transition period which connects the two has been called *Semi-Saxon*. This view had the justification that, looked upon by themselves, either as vehicles of thought or as objects of study and analysis, Old English, or Anglo-Saxon, and Modern English are, for all practical ends, distinct languages,—as much so, for example, as Latin and Spanish. No amount of familiarity with Modern English, including its local dialects, would enable the student to read Anglo-Saxon, three fourths of the vocabulary of which have perished and been reconstructed within 800 years; nor would a knowledge even of these lost words give him the power, since the grammatical system, alike in accidence and syntax, would be entirely strange to him. Indeed it is probable that a modern Englishman would acquire the power of reading and writing French in less time than it would cost him to attain to the same proficiency in Old English; so that if the test of distinct languages be their degree of practical difference from each other, it cannot be denied that Anglo-Saxon is a distinct language from Modern English. But when we view the subject historically, recognizing the fact that living speech is subject to continuous change in certain definite directions, determined by the constitution and circumstances of mankind, as an evolution or development of which we can trace the steps, and that, owing to the abundance of written materials, this evolution appears so gradual in English that we can nowhere draw distinct lines separating its successive stages, we recognize these stages as merely temporary phases of an individual whole, and speak of the English language as used alike by Cynewulf and by Tennyson, just as we include alike King Alfred and Mr Bright as members of the English race. It must not be forgotten, however, that in this wide sense the English language includes, not only the literary or courtly forms of speech used at successive periods, but also the popular and, it may be, altogether unwritten dialects that exist by their side. Only on this basis, indeed, can we speak of Old, Middle, and Modern English as the same *language*, since in actual fact the precise *dialect* which is now the cultivated language, or 'English' par excellence, is not the descendant of that dialect which was the cultivated language or English of Alfred, but of a sister dialect then sunk in obscurity, — even as the direct descendant of Alfred's 'Englisc' is now to be found in the neglected and non-literary rustic speech of Wiltshire and Somersetshire.

[Murray goes on to discuss Anglo-Saxon.]

As already hinted, the English language, in the wide sense, presents three main stages of development — Old, Middle, and Modern — distinguished by their inflexional characteristics. The latter can be best summarized in the words of Mr Henry Sweet, in his *History of English Sounds*: 'Old English is the period of *full* inflexions (*name, gifan, caru*), Middle English of *levelled* inflexions (*naame, given, caare*), and Modern English of *lost* inflexions (*name, give, care = nām, giv, cār*). We have besides two periods of *transition*, one in which *nama* and *name* exist side by side, and another in which final *e* [with other endings] is beginning to drop'.[26] By *lost* inflexions it is meant that only very few remain, and these mostly non-syllabic, as the -*s* in stone*s*, the -*ed* in lov*ed*, the -*r* in thei*r*, as contrasted with the plain Old English stán-*as*, luf-*od-e* and luf-*od-on*, þá-*ra*. Each of these periods may also be divided into two — an early and a late; but from the want of materials this division may be waived in regard to the first. We have thus the following divisions, with the approximate dates, which, however, varied considerably for different dialects and parts of the country: —

Old English or Anglo-Saxon........................ to 1100

Transition Old English, or 'Semi-Saxon' .... 1100 to 1200

Early Middle English, or 'Early English' .... 1200 to 1300

Late Middle English .... 1300 to 1400

Transition Middle English .... 1400 to 1485

---

[26] See the extract from Sweet. p. 53. The brackets are Murray's.

Early Modern English, 'Tudor English'............ 1485 to 1611
Modern English .... 1611 onward.

Many writers carry the Transition Old English down to 1250, Early
Middle English thence to 1350, and Late Middle English 1350 to 1485,
absorbing the Second Transition period. But the division given above, which
was, I believe, first proposed by Mr Sweet, represents better the development
of the language.

[...]

[...] During the 12th century, while this change was going on [the
levelling of inflected terminations to unstressed *e*], we find a great confusion
of grammatical forms, the full inflexions of Old English standing side by side
in the same sentence with the levelled ones of Middle English. It is to this state
of the language that the names *Transition* and *Period of Confusion* (Dr
Abbott's appellation)[27] point; its appearance, as that of Anglo-Saxon broken
down in its endings, had previously given to it the suggestive if not strictly
logical title of Semi-Saxon. By most writers the close of the period has been
brought down to 1250; but very shortly after 1200 in the south, and
considerably before it in the north, the levelling of inflexions was complete,
and the language possessed of a tolerably settled system of new grammatical
forms, the use of which marks Middle English.

Although the written remains of the TRANSITION OLD ENGLISH are few,
sufficient exist to enable us to trace the course of linguistic change. Within
two generations after the Conquest, faithful pens were at work transliterating
the old homilies of Ælfric, and other lights of the Anglo-Saxon Church, into
the neglected idiom of their posterity. Twice during the period, in the reigns
of Stephen and Henry II., Ælfric's gospels were similarly modernized so as to
be 'understanded of the people'.[28] And shortly after 1100 appeared the great
work of the age, the versified *Chronicle* of Layamon, or Lawëman, a priest of
Ernely, on the Severn, who, using as his basis the French *Brut* of Wace,
expanded it by additions of his own to more than twice the extent; his work of
32,250 lines is a mine of illustration for the language of the period. While
these southern remains carry on in unbroken sequence the history of the Old
English of Alfred and Ælfric, the history of the northern English is an entire
blank from the 11th to the 13th century. The stubborn resistance of the north,
and the terrible retaliation inflicted by William, apparently effaced northern
English culture for centuries. If anything was written in the vernacular in the
kingdom of Scotland during the same period, it probably perished during the

---

[27] Edwin A. Abbott, *How to Parse* (London: Seeley, Jackson and Halliday, 1875), p. 299.

[28] Aelfric's sermons were copied until well into the twelfth century, as for example in the
Lambeth and Vespasian homiliaries, in MS Lambeth Palace 487, Cotton MS Vespasian A XXII.

calamities to which that country was subjected during the half century of struggle for independence. In reality, however, the northern English had entered its Transition or 'Semi-Saxon' stage two centuries earlier; the glosses of the 10th century show that the Danish inroads had there anticipated the results hastened by the Norman Conquest in the south. Meanwhile a dialect was making its appearance in another quarter of England, destined to overshadow the old literary dialects of north and south alike, and become the English of the future. The Mercian kingdom, which, as its name imports, lay along the *marches* of the earlier states, and was really a congeries of the outlying members of many tribes, must have presented from the beginning a linguistic mixture and transition; and it is probable that more than one intermediate form of speech arose within its confines, between Lancashire and the Thames. But the only specimen of such we can with some degree of certainty produce comes towards the close of the Old English period, in the gloss to the Rushworth Gospels, which, so far as concerns St Matthew, and a few verses of St John xviii., is probably in a Mercian dialect.[29] At least it presents a phase of the language which in inflexional decay stands about midway between the West-Saxon and the Northumbrian glosses, to which it is yet posterior in time. But soon after the Conquest we find an undoubted midland dialect in the Transition stage from Old to Middle English, in the south-eastern part of ancient Mercia, in a district bounded on the south and south-east by the Saxon Middlesex and Essex, and on the east and north by the East Anglian Norfolk and Suffolk and the Danish settlements on the Trent and Humber. In this district, and in the monastery of Peterborough, one of the copies of the Old English Chronicle, transcribed about 1120, was written up by two succeeding hands to the death of Stephen in 1154. The section from 1122 to 1131, written in the latter year, shows the same confusion as in Layamon between Old English forms and those of a still simpler Middle English, impatient to rid itself of the inflexional trammels which were still, though in weakened forms, so tightly hugged south of the Thames. And in the concluding section written in 1154 we find Middle English fairly started on its career. [...]

The MIDDLE ENGLISH stage was pre-eminently the *Dialectal* period of the language. It was not till after the middle of the 14th century that English obtained official recognition as a language. For three centuries, therefore, there was no standard form of speech which claimed any pre-eminence over the others. The writers of each district wrote in the dialect familiar to them; and between extreme forms the difference was so great as to amount to unintelligibility; works written for southern Englishmen had to be translated

---

[29] The glosses in Bodl Auct. D.2.19 (3946) are by two OE scribes.

for the benefit of the men of the north: —

> 'In sotherin Inglis was it drawin,
> And turnid ic haue till ur awin
> Langage of þe northin lede
> That can na nothir Inglis rede'.
>
> *Cursor Mundi*, 20,064.[30]

Three main dialects were distinguished by contemporary writers, as in the often-quoted passage from Trevisa's translation of Higden's *Polychronicon* completed in 1387.[31]

[...]

In the productions of Caxton's press, we see the passage from Middle to Modern English completed. The earlier of these have still an occasional verbal plural in -*n*, especially in the word *they ben*; the southern *her* and *hem* of Middle English vary with the northern and Modern English *their*, *them*. In the late works, the older forms have been practically ousted, and the year 1485, which witnessed the establishment of the Tudor dynasty, may be conveniently put as that which closed the Middle English transition, and introduced Modern English. Both in the completion of this result, and in its comparative permanence, the printing press had an important share. By its exclusive patronage of the midland speech, it raised it still higher above the sister dialects, and secured its abiding victory. [...]

MODERN ENGLISH thus dates from Caxton. The language had at length reached the all but inflexionless state which it now presents. [...]

---

[30] Cf the lines in *Cursor Mundi*, ed. by Richard Morris, 7 vols. (London: EETS, 1874-93), IV (1877), 1148-49.

[31] Quotation omitted; cf Trevisa's statement in *Polychronicon Ranulphi Higden, Monachi Cestrensis; together with the English translations of John Trevisa [...]*, ed. by Churchill Babington and J. Rawson Lumby, 9 vols (London: HMSO, 1865-86), II (1869), 159, 161-63.

Part II: Literary criticism and commentary

1. Thomas Hearne (1678-1735)

Thomas Hearne is regarded by some as a founding figure in Middle English because of his impressive edition of the chronicle of Robert of Gloucester.[1] But Hearne did not create broad interest in his antiquarian studies and was memorialised in Alexander Pope's *Dunciad*: 'To future ages may thy dulness last, / As thou preserv'st the dulness of the past!'.[2] He was generally rejected by the antiquarians who began reviving Middle English later in the eighteenth century, his work deemed by them to be precisely what this form of study ought *not* to be. Thomas Warton certainly had Hearne in mind when he decried his predecessors for ignoring the romances in favour of 'obscure fragments of uninstructive morality or uninteresting history' (*HEP*, I, 209).

Hearne was a difficult man and it is generally agreed that he brought down on himself some of the considerable troubles he experienced. But there was also a political element to the rejection of Hearne by the usually conservative antiquarian clan. Hearne was born into a poor family but managed to go to Oxford. Having taken his M. A. in 1703, he continued his own studies in the Bodleian Library for several years. Recognized for his researches, he was made Second Keeper of the Library in 1712. But Hearne

---

[1] See for example Hudson, 'Middle English', p. 35; Hudson, 'Robert of Gloucester and the Antiquaries', p. 331 (full references are in the main text).

[2] *The Dunciad*, III, ll. 189-90, in *Alexander Pope*, ed. by Pat Rogers (Oxford: Oxford University Press, 1993), p. 504.

refused to swear allegiance to the Hanoverians and experienced persecution before being stripped of his post and refused entry to the Library in 1716. He remained in residence and at his antiquarian labours at St. Edmund Hall, refusing later offers of positions because of the allegiance requirement.

Hearne was somewhat indiscriminate in his publications, which he printed through public subscription, apparently successfully. He began principally with classical works, later printing great numbers of medieval chronicles. Most of these were in Latin; his edition of the chronicle of Robert of Gloucester is his major Middle English intervention.

For an assessment of Hearne's work in general see David C. Douglas, *English Scholars 1660-1730*, 2nd rev. edn (London: Eyre & Spottiswoode, 1951), chapter 9. On his edition of Robert of Gloucester and approach to editing, see Anne Hudson, 'Middle English' in *Editing Medieval Texts: English, French and Latin Written in England*, ed. by A. G. Rigg (New York: Garland, 1977), pp. 34-57, and Anne Hudson, 'Robert of Gloucester and the Antiquaries', *Notes and Queries* 214 (1969), 322-33.

Thomas Hearne, ed. *Robert of Gloucester's Chronicle. Transcrib'd, and now first publish'd, from a MS in the Harleyan Library*, 2 vols (Oxford: Sheldonian Theatre, 1724).

The edition was republished in 1810; the *Chronicle* was re-edited by William Aldis Wright as part of the Rolls Series in 1887.

From: 'The Publisher's Preface', l-lxxxv.

IX. I am here very sensible, that an Objection against Robert of Gloucester will be started by several upon the score of his Poëtry, as if that were a very cogent Argument to make him neglected and despised. But he (and not Chaucer, as Dr. Thomas Fuller,[3] and some others would have it,) is the Ennius of the English Nation, and he is, on that account, to be as much respected, as even Ennius himself was among the Romans, and I have good reason to think, that he will be so by Friends to our Antiquities, and our old History. 'Tis the Genius of the Age that is to be regarded in such Pieces of Poëtry. The Poëtry of those times consisted of Rhythms both here and in other Countries, and the Poëts thought they had done their Parts well, if their Rhythms, however mean otherwise, related matter of Fact, and were agreeable to Truth. And truly this exactly corresponded with the Rules of the ancient Pythagoræans. For even

---

[3] Thomas Fuller, *The Church-History of Britain* (London, 1655), bk VI, p. 268. tho' he had before told us, bk III, p. 4 that *he was counted the* Virgil *of his age, and the* Ennius *in ours.* – H.

Tully tells us, at the Beginning of the IVth. Book of his Tusculan Questions, that the Pythagoræans us'd to put their Precepts and other Things of moment (among which, to be sure, are to be reckon'd the famous Acts of their Ancestors) into Verse, and that it was usual with the old Romans, according to the Custom of the Pythagoræans, when they sat at Banquets, to recite the Virtues and Praises of Great Men in Verse, and to sing and play upon the Pipe upon such occasions, and thence, as I take it, even the old Britains, who followed the Pythagoræan Doctrines, addicted themselves so much to Verse, tho' as well the Pythagoræans, as Romans and Britains, took care, that no Verse should tend to the Injury of another, one of the Laws of the XII. Tables expressly forbidding any such Indecency, and some of our old Rhythms laying down Rules against any unbecoming Expressions in Poëtry, such as may conduce to Immorality; and in this, as well as his unaffected way of relating matter of Fact in Rhythm, our Author is to be commended, as a true Picture of Antiquity.

X. Since, therefore, Robert of Gloucester appears, on all accounts, to be so valuable an Author, what reason can be assign'd, that he hath been so much neglected, and that he was not long since published to the World? 'Tis probable the Obsoleteness of the Language might be the main reason, or, at least, 'tis likely, that some Persons of Distinction, not pleased with several of his honest Relations of Things, might characterize him as an insignificant Writer, and prejudice the Readers so much against him, that they were not at all sollicitous about an Edition. Be this as it will, as I look upon him to be one of the first Rank in our old Historians, so I, many Years agoe, had thoughts of publishing him according to the Bodleian MS. to which I had then daily access. But finding afterwards, that there are much better Copies in the World, I laid aside my Design of publishing this Author, and did not resume it 'till above a Year agoe, when the Loan of a MS. that formerly belong'd to Sir Simonds D'Ewes, (whose MSS. the Earl of Oxford purchas'd) was procured for me out of the Harleyan Library by that most eminent Physician the learned Dr. Richard Mead, who is my very great Friend.[4] It came to me, accompanied with another MS. of Robert of Gloucester, the Loan of which was obtain'd for me out of the Heralds Office by another great Friend, the learned John Bridges, Esq. who was at the trouble of transmitting both these MSS. to me. As soon as I saw the Harleyan MS. I presently concluded, that it was a very good one and authentick, and therefore I immediately transcrib'd it, and resolved to make it my Text. But then as to that of the Heralds Office, I

---

[4] Sir Simonds D'Ewes (1602-50), antiquary and diligent collector and copyist. The Earl of Oxford mentioned here as purchaser of his manuscripts was Sir Robert Harley (1661-1724), who began the famous library augmented by his son.

found not only the Language of Robert of Gloucester to be altered throughout in it, but the Work quite changed in several respects, by having some Passages transposed, others omitted, and divers inserted that were never written by Robert of Gloucester, who was of different Principles from this Author.[5] A great deal of Prose History in English (partly taken from Geffry of Monmouth, partly from William of Malmsbury, partly from Brute of England, *Polychronicon, &c.*) is intermix'd in this MS. with what is in Rhythm, but as the Substance of most of this is already published in Stowe (who had seen this MS.) and other Books,[6] I have left out much the greatest part of it, and confin'd my self to the genuine Work of Robert of Gloucester, which, however, I have carefully compar'd with this MS. of the Heralds Office, and taken notice of what I thought proper, and have inserted my Observations from it (among which are to be reckon'd also those of the Prose part) at the bottom of the page, always subjoyning *Ar.* [i.e. *the MS. of the College of Arms*] to them.[7] Who the Author was, that took such a liberty with Robert of Gloucester (a thing that hath happened to many other ancient Remains) I will not pretend, at present, to determine; but this is certain, that he both lived and wrote in the time of Hen. VI. as appears from this *Memorandum*, (written all [excepting M.cccc.xlviii.] in red Letters, but in the same Hand with the Book) at the Beginning of the Work: A petegreu, fro William Conquerour, of the Crowne of Engelonde, lynnyally descendyng, un to kyng Henry the vi. in the end of thys boke lymned in fygurs. Thys boke, with hys Antecedens and consequens, was ful ended the vi. day offe August, the ȝere of oure lorde a M.cccc.xlviii. and the yere of oure souerayn lorde kyng Harry the vi. affter the conquest the xxvi.

Tho' this MS. of the Heralds Office [...] be in several Places imperfect, and hath some of the Leaves transpos'd (as a few Leaves are also transpos'd in the Harleyan MS.) yet 'tis, as I judge, the very original Book. The Author, undoubtedly, took a great deal of pains in new modelling Robert of Gloucester, and in adapting every Thing to his own Scheme. He divers times introduceth the Rhythms by the Name of old Rhythms, but never so much as

---

[5] MS Harl 201 is defective, but for Hearne it had the advantage of being available to him for loan, unlike the earlier and more complete MS Cotton Caligula A XI from which William Aldis Wright printed in 1887. The College of Arms MS (now Magdalene College, Cambridge, no. 2833) is a late seventeenth-century copy.

[6] John Stow (1525?-1605), antiquary, edited Chaucer's works in 1561; his *Summarie of Englyshe Chronicles* (1565) was a digest of British history drawn from chronicles, and formed the basis of later, augmented publications under the titles *The Chronicles of England* and *The Annales of England*, updated and printed many times in the late sixteenth and early seventeenth centuries.

[7] Hearne's square brackets here and in the following sentence.

once mentions the Name of Robert of Gloucester, or pretends to discover what his own Name was. Mr. Weever had diligently perus'd this MS. and quotes it sometimes as if the whole were Robert of Gloucester's, a mistake that some great Men besides have been guilty of with respect to other Writers, as may plainly appear, as well from other Instances, as from what I observ'd lately with regard to Fordun's *Scotichronicon*.[8] The Petegreu mentioned in the Note abovesaid is still to be seen at the end of the MS. together with the Limnings or Pictures (all but that of William Rufus and Henry I. which are cut out) of the Kings of England from William the Conqueror to Hen. VI. inclusively, and this additional Part is also cited by Weever, but in that he happens to distinguish rightly, making it, as it is, quite different from any Piece of Robert of Gloucester's Writings. The Pictures I have omitted, but the rest I have printed in my Appendix, and, I hope, I have thereby obliged those that have any respect for our Antiquities.

[...]

I am very sensible, that the Obsoleteness of the Language will deterr many from Reading this very usefull Historian; but to such, as shall be pleased to make themselves acquainted with him (in order to which the Glossary, I have drawn up and subjoyn'd, may be of some service) he will appear very pleasant, entertaining and diverting, and they will value him the more, as he comes out in his primitive Dress. As it is a Reproach to us, that the Saxon Language should be so forgot, as to have but few (comparatively speaking) that are able to read it; so 'tis a greater Reproach, that the black Letter, which was the Character so much in use in our Grandfathers days, should be now (as it were) disus'd and rejected, especially when we know, the best Editions of our English Bible and Common Prayer (to say nothing of other Books) are printed in it.

Oxford April 14.
1724.

---

[8] John Weever (1576-1632), poet and antiquary, was a friend of Simonds D'Ewes who frequented the College of Arms and so was able to draw on the chronicle extensively in his *Ancient Funerall Monuments with in the united Monarchie of Great Britaine, Ireland, and the Ilands adjacent [...]* (London: Harper, 1631). Hearne had edited Fordun's *Scotichronicon*, with its continuation by Walter Bower, in 1722.

2. Thomas Percy (1729-1811)

The career of Thomas Percy in the Church eventually led to the bishopric of Dromore. He was famous in his time and best known today for the popular *Reliques of Ancient English Poetry* (1765), a collection of ballads and romances based partly on the manuscript known as the Percy Folio (now BL Add MS 27,879). This manuscript is of the mid-seventeenth century and although it contains some late medieval material, most of it was dressed to advantage by its editor. Nevertheless, Percy framed the work principally as commentary on the Middle Ages with three of the four scholarly essays in the work focusing on medieval literary topics. In these essays, and in his tastefully edited ballads, Percy conjured up a romantic world of chivalry, feudal pomp, and minstrel composers patronised by the aristocracy. In amongst the romantic flights of fancy, there was much new information for the prospective reader of medieval literature. Percy's essay on *Piers Plowman* contributed to a broader understanding of alliterative poetry. The *Reliques* (particularly the second edition), was also a major bibliographical resource; as Joseph M. P. Donatelli points out, Percy published the first bibliography of Middle English romance, at the end of the essay on metrical romances (Donatelli, p. 226).

The extracts are from the essays on ancient minstrels, metrical romances, and the metre of *Piers Plowman* which all appeared in the first edition of the *Reliques* (1765) along with an essay on the English stage. However, they are here taken from the second edition of 1767. The earlier versions may now be easily viewed in Nick Groom's facsimile of the first edition. The essays on romance and the alliterative metre are much as they appeared in 1765, but the essay on minstrels, which opened *Reliques* and stood as its scholarly centrepiece, was substantially revised for the second publication. Its first section is expanded, in order to make even stronger claims for the status of the minstrels. More examples are given, and the essay is followed by 38 pages of dense bibliographical notes (most of them cut here). The immediate occasion for the revision was a critique of parts of the first version of the essay in a paper read by the antiquarian Samuel Pegge to the Society of Antiquaries in 1766 (Davis, pp. 153-55; Friedman, p. 202). In their 1767 form, the essays were widely influential. Percy's publisher, Dodsley, put the four essays of the second edition together as a free-standing book, also in 1767. The essays on minstrels and metrical romances, the English stage and the metre of *Piers Plowman*, formed, as Bertram Davis points out, 'the most comprehensive and authoritative literary history that Percy's contemporaries could turn to' before Warton's *History of English Poetry* (Davis, p. 155).

On Percy's alterations to manuscript material, see Walter Jackson Bate, 'Percy's Use of his Folio-Manuscript', *Journal of English and Germanic Philology* 43 (1944), 337-48 and Joseph M. P. Donatelli, 'Old Barons in New Robes: Percy's Use of the Metrical Romances in the *Reliques of Ancient*

English Poetry', in *Hermeneutics and Medieval Culture*, ed. by Patrick J. Gallacher and Helen Damico (Albany: SUNY Press, 1989), pp. 225-35. On the *Reliques* see Albert B. Friedman, *The Ballad Revival: Studies in the Influence of Popular on Sophisticated Poetry* (Chicago: University of Chicago Press, 1961), ch. 7; Nick Groom, introduction, Thomas Percy, *Reliques of Ancient English Poetry*, facsimile of 1st edn (London: Routledge/Thoemmes Press, 1996), and *MME*, ch. 1. For biography see Bertram H. Davis, *Thomas Percy: A Scholar-Cleric in the Age of Johnson* (Philadelphia: University of Pennsylvania Press, 1989).

Thomas Percy, *The Reliques of Ancient English Poetry*, 2nd edn, 3 vols (London: Dodsley, 1767).

After its first appearance in 1765, the *Reliques* went through many editions; the third appeared in 1790, the fourth (and last in Percy's lifetime) in 1794. In 1891 the work was re-edited by Henry Wheatley, and this is the form in which it is most often seen today.

From: 'An Essay on the Ancient English Minstrels', (I, xix-xxxviii).

I. The minstrels were an order of men in the middle ages, who united the arts of poetry and music, and sung verses to the harp of their own composing. They also appear to have accompanied their songs with mimicry and action; and to have practised such various means of diverting as were much admired in those rude times, and supplied the want of more refined entertainments. These arts rendered them extremely popular and acceptable in this and all the neighbouring countries; where no high scene of festivity was esteemed complete, that was not set off with the exercise of their talents; and where, so long as the spirit of chivalry subsisted, they were protected and caressed, because their songs tended to do honour to the ruling passion of the times, and to encourage and foment a martial spirit.

The MINSTRELS seem to have been the genuine successors of the ancient BARDS, who under different names were admired and revered, from the earliest ages, among the people of Gaul, Britain, Ireland and the North; and indeed by almost all the first inhabitants of Europe, whether of Celtic or Gothic race; but by none more than by our own Teutonic ancestors, particularly by all the Danish tribes. By these they were distinguished by the name of SCALDS, a word which denotes 'Smoothers and Polishers of language'.[9] The origin of

---

[9] Percy here refers the reader to his own *Five Pieces of Runic Poetry Translated from the Islandic Language* (London: Dodsley, 1763); see in particular pp. A2-A3. The definition of 'scald' he takes from Thormodus Torfaeus, *Orcades seu Rerum Orcadensium Historiae Libri Tres* (1697); see the preface, C1. Percy's interest in this area was extensive; at the same time as he

their art was attributed to ODIN or WODEN, the father of their Gods; and the professors of it were held in the highest estimation. Their skill was considered as something divine; their persons were deemed sacred; their attendance was solicited by kings; and they were every where loaded with honours and rewards. In short, poets and their art were held among them in that rude admiration, which is ever shown by an ignorant people to such as excel them in intellectual accomplishments.

As these honours were paid to Poetry and Song, from the earliest times, in those countries which our Anglo-Saxon ancestors inhabited before their removal into Britain, we may reasonably conclude, that they would not lay aside all their regard for men of this sort immediately on quitting their German forests. At least so long as they retained their ancient manners and opinions, they would still hold them in high estimation. But as the Saxons, soon after their establishment in this island, were converted to Christianity; in proportion as literature prevailed among them, this rude admiration would begin to abate; and Poetry would be no longer a peculiar profession. Thus the POET and the MINSTEL [sic] early with us became two persons. Poetry was cultivated by men of letters indiscriminately; and many of the most popular rhimes were composed amidst the leisure and retirement of monasteries. But the Minstrels continued a distinct order of men for many ages after the Norman conquest; and got their livelihood by singing verses to the harp at the houses of the great. There they were still hospitably and respectfully received, and retained many of the honours shewn to their predecessors the BARDS and SCALDS. And tho', as their art declined, some of them only recited the compositions of others, many of them still composed songs themselves, and all of them could probably invent a few stanzas on occasion. I have no doubt but most of the old heroic Ballads in this collection were composed by this order of men. For altho' some of the larger metrical Romances might come from the pen of the monks or others, yet the smaller narratives were probably composed by the Minstrels, who sung them. From the amazing variations which occur in different copies of these old pieces, it is evident they made no scruple to alter each others productions; and the reciter added or omitted whole stanzas according to his own fancy or convenience.

In the early ages, as was hinted above, the profession of oral itinerant Poet was held in the utmost reverence among all the Danish tribes; and therefore we might have concluded, that it was not unknown or unrespected among

---

was assembling *Reliques*, he was also working on what was to be a less popular, but still important book, *Northern Antiquities* (1770), a translation of Paul-Henri Mallet's *Introduction à l'Histoire de Dannemarc* (1755-6; second edition 1763). On this see Margaret Clunies Ross, *The Norse Muse in Britain, 1750-1820* (Trieste: Edizioni Parnaso, 1998), chs. 1-3.

their Saxon brethren in Britain, even if History had been altogether silent on this subject. The original country of our Anglo-Saxon Ancestors is well known to have lien chiefly in the Cimbric Chersonese, in the tracts of land since distinguished by the names of Jutland, Angelen, and Holstein. The Jutes and Angles in particular, who composed two thirds of the conquerors of Britain, were a Danish people, and their country at this day belongs to the crown of Denmark; so that when the Danes again infested England, three or four hundred years after, they made war on the descendents of their own ancestors. From this near affinity we might expect to discover a strong resemblance between both nations in their customs, manners, and even language; and in fact we find them to differ no more, than would naturally happen between a parent country and its own colonies, that had been severed in a rude uncivilised state, and had dropt all intercourse for three or four centuries. Especially if we reflect, that the colony here settled had adopted a new Religion, extremely opposite in all respects to the ancient Paganism of the mother-country; and that even at first, along with the original Angli, had been incorporated a large mixture of Saxons from neighbouring parts of Germany; as afterwards, among the Danish invaders, had come vast multitudes of adventurers from the more northern parts of Scandinavia. But all these were only different tribes of the same common Teutonic Stock, and spoke only different dialects of the same Gothic Language.

From this sameness of original and similarity of manners, we might justly have wondered, if a character so dignified and distinguished among the ancient Danes, as the SCALD or BARD, had been totally unknown or unregarded in this sister nation. And indeed this argument is so strong, and, at the same time, the early annals of the Anglo-Saxons are so scanty and defective, that no objections from their silence could be sufficient to overthrow it. For if these popular bards were confessedly revered and admired, in those very countries which the Anglo-Saxons inhabited before their removal into Britain; and if they were afterwards common and numerous among their own descendents here after the Norman Conquest, what could have become of them in the intermediate time? Can we do otherwise than conclude, that this order of men still subsisted here, though perhaps with less splendour than in the North; and that there never was wanting a succession of them to hand down the art, though some particular conjunctures may have rendered it more respectable at one time than another? And this was really the case. For though much greater honours seem to have been heaped upon the Northern SCALDS, in whom the characters of historian, genealogist, poet, and musician were all united, than appear to have been paid to the MINSTRELS and HARPERS of the Anglo-Saxons, whose talents were chiefly calculated to entertain and divert; while the Scalds professed to inform and instruct, and were at once the moralists and theologues of their Pagan countrymen: yet the Anglo-Saxon Minstrels continued to possess no small portion of public favour; and the arts they professed were so extremely acceptable to our ancestors, that the word which peculiarly denoted their art, continues still in our language to be of all others the most expressive of that popular mirth and jollity, that strong sensation of delight, which is felt by unpolished and simple minds.[10]

[In the second section of the essay, Percy gives various examples of Anglo-Saxon minstrels and the regard in which they were held. He notes that in 878 King Alfred, 'being desirous to learn the true situation of the Danish army [...] assumed the dress and character of a Minstrel'. In this guise he went safely into a Danish camp: 'though he could not but be known to be a Saxon by his dialect, the character he had assumed procured him a hospitable reception'.[11] Having argued for the primacy of minstrels in Anglo-Saxon royal households, he proceeds to the Middle English period.]

III. We have now brought the inquiry down to the Norman conquest: and as the Normans had been a late colony from Norway and Denmark, where the SCALDS had arrived to the highest pitch of credit before Rollo's expedition into France, we cannot doubt but this adventurer, like the other northern princes, had many of these men in his train, who settled with him in his new duchy of Normandy, and left behind them successors in their art: So that, when his descendant, WILLIAM the BASTARD, invaded this kingdom in the following century, that mode of entertainment could not but be still familiar with the Normans. [...]

We see then that the Norman conquest was rather likely to favour the establishment of the minstrel profession in this kingdom, than to suppress it: and we may even conclude, that, after that period, this order of men would grow into more favour and repute; and the profession itself acquire new privileges.

IV. After the Norman conquest I have not met with any very particular fact concerning the MINSTRELS, till we come down to the reign of Richard the first: and under him their profession seems to have revived with additional splendor. Richard, who was the great restorer and hero of Chivalry, was also the distinguished patron of Poets and Minstrels: He was himself of their number, and some of his verses are still extant. As the Provençal Bards were in his time in high request for the softness of their language, and the superior elegance of their compositions, Richard invited multitudes of them to his court, where he loaded them with honours and rewards: and they in return

---

[10] i.e., 'glee'.

[11] Percy took the story from William of Malmesbury; see *Willelmi Malmesbiriensis Monachi De Gestis Regum Anglorum*, ed. by William Stubbs, 2 vols, RS 90 (London: HMSO, 1887-89), I, 126.

celebrated him as the most accomplished monarch in the world. The distinction and respect which Richard showed to men of this profession, although his favours were chiefly heaped upon foreigners, could not but recommend the profession itself among his own subjects: and therefore we may conclude, that English Minstrelsy would, in a peculiar manner, flourish in his time: and probably it is from this æra, that we are to date that remarkable intercommunity and exchange of each other's compositions, which we discover to have taken place at some early period between the French and English Minstrels: the same set of phrases, the same species of characters, incidents, and adventures, and often the same identical stories, being found in the old metrical Romances of both nations.[12]

[Percy then gives examples of minstrels, beginning with Blondel and his rescue of Richard I, throughout the Middle English period and up to the time of Elizabeth I when, although 'they had lost much of their dignity, and were sinking into contempt and neglect', they still 'sustained a character far superior to any thing we can conceive at present of the singers of old ballads'.]

V. I cannot conclude this account of the ancient MINSTRELS, without remarking that they are most of them represented to have been of the North. There is hardly an ancient Ballad or Romance, wherein a Minstrel or Harper appears, but he is characterized by way of eminence to have been 'OF THE NORTH COUNTRYE': and indeed the prevalence of the Northern dialect in such kind of poems, shews that this representation is real. The reason of which seems to be this; the civilizing of nations has begun from the South: the North would therefore be the last civilized, and the old manners would longest subsist there.[13] With the manners, the old poetry that painted these manners would remain likewise; and in proportion as their boundaries became more contracted, and their neighbours refined, the poetry of those rude men would be more distinctly peculiar, and that peculiarity more strikingly remarked.

[...] For it is to be observed, that so long as the Minstrels subsisted, they seem never to have designed their rhimes for literary publication, and probably never committed them to writing themselves: what copies are

---

[12] What is skirted round in this passage is the question of the language in which these supposed English minstrels composed. Percy is on much firmer ground arguing for the existence of French minstrels than he is when he argues that there must also have been a parallel class of English minstrels composing in English. The 'intercommunity and exchange' seems to have consisted chiefly of English writers translating from French.

[13] This accorded well with the belief, evident in Percy's writing and further developed by Scott, that the Border country was the true repository of 'bardic' literature, the scene of the 'romantic wildness' he mentions a little further on.

preserved of them were doubtless taken down from their mouths.[14] But as the old Minstrels gradually wore out, a new race of Ballad-writers succeeded, an inferior sort of minor poets, who wrote narrative songs merely for the press. [...]

The old Minstrel-ballads are in the northern dialect, abound with antique words and phrases, are extremely incorrect, and run into the utmost licence of metre; they have also a romantic wildness, and are in the true spirit of chivalry. [...]

From: 'On the Metre of Pierce Plowman's Visions', *Reliques*, II, 268-80.

[Percy opens by noting that the ancient Icelandic poets depended neither on rhyme nor quantity of syllables, but on 'alliteration, or a certain artful repetition of the sounds in the middle of the verses. This was adjusted according to certain rules of their prosody, one of which was, that every distich should contain at least three words beginning with the same letter or sound. Two of these correspondent sounds might be placed either in the first or second line of the distich, and one in the other: but all three were not regularly to be crowded into one line'.]

Their brethren the Anglo-saxon poets occasionally used the same kind of alliteration, and it is common to meet in their writings with similar examples of the foregoing rules. Take an instance or two in modern characters:

> *Sk*eop tha and *Sk*yrede   *H*am and *H*eahfetl
> *Sk*yppend ure.   *H*eofena rikes.[15]

I know not however that there is any where extant an entire Saxon poem all in this measure. But distichs of this sort perpetually occur in all their poems of any length.

Now if we examine the versification of PIERCE PLOWMAN'S VISIONS, we shall find it constructed exactly by these rules; and therefore each line, as printed, is in reality a distich of two verses, and will, I believe, be found distinguished as such, by some mark or other in all the ancient MSS. viz.

---

[14] This argument, or one like it, would often be used by later writers to account for the otherwise embarrassing gap between the great dignity and poetic skill they were claiming for their minstrel authors, and the evident barbarity and corruption of the actual text. The corruption was deemed to have happened in the process of transmission, giving rise to the prevalent notion that behind Middle English texts as they existed in manuscripts there must once have been purer, truer versions.

[15] Hickes, *Thesaurus*, I, 217. – P. [The verses are from *Genesis*, ll. 65, 33; see *The Junius Manuscript*, ed. by George Philip Krapp (London: Routledge, 1931), p. 4. The eccentric spelling is Percy's, and he owes the comparison of the Anglo-Saxon with *Piers* to Hickes.]

In a *Som*er *S*eason, | when 'hot[16] was the *S*unne,
I *Sh*ope me into *Sh*roubs, | as I a *Sh*epe were;
In *H*abite as an *H*armet | un*H*oly of werkes,
*W*ent *W*yde in thys world | *W*onders to heare, &c.

So that the author of this poem will not be found to have invented any new mode of versification, as some have supposed, but only to have retained that of the old Saxon and Gothic poets; which was probably never wholly laid aside, but occasionally used at different intervals; tho' the ravages of time will not suffer us now to produce a regular series of poems entirely written in it.

There are some readers, whom it may gratify to mention, that these VISIONS OF PIERCE [i.e. Peter] the PLOWMAN, are attributed to Robert Langland, a secular priest, born at Mortimer's Cleobury in Shropshire, and fellow of Oriel College in Oxford, who flourished in the reigns of Edward III. and Richard II. and published his poems a few years after 1350.[17] It consists of xx PASSUS or Breaks, exhibiting a series of visions, which he pretends happened to him on Malvern hills in Worcestershire. The author excells in strong allegoric painting, and has with great humour spirit and fancy, censured most of the vices incident to the several professions of life; but he particularly inveighs against the corruptions of the clergy, and the absurdities of superstition.

[Percy then discusses other poems in the alliterative metre, quoting from them in illustration, including *Piers the Plowman's Creed*, *The Siege of Jerusalem*,

---

[16] So I would read with Mr. Warton, rather than either 'soft', as in MS, or 'set' as in PCC. – P. [The floating quotation mark here (the lack of a closing mark is probably a typsesetter's error) is Percy's chief way of indicating an emendation; a practice that, inconsistently applied throughout the *Reliques*, would later attract strong criticism. What Percy intends by 'PCC' is unclear; it seems to be a reference to the Crowley texts of *Piers*, which all read 'set' in the first line of the poem.]

[17] Square brackets are Percy's. This information was a commonplace of eighteenth-century belief about Langland; it will be seen again in the extracts from Warton, Ritson, and Ellis. It is ultimately based on John Bale's *Index Britanniae Scriptorum*, written after 1546, unpublished, but held in manuscript in the Bodleian library. This was probably the source for the very similar information recorded in Robert Crowley's three printings of *Piers Plowman* (1550) and a similar account appears in Bale's *Scriptorum Illustrium Maioris Brytanniae [...]* (Basle, 1557-59). See *Index Britanniae Scriptorum [...] John Bale's Index of British and Other Writers*, ed. by Reginald Lane Poole (Oxford: Clarendon Press, 1902), pp. 383, 509, 510. See also Charlotte Brewer, *Editing 'Piers Plowman': The Evolution of the Text* (Cambridge: Cambridge University Press, 1996), p. 11. On the confusion over 'Robert' and 'William' see George Kane, *Piers Plowman: The Evidence for Authorship* (London: Athlone, 1965), pp. 37-46.

and *Chevalere Assigne*. Then, noting a poem about Flodden Field in alliterative metre, he continues:]

Thus have we traced the Alliterative Measure so low as the sixteenth century. It is remarkable that all such poets as used this kind of metre, retained along with it many peculiar Saxon idioms, particularly such as were appropriated to poetry: this deserves the attention of those, who were desirous to recover the laws of the ancient Saxon Poesy, usually given up as inexplicable: I am of opinion that they will find what they seek in the Metre of Pierce Plowman.

[...]

To conclude; the metre of Pierce Plowman's Visions has no kind of relation with what is commonly called Blank Verse; yet has it a sort of harmony of its own, proceeding not so much from its alliteration, as from the artful disposal of its cadence, and the contrivance of its pause. So that when the ear is a little accustomed to it, it is by no means unpleasing; but claims all the merit of the French heroic numbers, only far less polished; being sweetened, instead of their final rhymes, with the internal recurrence of similar sounds.

From: 'On the Ancient Metrical Romances', *Reliques*, III, ii-xxi.

I. The first attempts at composition among all barbarous nations are ever found to be Poetry and Song. The praises of their Gods, and the atchievements of their heroes, are usually chanted at their festival meetings. These are the first rudiments of History. It is in this manner that the savages of North America preserve the memory of past events: and the same method is known to have prevailed among our Saxon Ancestors, before they quitted their German forests. The ancient Britons had their BARDS and the Gothic nations their SCALDS or popular poets, whose business it was to record the victories of their warriors, and the genealogies of their Princes, in a kind of narrative songs, which were committed to memory, and delivered down from one Reciter to another. So long as Poetry continued a distinct profession, and while the Bard, or Scald was a regular and stated officer in the King's court, these men are thought to have performed the functions of the historian pretty faithfully; for tho' their narrations would be apt to receive a good deal of embellishment, they are supposed to have had at the bottom so much of truth as to serve for the basis of more regular annals. At least succeeding historians have taken up with the relations of these rude men, and for want of more authentic records, have agreed to allow them the credit of true history.[18]

---

[18] This argument, that behind any poetic fancy of the romancers there lay realistic historical representations, was later developed further by Warton and was crucial to the revival

After letters began to prevail, and history assumed a more stable form, by being committed to plain simple prose; these Songs of the Scalds or Bards began to be more amusing, than useful. And in proportion as it became their business chiefly to entertain and delight, they gave more and more into embellishment, and set off their recitals with such marvelous fictions, as were calculated to captivate gross and ignorant minds. Thus began stories of adventures with Giants and Dragons, and Witches and Enchanters, and all the monstrous extravagances of wild imagination, unguided by judgment, and uncorrected by art.

This is the true origin of that species of Romance, which so long celebrated feats of Chivalry, and which at first in metre and afterwards in prose, was the entertainment of our ancestors, in common with their contemporaries on the continent, till the satire of Cervantes, or rather the increase of knowledge and classical literature, drove them off the stage, to make room for a more refined species of fiction, under the name of French Romances, copied from the Greek.

That our old Romances of Chivalry may be derived in a lineal descent from the ancient historical songs of the Gothic bards and Scalds, will be shown below, and indeed appears the more evident as many of those Songs are still preserved in the north, which exhibit all the seed of Chivalry before it became a solemn institution. 'CHIVALRY, as a distinct military order, conferred in the way of investiture, and accompanied with the solemnities of an oath, and other ceremonies', was of later date, and sprung out of the feudal constitution, as an elegant writer has lately shown.[19] But the ideas of Chivalry prevailed long before in all the Gothic nations, and may be discovered as in embrio in the customs, manners, and opinions, of every branch of that people. That fondness of going in quest of adventures, that spirit of challenging to single combat, and that respectful complaisance shewn to the fair sex, (so different from the manners of the Greeks and Romans), all are of Gothic origin, and may be traced up to the earliest times among all the northern nations. These existed long before the feudal ages, tho' they were called forth and strengthened in a peculiar manner under that constitution, and at length arrived to their full maturity in the times of the Crusades, so replete with romantic adventures.

Even the common arbitrary fictions of Romance were (as is hinted above) most of them familiar to the ancient Scalds of the north, long before the time of the Crusades. They believed the existence of Giants and Dwarfs, they had

---

of interest in romance.
[19] Richard Hurd, in *Letters on Chivalry and Romance* (London, 1762), pp. 6-7, from which these slightly misquoted words are taken.

some notion of Fairies, they were strongly possessed with the belief of spells and inchantment, and were fond of inventing combats with Dragons and Monsters.

[...]

It was probably not till after the historian and the bard had been long disunited, that the latter ventured at pure fiction. At length when their business was no longer to instruct or inform, but merely to amuse, it was no longer needful for them to adhere to truth. Then began fabulous and romantic songs which for a long time prevailed in France and England before they had books of Chivalry in prose. Yet in both these countries the Minstrels still retained so much of their original institution, as frequently to make true events the subject of their Songs; and indeed, as during the barbarous ages, the regular histories were almost all written in Latin by the Monks, the memory of events was preserved and propagated among the ignorant laity by scarce any other means than the popular songs of the Minstrels.

[In the second section of the essay, Percy begins by discussing the Normans, noting that the term 'romance' derives from 'what was called the ROMANCE Tongue, a mixture of the language of the Franks and bad Latin'. The romances of Chivalry, he continues, are to be found as early as the eleventh century, and notes the story of Taillefer, the minstrel who supposedly marched into the Battle of Hastings recounting the deeds of Roland.]

So early as this I cannot trace the Songs of Chivalry in English. The most ancient I have seen, is that of HORNECHILD described below, which seems not older than the twelfth century.[20] However, as this rather resembles the Saxon poetry, than the French, it is not certain that the first English Romances were translated from that language. We have seen above, that a propensity to this kind of fiction prevailed among all the Gothic nations; and, tho' after the Norman Conquest, both the French and the English translated each others [sic] Romances, there is no room to doubt, but both of them composed original pieces of their own.

The stories of King Arthur and his Round Table, may be reasonably supposed of the growth of this island; both the English and the French had them from the Britons. The stories of Guy and Bevis, with some others, were probably the invention of English Minstrels. On the other hand, the English procured translations of such Romances as were most current in France; and in the List given at the conclusion of these Remarks, many are doubtless of

---

[20] Percy is referring to *King Horn*, the oldest extant English romance with its composition thought to be c. 1220-25; the title *Horn Child*, often given by the antiquarians to this romance, is now the title given to the late version of the story found in the Auchinleck manuscript.

French original.

The first PROSE books of Chivalry that appeared in our language, were those printed by Caxton; at least, these are the first I have been able to discover, and these are all translations from the French. Whereas Romances of this kind had been long current in metre, and were so generally admired in the time of Chaucer, that his Rhyme of Sir Thopas was evidently written to ridicule and burlesque them.

He expressly mentions several of them by name in a stanza, which I shall have occasion to quote more than once in this volume.

> Men speken of Romaunces of Price,
> Of Horne-Child, and Ipotis,
>   Of Bevis, and Sir Guy,
> Of Sir Libeaux and Blandamoure,
> But Sir Thopas bereth the floure,
>   Of riall chevallrie.[21]

Most, if not all of these are still extant in MS. in some or other of our libraries, as I shall shew in the conclusion of this slight Essay, where I shall give a list of such metrical Histories and Romances as have fallen under my observation.

As many of these contain a considerable portion of poetic merit, and throw great light on the manners and opinions of former times, it were to be wished that some of the best of them were rescued from oblivion. A judicious collection of them accurately published with proper illustrations, would be an important accession to our stock of ancient English Literature. Many of them exhibit no mean attempts at Epic Poetry, and tho' full of the exploded fictions of Chivalry, frequently display great descriptive and inventive powers in the Bards, who composed them. They are at least generally equal to any other poetry of the same age. They cannot indeed be put in competition with the nervous productions of so universal and commanding a genius as Chaucer, but they have a simplicity that makes them be read with less interruption, and be more easily understood: and they are far more spirited and entertaining than the tedious allegories of Gower, or the dull and prolix legends of Lydgate. Yet, while so much stress is laid upon the writings of these last, by such as treat of English poetry, the old metrical Romances, tho' far more popular in their time, are hardly known to exist. But it has happened unluckily, that the antiquaries, who have revived the works of our ancient writers, have been for the most part men void of taste and genius, and

---

[21] Cf *Sir Thopas, CT,* VII, 897-902.

therefore have always fastidiously rejected the old poetical Romances, because founded [*sic*] on fictitious or popular subjects, while they have been careful to grub up every petty fragment of the most dull and insipid rhymist, whose merit it was to deform morality, or obscure true history. Should the public encourage the revival of some of those ancient Epic Songs of Chivalry, they would frequently see the rich ore of an Ariosto or a Tasso, tho' buried it may be among the rubbish and dross of barbarous times.

Such a production would answer many important uses: It would throw new light on the rise and progress of English poetry, the history of which can be but imperfectly understood, if these are neglected: It would also serve to illustrate innumerable passages in our ancient classic poets, which without their help must be for ever obscure. For not to mention Chaucer and Spencer, who abound with perpetual allusions to them, I shall give an instance or two from Shakespeare, by way of specimen of their use.

[Percy gives an example of what he believes to be Shakespeare's referring to the romance of *Richard Coer de Lyon*, which he summarises and quotes from.[22] In the third section of the essay, he goes on to discuss *Libeaus Desconus*, summarising the plot of the romance at length.]

Such is the fable of this ancient piece: which the reader may observe, is as regular in its conduct, as any of the finest poems of classical antiquity. If the execution, particularly as to the diction and sentiments, were but equal to the plan, it would be a capital performance; but this is such as might be expected in rude and ignorant times, and in a barbarous unpolished language.

IV. I shall conclude this prolix account, with a LIST of such old METRICAL ROMANCES as are still extant: beginning with those mentioned by Chaucer.

[Percy then lists around 30 romances known to him, giving a short comment on each and providing bibliographical information.]

---

[22] *King John* I. 1. 267.

3. Thomas Warton (1728-90)

Many eighteenth-century scholars and writers felt the need of a comprehensive history of English poetry, but little beyond the planning was done before Thomas Gray began research for such a work in 1753. Gray gave up, but sent his plan to Thomas Warton, on hearing that Warton was engaged on a similar enterprise (see Fairer, Introduction (1998), pp. 7-8). With the *History of English Poetry* Warton provided a second great resource, after Percy's *Reliques*, for the study of the later medieval literature. He excluded Anglo-Saxon from his researches, ostensibly because it had 'no connection' with his subject, which began with 'that era, when our national character began to dawn' (*HEP*, I, vi); implicitly, that national character does not derive from the Germanic nation that preceded the Conquest. The plan was to bring the history up to Warton's own time, but only a few pages of the projected fourth volume were printed. By default, the *History* became a study of late medieval and early modern literature; like the *Reliques*, it popularised a vision of a Middle Ages of feudal pomp and glamorous chivalry and saw the chivalric romances, however fanciful they were, as reflections of real life. The *History* gave readers (more or less) direct access to texts in hundreds of manuscripts, many of which had been forgotten for centuries. Amongst other things, Warton discovered the romance of *Ywain and Gawain*, and also found *Pearl* and *Cleanness*, including only short extracts from those poems (and missing *Sir Gawain and the Green Knight* altogether). He gave the first extended critical accounts of the Scottish Chaucerians, and of Gower, Lydgate, Hoccleve and Hawes. One biographer noted that Warton had gone to 4000 authorities in compiling the history (Rinaker, p. 124).

The sheer utility of the work outweighed its many and considerable shortcomings. Succeeding literary antiquarians would complain about its inadequacy, but it was too useful to ignore or to replace. Consequently, it was revised once a generation or so in the nineteenth century: by Richard Price in 1824 with notes by Ritson, Francis Douce, and others; by Richard Taylor in 1840, with help from Frederic Madden, Thomas Wright, Richard Garnett, the Anglo-Saxonists Benjamin Thorpe and J. M. Kemble, and others; and by W. Carew Hazlitt, in 1871. Hazlitt's revision included work by Madden and Wright — by then very much of the older generation of scholars — and from the new medievalists, Walter Skeat, Richard Morris, and Frederic Furnivall. In addition, George Ellis's *Specimens of the Early English Poets* (see section on Ellis) is explicitly in the tradition of Warton, and can be regarded as a kind of supplement to his history. (See also the introductory note to Warton in Part 1.)

For biography on Warton, see Clarissa Rinaker, *Thomas Warton: A Biographical and Critical Study* (Urbana: University of Illinois, 1916), John A. Vance, *Joseph and Thomas Warton* (Boston: Twayne, 1983) and David

Fairer ed., *The Correspondence of Thomas Warton* (Athens, GA: University of Georgia Press, 1995); on the *History*, its genesis and its nature, see Joseph M. P. Donatelli, 'The Medieval Fictions of Thomas Warton and Thomas Percy', *University of Toronto Quarterly* 60 (1991), 435-51; David Fairer, 'The Origin of Warton's History of English Poetry', *Review of English Studies* 32 (1981), 37-63; David Fairer, 'Introduction', *Thomas Warton's History of English Poetry*. 4 vols. (London: Routledge/Thoemmes, 1998); *EG*, ch. 4, and *MME*, ch. 2.

Thomas Warton, *The History of English Poetry*, 3 vols (London, 1774-81).

From: volumes 1 and 2 (1774 and 1778), various.
Warton on early Middle English (pp. 37-42)

[After the discussion of linguistic change with which he opens the *History* proper — see Part I — Warton begins detailing the poetic contents of various manuscripts and quoting at length from poems. These he ornaments with commentary, which is essentially his method throughout the work. He begins with passages from the satire, 'The Land of Cokaygne', and then quotes from several saints' lives and the Harley lyrics, before passing to the topic of romance.]

When we consider the feudal manners, and the magnificence of our Norman ancestors, their love of military glory, the enthusiasm with which they engaged in the crusades, and the wonders to which they must have been familiarised from those eastern enterprises, we naturally suppose, what will hereafter be more particularly proved, that their retinues abounded with minstrels and harpers, and that their chief entertainment was to listen to the recital of romantic and martial adventures. But I have been much disappointed in my searches after the metrical tales which must have prevailed in their times. Most of those old heroic songs are perished, together with the stately castles in whose halls they were sung. Yet they are not so totally lost as we may be apt to imagine. Many of them still partly exist in the old English metrical romances, which will be mentioned in their proper places; yet divested of their original form, polished in their style, adorned with new incidents, successively modernised by repeated transcription and recitation, and retaining little more than the outlines of the original composition. This has not been the case of the legendary and other religious poems written soon after the conquest, manuscripts of which abound in our libraries. From the nature of their subject they were less popular and common; and being less frequently recited, became less liable to perpetual innovation or alteration.

The most antient English metrical romance which I can discover, is entitled the GESTE OF KING HORN. It was evidently written after the crusades had begun, is mentioned by Chaucer, and probably still remains in its original state.[23] I will first give the substance of the story, and afterwards add some specimens of the composition. But I must premise, that this story occurs in very old French metre in the manuscripts of the British Museum, so that probably it is a translation:[24] a circumstance which will throw light on an argument pursued hereafter, proving that most of our metrical romances are translated from the French.

[Warton then summarises the story, and quotes at some length from the poem.]

It is the force of the story in these pieces that chiefly engages our attention. The minstrels had no idea of conducting and describing a delicate situation. The general manners were gross, and the arts of writing unknown. Yet this simplicity sometimes pleases more than the most artificial touches. In the mean time, the pictures of antient manners presented by these early writers, strongly interest the imagination: especially as having the same uncommon merit with the pictures of manners in Homer, that of being founded in truth and reality, and actually painted from the life. To talk of the grossness and absurdity of such manners is little to the purpose; the poet is only concerned in the justness and faithfulness of the representation.

Warton on later Middle English (pp. 43-92)

Hitherto we have been engaged in examining the state of our poetry from the conquest to the year 1200, or rather afterwards. It will appear to have made no very rapid improvement from that period. Yet as we proceed, we shall find the language losing much of its antient barbarism and obscurity, and approaching more nearly to the dialect of modern times.

[...]

The first poet whose name occurs in the reign of Edward the first, and indeed in these annals, is Robert of Glocester, a monk of the abbey of Glocester. He has left a poem of considerable length, which is a history of England in verse, from Brutus to the reign of Edward the first.[25] It was evidently written after the year 1278, as the poet mentions king Arthur's

---

[23] *Sir Thopas*, CT, VII, 898; it is in fact *Horn Child* that is mentioned in *Thopas*, which Chaucer perhaps knew from the Auchinleck manuscript. This title was, however, regularly used for *King Horn* in the eighteenth and early nineteenth century. *King Horn* is still believed to be the oldest English romance. Warton knew it from BL MS Harl 2253; it also exists in a manuscript probably slightly earlier, Bodl Laud Misc. 108.

[24] The late twelfth-century AN *Horn et Rimenhild*, known by Warton to be in BL MS Harl 527; *King Horn* is not a direct translation from this poem and the exact relation of the two is unclear.

[25] See *The Metrical Chronicle of Robert of Gloucester*, ed. by William Aldis Wright, 2 vols, RS 86 (London: HMSO, 1887).

sumptuous tomb, erected in that year before the high altar of Glastenbury church: and he declares himself a living witness of the remarkably dismal weather which distinguished the day on which the battle of Evesham abovementioned was fought, in the year 1265. From these and other circumstances this piece appears to have been composed about the year 1280.[26] [...] This rhyming chronicle is totally destitute of art or imagination. The author has cloathed the fables of Geoffrey of Monmouth in rhyme, which have often a more poetical air in Geoffrey's prose. The language is not much more easy or intelligible than that of many of the Norman Saxon poems quoted in the preceding section: it is full of Saxonisms, which indeed abound, more or less, in every writer before Gower and Chaucer. But this obscurity is perhaps owing to the western dialect, in which our monk of Glocester was educated. Provincial barbarisms are naturally the growth of extreme counties, and of such as are situated at a distance from the metropolis: and it is probable, that the Saxon heptarchy, which consisted of a cluster of seven independent states, contributed to produce as many different provincial dialects.

[...]

At the close of the reign of Edward the first, and in the year 1303, a poet occurs named Robert Mannyng, but more commonly called Robert de Brunne. He was a Gilbertine monk in the monastery of Brunne, or Bourne, near Depyng in Lincolnshire: but he had been before professed in the priory of Sixhille, a house of the same order, and in the same county. He was merely a translator. He translated into English meter, or rather paraphrased, a French book, written by Grosthead bishop of Lincoln, entitled, MANUEL PECHE, or MANUEL de PECHE, that is, the MANUAL OF SINS.[27] This translation was never printed.[28] It is a long work, and treats of the decalogue, and the seven deadly sins, which are illustrated with many legendary stories. [...] From the Prologue, among other circumstances, it appears that Robert de Brunne designed this performance to be sung to the harp at public entertainments, and that it was written or begun in the year 1303.
[Warton quotes from the work.]

---

[26] Douglas Gray suggests that the chronicle, which is now believed to be the work of more than one contributor, might not have been 'completed much before 1325' (MEL, p. 92).

[27] Robert Grosseteste, bishop of Lincoln (1235-53), is attributed with the authorship of Le Manuel des Pechiez in two manuscripts of Mannyng's Handlyng Synne but is not now thought to be the author. The work is sometimes attributed to a William of Wadington; see MEL, pp. 46, 41.

[28] Edited by Frederick Furnivall for the EETS in 1901-03, it is now available in Idelle Sullens, ed. Handlyng Synne, MRTS 14 (Binghamton, N.Y.: State University of New York, 1983).

But Robert de Brunne's largest work is a metrical chronicle of England. The former part, from Æneas to the death of Cadwallader, is translated from an old French poet called MAISTER WACE or GASSE, who manifestly copied Geoffry of Monmouth, in a poem commonly entitled ROMAN DE ROIS D'ANGLETERRE. It is esteemed one of the oldest of the French romances; and begun to be written by Eustace [...] who finished his part under the title of BRUT D'ANGLETERRE, in the year 1155. Hence Robert de Brunne, somewhat inaccurately, calls it simply the BRUT.

[...]

The second part of Robert de Brunne's CHRONICLE, beginning from Cadwallader, and ending with Edward the first, is translated, in great measure, from the second part of a French metrical chronicle, written in five books, by Peter Langtoft, an Augustine canon of the monastery of Bridlington in Yorkshire, who wrote not many years before his translator.

[Warton gives extracts from Mannyng's works and, in an aside that would cause much later speculation, surmises that the poet Thomas of Erceldoune mentioned by Mannyng is the same as the semi-legendary Thomas the Rhymer. He continues:]

But I forbear to give further extracts from this writer, who appears to have possessed much more industry than genius, and cannot at present be read with much pleasure. Yet it should be remembered, that even such a writer as Robert de Brunne, uncouth and unpleasing as he naturally seems, and chiefly employed in turning the theology of his age into rhyme, contributed to form a style, to teach expression, and to polish his native tongue. In the infancy of language and composition, nothing is wanted but writers: at that period even the most artless have their use.

[...]

It is at least probable, that the leisure of monastic life produced many rhymers. From proofs here given we may fairly conclude, that the monks often wrote for the minstrels: and although our Gilbertine brother of Brunne chose to relate true stories in plain language, yet it is reasonable to suppose, that many of our antient tales in verse containing fictitious adventures, were written, although not invented, in the religious houses. The romantic history of *Guy earl of Warwick*, is expressly said, on good authority, to have been written by Walter of Exeter, a Franciscan Friar of Carocus in Cornwall, about the year 1292.[29] The libraries of the monasteries were full of romances. *Bevis*

---

[29] The authority is Bale, in his *Index Britanniae Scriptorum* (after 1546); see *Index Britanniae Scriptorum [...] John Bale's Index of British and Other Writers*, ed. by Reginald Lane Poole (Oxford: Clarendon Press, 1902), p. 104. But there is nothing to suggest that this Walter of Exeter's life of Guy was the *romance*. Ritson is more sceptical; see pp. 112-114.

of Southampton, in French, was in the library of the abbey of Leicester.
[...]
Nor is it improbable, that some of our greater monasteries kept minstrels of their own in regular pay.

Warton on romance (pp. 109-209)

We have seen, in the preceding section, that the character of our poetical composition began to be changed about the reign of the first Edward: that either fictitious adventures were substituted by the minstrels in the place of historical and traditionary facts, or reality disguised by the misrepresentations of invention; and that a taste for ornamental and even exotic expression gradually prevailed over the rude simplicity of the native English phraseology. This change, which with our language affected our poetry, had been growing for some time; and among other causes was occasioned by the introduction and increase of the tales of chivalry.

The ideas of chivalry, in an imperfect degree, had been of old established among the Gothic tribes. The fashion of challenging to single combat, the pride of seeking dangerous adventures, and the spirit of avenging and protecting the fair sex, seem to have been peculiar to the northern nations in the most uncultivated state of Europe. All these customs were afterwards encouraged and confirmed by corresponding circumstances in the feudal constitution. At length the crusades excited a new spirit of enterprise, and introduced into the courts and ceremonies of European princes a higher degree of splendor and parade, caught from the riches and magnificence of eastern cities. These oriental expeditions established a taste for hyperbolical description, and propagated an infinity of marvellous tales, which men returning from distant countries easily imposed on credulous and ignorant minds. The unparalleled emulation with which the nations of christendom universally embraced this holy cause, the pride with which emperors, kings, barons, earls, bishops, and knights strove to excel each other on this interesting occasion, not only in prowess and heroism, but in sumptuous equipages, gorgeous banners, armorial cognisances, splendid pavilions, and other expensive articles of a similar nature, diffused a love of war, and a fondness for military pomp. Hence their very diversions became warlike, and the martial enthusiasm of the times appeared in tilts and tournaments. These practices and opinions co-operated with the kindred superstitions of dragons, dwarfs, fairies, giants, and enchanters, which the traditions of the Gothic scalders had already planted; and produced that extraordinary species of composition which has been called ROMANCE.[30]

---

[30] The account of chivalry in this paragraph is essentially a digest of the arguments of

[...]

But not only the pieces of the French minstrels, written in French, were circulated in England about this time [1200]; but translations of these pieces were made into English, which containing much of the French idiom, together with a sort of poetical phraseology before unknown, produced various innovations in our style. These translations, it is probable, were enlarged with additions, or improved with alterations of the story. Hence it was that Robert de Brunne, as we have already seen, complained of *strange* and *quaint* English, of the changes made in the story of SIR TRISTRAM, and of the liberties assumed by his cotemporary minstrels in altering facts and coining new phrases.[31] Yet these circumstances enriched our tongue, and extended the circle of our poetry. And for what reason these fables were so much admired and encouraged, in preference to the languid poetical chronicles of Robert of Gloucester and Robert of Brunne, it is obvious to conjecture. The gallantries of chivalry were exhibited with new splendour, and the times were growing more refined.

[...]

Tilts and tournaments, after a long disuse, were revived with superior lustre in the reign of Edward the first. Roger earl of Mortimer, a magnificent baron of that reign, erected in his stately castle of Kenelworth a Round Table, at which he restored the rites of king Arthur. He entertained in this castle the constant retinue of one hundred knights, and as many ladies; and invited thither adventurers in chivalry from every part of christendom. These fables were therefore an image of the manners, customs, mode of life, and favourite amusements, which now prevailed, not only in France but in England, accompanied with all the decorations which fancy could invent, and recommended by the graces of romantic fiction. They complimented [*sic*] the ruling passion of the times, and cherished in a high degree the fashionable sentiments of ideal honour, and fantastic fortitude.

[Warton now warms to his main subject, romance, quoting and summarising from several metrical romances for many pages, and explicitly recommending romance over the 'obscure fragments of uninstructive morality or

---

Richard Hurd in his *Letters on Chivalry and Romance* (London, 1762), and testifies to the prevalence at the time of the notion that chivalric romance derived from the north; see also Percy's essay on metrical romances. It was furthermore thought by many scholars that the northern, 'Gothic' tribes derived ultimately from the east. The medieval Icelandic connection of the Norse Æsir (the Old Norse name for the pagan gods) with Asia had been restated by Paul-Henri Mallet in his *Introduction à l'Histoire de Dannemarc*, 2 vols. (Copenhagen, 1755-6) and 2nd. edn (Geneva, 1763), translated by Percy as *Northern Antiquities* (1770), esp. 37.

[31] See Idelle Sullens, ed. *Robert Mannyng of Brunne: Chronicle*, MRTS 153 (Binghamton, N.Y.: Binghamton University, 1996), p. 93, ll. 93-102.

uninteresting history' that earlier antiquarians had favoured. 'But in the present age we are beginning to make ample amends: in which the curiosity of the antiquarian is connected with taste and genius, and his researches tend to display the progress of human manners, and to illustrate the history of society'.]

Warton on Langland (pp. 266-67)

The next poet in succession is one who deserves more attention on various accounts. This is Robert Longlande, author of the poem called the VISION OF PIERCE PLOWMAN, a secular priest, and a fellow of Oriel college, in Oxford. He flourished about the year 1350.[32] This poem contains a series of distinct visions, which the author imagines himself to have seen, while he was sleeping, after a long ramble on Malverne-hills in Worcestershire. It is a satire on the vices of almost every profession: but particularly on the corruptions of the clergy, and the absurdities of superstition. These are ridiculed with much humour and spirit, couched under a strong vein of allegorical invention. But instead of availing himself of the rising and rapid improvements of the English language, Longland prefers and adopts the style of the Anglo-Saxon poets. Nor did he make these writers the models of his language only: he likewise imitates their alliterative versification, which consisted in using an aggregate of words beginning with the same letter. He has therefore rejected rhyme, in the place of which he thinks it sufficient to substitute a perpetual alliteration. But this imposed constraint of seeking identical initials, and the affectation of obsolete English, by demanding a constant and necessary departure from the natural and obvious forms of expression, while it circumscribed the powers of our author's genius, contributed also to render his manner extremely perplexed, and to disgust the reader with obscurities. The satire is conducted by the agency of several allegorical personages, such as Avarice, Bribery, Simony, Theology, Conscience, &c.

Warton on Chaucer (pp. 339-44)

As we are approaching to Chaucer, let us here stand still, and take a retrospect of the general manners. The tournaments and carousals of our antient princes, by forming splendid assemblies of both sexes, while they inculcated the most liberal sentiments of honour and heroism, undoubtedly contributed to introduce ideas of courtesy, and to encourage decorum. Yet the national manners still retained a great degree of ferocity, and the ceremonies of the most refined courts in Europe had often a mixture of barbarism, which rendered them ridiculous. This absurdity will always appear at periods when

---

[32] See above, note 17.

men are so far civilised as to have lost their native simplicity, and yet have not attained just ideas of politeness and propriety. Their luxury was inelegant, their pleasures indelicate, their pomp cumbersome and unwieldy. In the mean time it may seem surprising, that the many schools of philosophy which flourished in the middle ages, should not have corrected and polished the times. But as their religion was corrupted by superstition, so their philosophy degenerated into sophistry. Nor is it science alone, even if founded on truth, that will polish nations. For this purpose, the powers of imagination must be awakened and exerted, to teach elegant feelings, and to heighten our natural sensibilities. It is not the head only that must be informed, but the heart must also be moved.[33] Many classic authors were known in the thirteenth century, but the scholars of that period wanted taste to read and admire them. The pathetic or sublime strokes of Virgil would be but little relished by theologists and metaphysicians.

Sect. XII

The most illustrious ornament of the reign of Edward the third, and of his successor Richard the second, was Jeffrey Chaucer; a poet with whom the history of our poetry is by many supposed to have commenced; and who has been pronounced, by a critic of unquestionable taste and discernment, to be the first English versifier who wrote poetically.[34] He was born in the year 1328, and educated at Oxford, where he made a rapid progress in the scholastic sciences as they were then taught:[35] but the liveliness of his parts, and the native gaiety of his disposition, soon recommended him to the patronage of a magnificent monarch, and rendered him a very popular and acceptable character in the brilliant court which I have above described.[36] In

---

[33] The tension between head and heart, reason and emotion, is a key Wartonian theme; these oppositions, for Warton, parallel the opposition between modernity and the Middle Ages. While he views his own modernity as a time of unexampled refinement, Warton feels there is something of imaginative value in the Middle Ages that has been lost and that can be partially recovered through the romances.

[34] Samuel Johnson, *A Dictionary of the English Language*, 2 vols (London, 1755), I, F1[v].

[35] 'For Chaucer's early biographers it was, of course, very desirable that the poet should have attended one or other of the ancient universities; conscious of the invidiousness of choice, they compromised by sending him to both'. Derek Pearsall, *The Life of Geoffrey Chaucer: A Critical Biography* (Oxford: Blackwell, 1992), p. 29. Speght, in 1598, argued that Chaucer was born in London on the basis of the *Testament of Love* (included in William Thynne's Chaucer edition of 1532) and gave a date of 1328 or 1329 that seems to rely on guesswork. But 1328 was accepted until the discovery of life-records disproved it late in the nineteenth century. Thomas Speght, *The Workes of [...] Geffrey Chavcer* (London, 1598), Bii[r]; cf *Testament of Love* 1.6.97-99, in *The Complete Works of Geoffrey Chaucer*, ed. by W. W. Skeat, 7 vols (Oxford: Clarendon Press, 1894-97), VII (1897), 27-28.

[36] Note that Warton's phrase concerning Chaucer here is a direct echo of Percy's

the mean time, he added to his accomplishments by frequent tours into France and Italy, which he sometimes visited under the advantages of a public character. Hitherto our poets had been persons of a private and circumscribed education, and the art of versifying, like every other kind of composition, had been confined to recluse scholars. But Chaucer was a man of the world: and from this circumstance we are to account, in great measure, for the many new embellishments which he conferred on our language and our poetry. The descriptions of splendid processions and gallant carousals, with which his works abound, are a proof that he was conversant with the practices and diversions of polite life. Familiarity with a variety of things and objects, opportunities of acquiring the fashionable and courtly modes of speech, connections with the great at home, and a personal acquaintance with the vernacular poets of foreign countries, opened his mind and furnished him with new lights. In Italy he was introduced to Petrarch, at the wedding of Violante, daughter of Galeazzo duke of Milan, with the duke of Clarence: and it is not improbable that Boccacio [sic] was of the party. Although Chaucer had undoubtedly studied the works of these celebrated writers, and particularly of Dante, before this fortunate interview; yet it seems likely, that these excursions gave him a new relish for their compositions, and enlarged his knowledge of the Italian fables. His travels likewise enabled him to cultivate the Italian and Provencial languages with the greatest success; and induced him to polish the asperity, and enrich the sterility of his native versification, with softer cadences, and a more copious and variegated phraseology. In this attempt, which was authorised by the recent and popular examples of Petrarch in Italy and Alain Chartier in France, he was countenanced and assisted by his friend John Gower, the early guide and encourager of his studies. The revival of learning in most countries appears to have first owed its rise to translation. At rude periods the modes of original thinking are unknown, and the arts of original composition have not yet been studied. The writers therefore of such periods are chiefly and very usefully employed in importing the ideas of other languages into their own. They do not venture to think for themselves, nor aim at the merit of inventors, but they are laying the foundations of literature: and while they are naturalising the knowledge of more learned ages and countries by translation, they are imperceptibly improving the national language. This has been remarkably the

---

contention that the minstrels were 'extremely popular and acceptable' in aristocratic courts (see the first paragraph of Percy's essay on minstrels). The obvious implication is that Chaucer shared the minstrels' exalted and protected position; behind the echo there is also perhaps a sense that Chaucer is the inheritor of the role of Percy's minstrels just as the minstrels were seen in a lineage going back to the ancient bards.

case, not only in England, but in France and Italy. In the year 1387, John Trevisa canon of Westbury in Wiltshire, and a great traveller, not only finished a translation of the Old and New Testaments, at the command of his munificent patron Thomas lord Berkley, but also translated Higden's POLYCHRONICON, and other Latin pieces. But these translations would have been alone insufficient to have produced or sustained any considerable revolution in our language: the great work was reserved for Gower and Chaucer. Wickliffe had also translated the bible: and in other respects his attempts to bring about a reformation in religion at this time proved beneficial to English literature. The orthodox divines of the period generally wrote in Latin: but Wickliffe, that his arguments might be familiarised to common readers and the bulk of the people, was obliged to compose in English his numerous theological treatises against the papal corruptions. Edward the third, while he perhaps intended only to banish a badge of conquest, greatly contributed to establish the national dialect, by abolishing the use of the Norman tongue in the public acts and judicial proceedings, as we have before observed, and by substituting the natural language of the country. But Chaucer manifestly first taught his countrymen to write English; and formed a style by naturalising words from the Provencial, at that time the most polished dialect of any in Europe, and the best adapted to the purposes of poetical expression.

It is certain that Chaucer abounds in classical allusions: but his poetry is not formed on the antient models. He appears to have been an universal reader, and his learning is sometimes mistaken for genius: but his chief sources were the French and Italian poets.

Warton on a Canterbury Tale (I, 423-32)

[...] But I am of opinion that the MILLER'S TALE has more true humour than either [the Nun's Priest's or Merchant's tales]. Not that I mean to palliate the levity of the story, which was most probably chosen by Chaucer in compliance with the prevailing manners of an unpolished age, and agreeable to ideas of festivity not always the most delicate and refined. Chaucer abounds in liberties of this kind, and this must be his apology.

[...]

[...] The character of the Clerke of Oxford, who studied astrology, a science then in high repute, but under the specious appearance of decorum, and the mask of the serious philosopher, carried on intrigues, is painted with these lively circumstances. [Warton quotes the description of Nicholas, *CT*, I, 3199-3216.]

In the description of the young wife of our philosopher's host, there is great elegance with a mixture of burlesque allusions. Not to mention the curiosity of a female portrait, drawn with so much exactness at such a distance of time. [Warton quotes *CT*, I, 3233-67.]

Nicholas, as we may suppose, was not proof against the charms of his blooming hostess. He has frequent opportunities of conversing with her: for her husband is the carpenter of Oseney Abbey near Oxford, and often absent in the woods belonging to the monastery. His rival is Absalom, a parish-clerk, the gaiest of his calling, who being amorously inclined, very naturally avails himself of a circumstance belonging to his profession: on holidays it was his business to carry the censer about the church, and he takes this opportunity of casting unlawful glances on the handsomest dames of the parish. His gallantry, agility, affectation of dress and personal elegance, skill in shaving and surgery, smattering in the law, taste for music, and many other accomplishments, are thus inimitably represented by Chaucer, who must have relished so ridiculous a character. [Warton quotes *CT*, I, 3312-32, 3373-84, 3687-94, in this way summarising the plot, with quotations.]

[...] He [John the carpenter] is soon persuaded to believe the prediction: and in the sequel, which cannot be repeated here, this humourous contrivance crowns the scholar's schemes with success, and proves the cause of the carpenter's disgrace. In this piece the reader observes that the humour of the characters is made subservient to the plot.

I have before hinted, that Chaucer's obscenity is in great measure to be imputed to his age. We are apt to form romantic and exaggerated notions about the moral innocence of our ancestors. Ages of ignorance and simplicity are thought to be ages of purity. The direct contrary, I believe, is the case. Rude periods have that grossness of manners which is not less friendly to virtue than luxury itself. In the middle ages, not only the most flagrant violations of modesty were frequently practised and permitted, but the most infamous vices. Men are less ashamed as they are less polished. Great refinement multiplies criminal pleasures, but at the same time prevents the actual commission of many enormities: at least it preserves public decency, and suppresses public licentiousness.

Warton on realism and character in the *Canterbury Tales* (p. 435)

But Chaucer's vein of humour, although conspicuous in the CANTERBURY TALES, is chiefly displayed in the Characters with which they are introduced. In these his knowledge of the world availed him in a peculiar degree, and enabled him to give such an accurate picture of antient manners, as no cotemporary nation has transmitted to posterity. It is here that we view the pursuits and employments, the customs and diversions, of our ancestors, copied from the life, and represented with equal truth and spirit, by a judge of mankind, whose penetration qualified him to discern their foibles or discriminating peculiarities; and by an artist, who understood that proper selection of circumstances, and those predominant characteristics, which form a finished portrait. We are surprised to find, in so gross and ignorant an age, such talents for satire, and for observation on life; qualities which usually exert themselves at more civilised periods, when the improved state of society, by subtilising our speculations, and establishing uniform modes of behaviour, disposes mankind to study themselves, and renders deviations of conduct, and singularities of character, more immediately and necessarily the objects of censure and ridicule. These curious and valuable remains are specimens of Chaucer's native genius, unassisted and unalloyed. The figures are all British, and bear no suspicious signatures of classical, Italian, or French imitation. The characters of Theophrastus are not so lively, particular, and appropriated.

In conclusion on Chaucer (p. 457)

It is not my intention to devote a volume to Chaucer, how much soever he may deserve it; nor can it be expected, that, in a work of this general nature, I should enter into a critical examination of all Chaucer's pieces. Enough has been said to prove, that in elevation, and elegance, in harmony and perspicuity of versification, he surpasses his predecessors in an infinite proportion: that his genius was universal, and adapted to themes of unbounded variety: that his merit was not less in painting familiar manners with humour and propriety, than in moving the passions, and in representing the beautiful or the grand objects of nature with grace and sublimity. In a word, that he appeared with all the lustre and dignity of a true poet, in an age which compelled him to struggle with a barbarous language, and a national want of taste; and when to write verses at all, was regarded as a singular qualification.

Warton on fifteenth-century verse (p. 51)

I consider Chaucer as a genial day in an English spring. A brilliant sun enlivens the face of nature with an unusual lustre: the sudden appearance of cloudless skies, and the unexpected warmth of a tepid atmosphere, after the gloom and the inclemencies of a tedious winter, fill our hearts with the visionary prospect of a speedy summer: and we fondly anticipate a long continuance of gentle gales and vernal serenity. But winter returns with redoubled horrors: the clouds condense more formidably than before; and those tender buds, and early blossoms, which were called forth by the transient gleam of a temporary sun-shine, are nipped by frost, and torn by tempests.

Most of the poets that immediately succeeded Chaucer, seem rather relapsing into barbarism, than availing themselves of those striking ornaments which his judgment and imagination had disclosed. They appear to have been insensible to his vigour of versification, and his flights of fancy. It was not indeed likely that a poet should soon arise equal to Chaucer: and it must be remembered, that the national distractions which ensued, had no small share in obstructing the exercise of those studies which delight in peace and repose. His successors, however, approach him in no degree of proportion.

4. Joseph Ritson (1752-1803)

Joseph Ritson, the firebrand of late eighteenth-century antiquarianism, was born in Durham and trained as a lawyer, but he seems to have devoted himself principally to his antiquarian researches after moving to Gray's Inn in London in 1775. Where most literary antiquarians tended to be politically conservative, Ritson was an avowed revolutionary, a sympathiser with the French cause in the 1790s, and for a time an associate of the radicals William Godwin, John Thelwall, and Thomas Holcroft. He took this adversarial stance into his literary scholarship, where his famously abrasive style earned him few friends and ensured his unpopularity and consequent poverty, which in turn contributed to his decline into illness, madness, and an early death.

The hallmark of Ritson's editorial approach was accuracy. He decried the common eighteenth-century practice, represented particularly by Percy, of tastefully improving early literature. His approach found little favour, and although he produced many carefully designed works of early literature he converted few readers to his cause. In the nineteenth century, his reputation was partially rehabilitated by scholars who rejected the 'improvement' style of editing, and some of his works, particularly his *Robin Hood*, became very popular.

Ritson's principal Middle English works were *Poems on Interesting Events in the Reign of King Edward III [...] By Laurence Minot* (London, 1795), the first edition of that poet's work, and *Ancient Engleish Metrical Romanceës* in 3 volumes, (London, 1802), which contained the first editions of several works, including *Ywain and Gawain*. His *Ancient Songs, From the Time of King Henry the Third, to the Revolution* (London, 1790; not published until 1792), *Pieces of Ancient Popular Poetry* (London, 1791) and *Robin Hood* (London, 1795) all contained some medieval verse. Like Percy and other antiquarians, Ritson tended to be interested in genres and authors rather than periods. So, like the *Reliques*, his collections usually crossed the divide between medieval and early modern. *Ancient Engleish Metrical Romanceës* is one of his better known works, and remained useful for many years. However, Ritson's more characteristic concern was with popular poetry, the poetry he imagined to be that of the people.

For biography, see Bertrand H. Bronson, *Joseph Ritson: Scholar-at-Arms*, 2 vols (Berkeley: University of California Press, 1938); on Ritson's work and career see also *EG*, ch. 5, and *MME*, ch. 2; on his editing, see A. S. G. Edwards, 'Observations on the History of Middle English Editing', in *Manuscripts and Texts: Editorial Problems in Later Middle English Literature*, ed. by Derek Pearsall (Cambridge: Brewer, 1987), pp. 34-48.

[Joseph Ritson], ed. *A Select Collection of English Songs*, 3 vols. (London, 1783).

From: Preface (I, pp. ix-x).

[In this aside in what is otherwise a preface concerning his principles of selection, Ritson opens the attack he would later intensify on Percy's practices of editing.]

What is already said has been entirely confined to the three first parts of the collection; of PART THE FOURTH, therefor, a considerable, at least interesting portion of the work, not to be found in any former compilation of this nature, it still remains to be spoken. This department is engrossed by a select number, indeed ALL THE BEST, of our old popular tragic legends, and historical or heroic ballads: the genuine effusions of the English muse, unadulterated with the sentimental refinements of Italy or France. And without these (which would by no means assimilate or mix with the more polished contents of the preceding divisions) the collection, as professedly designed to comprehend every species of singing poetry, would, doubtless, have been imperfect. Every piece in this class has been transcribed from some old copy, generally in black letter; and has, in most cases, been collated with various others, preserved in different repositories. Many of them, however, it must be confessed, are printed in the *Reliques of ancient English Poetry*; a work which may, perhaps, be by some thought to have precluded every future attempt. But, in truth, there is not the least rivalship, or even connection, between the two publications. And, indeed, if the contrary had been the case, the inaccurate, and sophisticated manner in which every thing that had real pretensions to antiquity, has been printed by the right reverend editor of that admired and celebrated work, would be a sufficient apology for any one who might undertake to publish more faithful, though, haply, less elegant copies. No liberties, beyond a necessary modernisation of the orthography, have been taken with the language of these antique compositions, unless in a few instances, where a manifest blunder of the press at once required and justified the correction.

[The attack continues in a footnote:]

The truth of this charge [against the *Reliques*], which will not, it is believed, much surprise any person conversant in the illustrious editors authorities, may, on some future occasion, be more minutely exemplified, and satisfactorily proved. It will be, here, sufficient to observe, that frequent recourse has, in compiling materials for the present volumes, been necessarily had to many of the originals from which the *Reliques* are professedly printed; but not one has, upon examination, been found to be followed with either fidelity or correctness. That the above work is beautiful, elegant, and ingenious, it would be ridiculous to deny; but they who look into it to be acquainted with the state of ancient poetry, will be miserably disappointed or fatally misled. Forgery and imposition of every kind, ought to be universally execrated, and never more than when they are employed by persons high in rank or character, and those very circumstances are made use of to sanctify the deceit.[37]

From: 'A Historical Essay on the Origin and Progress of National Song' (I, pp. xlv-lviii).

It is not unreasonable to attribute the suppression of the romantic poems and popular songs of the Saxons, to the monks, who seem not only to have refused to commit them to writing, which few others were capable of doing, but to have given no quarter to any thing of the kind which fell into their hands. Hence it is, that, except the Saxon chronicle, and a few other historical fragments, together with many of their laws, and a number of charters, deeds, &c. all which are to be sure of some consequence, we have little or nothing original, in the language, but lying legends, glosses, homilies, charms, and such-like things, which evidently shew the people, from their conversion, at least, to have been gloomy, superstitious, and priest-ridden. What advantages Christianity brought them, how much it enlightened their understandings, or improved their morals, to counterbalance the destruction of their national genius and spirit, is not, perhaps, at this distance of time, altogether so easy to be discovered.

[...]

The Saxon language continued to be spoken by the old inhabitants for near a century and a half after their subduction, but, by a rapid, though, doubtless, gradual corruption, from an intermixture of Norman words, and the adoption of Norman idioms and modes of speaking, we may, in some, probably the earlier part of the long and turbulent reign of Henry III. pronounce it to have dyed a violent death; the written dialect we meet toward the end of his time, being essentially a different tongue: from this uncertain period, therefor, we date the birth and establishment of the English language.

[...]

These two songs [*The Battle of Otterburn* and *Chevy Chace*] are by this

---

[37] Ritson here implies that Percy used his position as bishop to carry off the 'deceit' in the editing of the *Reliques*, a charge that does not stand up. Percy was an almost unknown country vicar when the work first appeared and the first three editions long predated his elevation in the church. In addition, Ritson is asking that Percy conform to standards that barely existed in the 1760s. As Albert B. Friedman suggests, the *Reliques* 'was a victim of its own success: the respect which the *Reliques* won for popular poetry led eventually to higher standards in ballad-editing, against which the *Reliques* itself came to be measured and found seriously deficient' (*The Ballad Revival: Studies in the Influence of Popular on Sophisticated Poetry* [Chicago: University of Chicago Press, 1961.], p. 209.)

ingenious writer [Thomas Percy] ascribed to a body of men, who are supposed to have been, about this period, and for some preceding centuries, very numerous and respectable; and concerning whom he has favoured the world with a most ingenious and elegant essay. The reader will immediately recollect — the 'ancient English minstrels', of whom, before we advance further in our little history, it may not be impertinent or improper to take some notice.

Without attempting to controvert the slightest fact laid down by the learned prelate, one may well be permitted to question the propriety of his inferences, and, indeed, his general hypothesis. Every part of France, but more especially Normandy, seems to have formerly abounded in minstrels, whose profession has been already described. Many of these people, we can easily suppose, attended the Conqueror, and his Norman barons, in their expedition to England; and perhaps were provided for, or continued to gain a subsistence by their professional art among the settlers. The constant intercourse which so long subsisted between the two countries, that is, while the English monarchs had possessions in France, afforded the French and Norman minstrels constant opportunities of a free and unexpensive passage into England, where they were certain of a favorable reception and liberal rewards from the king, his barons, and other Anglo-Norman subjects. French or Norman minstrels, however, are not English ones. There is not the least proof that the latter were a respectable society, or that they even deserve the name of a society. That there were men in those times, as there are in the present, who gained a livelihood by going about from place to place, singing and playing to the illiterate vulgar, is doubtless true; but that they were received into the castles of the nobility, sung at their tables, and were rewarded like the French minstrels, does not any where appear, not is it at all credible. The reason is evident. The French tongue alone was used at court, and in the households of the Norman barons (who despised the Saxon manners and language), for many centuries after the Conquest, and continued till, at least, the reign of Henry VIII. the polite language of both court and country, and as well known as the English itsself: a fact of which (to keep to our subject) we need no other evidence than the multitude of French poems and songs to be found in every library. The learned treatise above noticed might, therefor, with more propriety, have been intitled 'An Essay on the ancient FRENCH Minstrels', whom the several facts and anecdotes there related alone concern. Of the English minstrels, all the knowledge we have of them is, that by a law of queen Elizabeth they were pronounced 'rogues, vagabonds, and sturdy beggars';[38] a sufficient proof

---

[38] Ritson refers to an act of the time of Elizabeth I, found in the standard source, *Pulton's Statutes* (39 Elizabeth, ch. 4, par. 2), perhaps read by Ritson in the edition prepared by Joseph

they were not very respectable in her time, how eminent soever they might
have been before. That such characters as these should have left us no
memorials of theirselves is not at all surprising. They could sing and play; but
it was none of their business to read or write. So that, whatever their songs
may have been, they seem to have perished along with them; for, excepting
the two ballads which have been mentioned (neither of which, unless it be
from the rude and barbarous jargon in which they are composed, are
necessarily ascribable to minstrels), we have not a single composition which
can, with any degree of certainty, or even plausibility, be given to a person of
this description.

[...]

What a treasure would it be to possess a collection of the vulgar songs
composed and sung during the civil wars of York and Lancaster, in which
almost every moment afforded some great, noble, interesting or pathetic
subject for the imagination of the poet! How delightful, how instructive, would
be the perusal of such a little history of that turbulent and bloody period! The
ponderous tomes of Lydgate and Occleve have descended to us in the highest
preservation; one would gladly sacrifice the whole for a single page! But the
songs of which we are speaking appear to have born so little resemblance to
the stile and manner of the old ballads with which we are now acquainted, and
from which a part of the present collection is formed, that we may fairly infer
that not one of the latter existed before the reign of the above princess
[Elizabeth I]. The learned and ingenious bishop Percy has, indeed, published
a work, in which a considerable number of songs and ballads, that have never
otherwise appeared, are ascribed to a very remote antiquity; an antiquity
altogether incompatible with the stile and language of the compositions
theirselves, most of which, one may be allowed to say, bear the strongest
intrinsic marks of a *very* modern date. But the genuineness of these pieces
cannot be properly investigated or determined without an inspection of the
original manuscript, from which they are said to be extracted.

[Joseph Ritson], ed. *Ancient Songs, From the Time of King Henry the Third, to the Revolution* (London, 1790).

[Ritson widened the attack on Percy's minstrel theory here, contrasting the
evidence for the existence of French minstrels with the paucity of evidence for
minstrels in England. Minstrels might have played the harp or fiddle in
England, but Ritson concluded that 'no English Minstrel was ever famous for
his composition or his performance; nor is the name of a single one
preserved'.]

Keble, *The Statutes at Large [...] from Magna Charta Until this Time* (London, 1681), p. 918.

From: 'Observations on the Ancient Minstrels' (pp. i-xxvi).

I. The Minstrels, by a learned, ingenious, and elegant writer, whom there will be frequent occasion to quote, are described to be 'an order of men in the middle ages, who united the arts of poetry and music, and sung verses to the harp of their own composing; who appear to have accompanied their songs with mimicry and action; and to have practised such various means of diverting as were much admired in those rude times, and supplied the want of more refined entertainment; whom these arts rendered extremely popular and acceptable, in this and all the neighbouring countries; where no high scene of festivity was esteemed complete, that was not set off with the exercise of their talents; and, where so long as the spirit of chivalry subsisted, they were protected and caressed, because their songs tended to do honour to the ruling passion of the times, and to encourage and foment a martial spirit'.[39] This is certainly a fine, and possibly an unflattering description of a set of men, who unquestionably existed and flourished in France for several centuries, and whom several ingenious writers have contributed to render famous. Numbers of these, no doubt, owing to the free intercourse between this country and the continent, so long as the English monarchs retained any of their Norman territories, were constantly flocking to their court and to the castles of their barons, where it may be easily believed they would enjoy the most favorable reception. They were still French, however; and it is to be remembered, that if this language were not the only, it was at least the usual one, spoken by the English monarchs and great men for several centuries after the conquest; a fact which, if not notorious, must be evident to every person in any degree conversant with the history of those times. If therefor, by 'Ancient English Minstrels', we are to understand a body of our own countrymen who united the arts of poetry and music, and got their livelihood by singing verses to the harp of their own composing in their native tongue, who were well known to the Saxons, 'continued a distinct order of men for many ages after the Norman conquest', and were hospitably and respectfully received at the houses of the great, all the facts, anecdotes and other circumstances which have been collected relative to the Provençal Troubadours or Norman Minstrels, however numerous or authentic, are totally foreign to the subject; and do not even prove the mere existence of the character supposed.

The incidents referred by the above learned writer to the times and manners of the Anglo-Saxons, though probably nothing more than the fictions of romance, do not seem to require examination;[40] since, allowing the

---

[39] See, in the extract from Percy, the first paragraph of the essay on minstrels.

[40] Ritson is referring here to the story of Alfred's incursion into the Danish camp in the

facts themselves, they by no means affect the question proposed to be here considered, which is, Whether at any time, since the Norman Conquest, there has existed a distinct order of men, who united the arts of poetry and music and got their livelihood by singing to the harp verses in their native tongue of their own composing? And if the elucidation of an obscure and interesting subject, or the attainment of just and distinct ideas of ancient characters and manners, be an object of any consequence, the discussion of this question will not be impertinent or useless.

[Beginning with the story of Richard I and his minstrel Blondel, Ritson then works through many of Percy's examples of English minstrelsy, in order to debunk them.]

II. It is somewhat remarkable, that we have yet seen no authority which should induce one to think, that there ever was a single Englishman, who 'united the arts of poetry and music, and sung verses to the harp of his own composing'; nor in fact is any such authority to be found. If those writers who have become the historians or panegyrists of the Provençal *troubadours*, or the French Minstrels, had been possessed of no better evidence than we are, the mere existence of such a body would not have been at present known. The *tensons*, the *sirventes*, the *pastourelles* of the former, the *lais*, *contes*, and *fabliaux* of the latter are innumerable, and not only prove their existence, but afford sufficient materials for their description and history. But this is by no means the case with the 'Ancient English Minstrels', of whom it is not pretended that we have any thing more than a few rude ballads, which prove nothing less than their origin. Not a single piece is extant in which an English Minstrel speaks of himself; whereas, the importance or vanity of the French Minstrel, for ever leads him to introduce himself or his profession, and to boast of his feats and his talents. That there did exist in this country an order of men called Minstrels, is certain; but then it is equally clear, that the word was never used by any English writer, for 'one who united the arts of poetry and music, and sung verses to the harp of his own composing', before the ingenious writer so often quoted; but, on the contrary, that it ever implied an instrumental performer, and generally a fidler, or such like base musician.

[Ritson quotes several glossarists and gives examples from medieval literature to the effect that 'minstrel' in English records refers to a musician.]

---

guise of a minstrel, and the similar story concerning the Dane Anlaf, who entered the Anglo-Saxon camp before the battle of Brunanburh as a minstrel; Percy had adduced both as testifying to the privileged position of minstrels (see on the former the extract from Percy's essay on ancient minstrels). Percy took the original stories from William of Malmesbury; see *Willelmi Malmesbiriensis Monachi De Gestis Regum Anglorum*, ed. by William Stubbs, 2 vols, RS 90 (London: HMSO, 1887-89), I, 126, 143.

III. That there were individuals formerly, who made it their business to wander up and down the country chanting romances, and singing songs and ballads to the harp, fiddle, or other more humble and less artificial instrument, cannot be doubted. These men were in all probability comprehended within the general term of Minstrels, but are by no means to be exclusively distinguished by that title; and indeed were generally denominated from the particular instruments on which they performed. It may be easily imagined, that many of these people, though entirely destitute of education, and probably unable either to write or read, possessed the talent of inventing historical or legendary songs, which would sometimes have merit; but it is to be observed, that all the minstrel songs which have found their way to us, are merely narrative; nothing of passion, sentiment, or even description, being to be discovered among them. Men equally ignorant, have in all ages and in all countries, been possessed of the same talent, and such a character is only rare at present, because it is become more difficult to please. It is however worthy of remark, that no English Minstrel was ever famous for his composition or his performance; nor is the name of a single one preserved.

[The essay closes by casting some doubt on the existence of the folio manuscript Percy claimed to have in his possession. Ritson does not, finally, accuse Percy of fraud (as is sometimes assumed) but he does argue, after analysis of several poems, that 'the learned collector has preferred his ingenuity to his fidelity, without the least intimation to the reader', by substantially altering the manuscript originals. 'It follows, from the manner in which this celebrated collection is avowedly published, even allowing the MS. to be genuine, and to contain what it is said to do, that no confidence can be placed in any of the "old Minstrel ballads" inserted in that collection, and not to be found elsewhere'.]

After all, the Minstrel songs, under the circumstances in which they were produced, are certainly both curious and valuable compositions, and could any further lights be thrown upon the history of those by or for whom they were invented, a collection of all that can be discovered would still be a very entertaining and interesting work; but if such a publication should ever appear, it is to be hoped that it will come from an Editor who prefers truth to hypothesis, and the genuine remains of the Minstrel Poets, however mutilated or rude, to the indulgence of his own poetical vein, however fluent or refined.

[Joseph Ritson, ed.] *Poems on Interesting Events in the Reign of King Edward III. Written, in the Year MCCCLII. By Laurence Minot* (London, 1795).

From: Preface (pp. v-xiv).

The neglect which writers of genius are occasionally condemned to experience, as well from their contemporaries as from posterity, was never exemplifyed, perhaps, in a more eminent degree than by the poet whose works are now offered to the public. His very name appears totally unknown to Leland, Bale, Pitts, and Tanner: it is mentioned, in short, by no one writer, till late in the present century, nor is found to occur in any catalogue: while the silence of the public records would induce us to believe that the great monarch whom he has so eloquently and earnestly panegyrised was either ignorant of his existence or insensible of his merit.

[Ritson then relates the circumstances of the discovery of Laurence Minot's poems in MS Cotton Galba E IX by Thomas Tyrwhitt in the course of his preparations for his edition of the *Canterbury Tales*.[41]]

Minot, of course, is to be regarded as a poet anterior not only to Chaucer, who, in 1352, was but 24 years of age,[42] and had not, so far as we know, given any proofs of a poetical imagination, but also to Gower, who, though he survived that writer, was probably his senior by some years. He cannot, at the same time, be considered as the first of English poets, since, not to mention the hermit of Hampole, the prolixity of whose compositions is compensated more by their piety than by their spirit, he is clearly posterior to Robert Mannyng (or of Brunne); whose namesake of Gloucester is, in fact, the Ennius of this numerous family.

It seems pretty clear, from our authors dialect and orthography, that he was a native of one of the northern counties, in some monastery whereof the manuscript which contains his poems, along with many others in the same dialect, is conjectured to have been written; and to which, at the same time, it is not improbable that he himself should have belonged. Chance, however, may one day bring us somewhat better acquainted with his history.[43]

The creative imagination and poetical fancy which distinguish Chaucer, who, considering the general barbarism of his age and country, may be regarded as a prodigy, admit, it must be acknowledged, of no competition; yet, if the truth may be uttered without offence to the established reputation of that preeminent genius, one may venture to assert that, in point of ease, harmony, and variety of versification, as well as general perspicuity of stile, Laurence Minot is, perhaps, equal, if not superior, to any English poet before the sixteenth, or even, with very few exceptions, before the seventeenth, century. There are, in fact, but two other poets who are any way remarkable for a particular facility of rimeing and happy choice of words: Robert of

---

[41] *CTC*, IV, 67 n.54.

[42] As the common belief had it; see above, note 35.

[43] Laurence Minot is now just as shadowy a figure as he was in Ritson's day. Although some references to actual Minots in the first half of the fourteenth century have been explored, 'the evidence', according to Rossell Hope Robbins, 'is illusory'. *MWME*, V (1975), 1412.

Brunne, already mentioned, who wrote before 1340, and Thomas Tusser, who wrote about 1560.

[Joseph Ritson], *Bibliographia Poetica: A Catalogue of Engleish Poets, of the Twelfth, Thirteenth, Fourteenth, Fifteenth, and Sixteenth Centurys, with a short account of their works* (London: Nicol, 1802).

From: pp. 24-25, 26-31

GOWER JOHN, wrote, in English metre, a prolix dialogue, of various argument, according to the fashion of his age, intitled '*Confessio amantis*, (that is to say in Englisshe, The confessyon of the lover)'; originally printed by William Caxton, in 1483, and reprinted by Thomas Berthelet, in 1532, and 1554, folio: also a long parasytical *balade* in praise of king Henry the fourth, inserted in several editions of Chaucer. In lord Gowers library, as we are told by Warton, there is a thin oblong manuscript on vellum, containing some of Gowers poems in Latin, French, and English.[44]

Some of his smaller poems are preserved in a MS. of Trinity-college, Cambridge; and, it may be, in other collections; but, possessing little or no merit,[45] are likely to remain in obscurity. He dyed, aged, in 1402, and was intered in the church of St. Mary-Overy, Southwark, where his monument, a curious piece of antiquity, still remains.

[...]

LANGELANDE ROBERT, 'a Shropshire man', it is sayed, borne in Cleybirie, aboute eight myles from Malverne hilles', wrote 'The vision of Pierce Plowman', a curious allegorical poem, first printed by Robert Crowley, vicar of Saint-Giles Cripplegate, in 1550 (of which there at least two, if not three editions), and, again, by Owen Rogers, in 1561 (all in quarto and black-letter).[46] The learned Tyrwhitt disputes our authors title, since in what he esteemed the best manuscripts (which, whether they be so or not, differ materially from the printed copys), the poet is expressly saluted by the name of 'WILLE', and the work itself intitled '*Visio* WILLELMI *de Petro Ploughman*'.[47] Now, unless the word WILLE be, as there is some reason to believe, no more than a personification of the mental faculty, and have,

---

[44] *HEP*, II, G1^v-G2^r. – R.

[45] His *Vox Clamantis* might have deserved publication, in a historical view, if he had not proved an ingrate to his lawful sovereign, and a sycophant to the usurper of his throne. – R.

[46] Crowley printed three editions in 1550; Rogers reprinted Crowley's third impression and added *Pierce the Plowman's Creed*. Ritson quotes from the prefaced note, 'The Printer to the Reader', *The Vision of Pierce Plowman*, 1st printing (London, 1550), p. ii^r.

[47] *CTC*, IV, 74 n.57.

consequently, been misapprehended by the writer of that title, it should follow
that the authors name was WILLIAM, and that his surname and quality are
totally unknown. However this may be, the work itself, a very curious and
masterly production, appears to have been composed in, or soon after, the
year 1362. It is a kind of religious allegorical satire; in which Pierce the
ploughman, the principal personage, seems to be intended for the pattern of
Christian perfection, if not, occasionally for Jesus Christ himself. The mode of
versification adopted by this writer (an alliterative metre of 9 and 11 syllables
without rime) is originally Gothick, and, from the many other instances which
occur in MS. is conjectured to have been a favourite poetick stile with the
common people (as they are called) down to late period.[48] Our author became
popular, about the time of the reformation, from his haveing lashed the vices
of the clergy, both regular and secular, with a just severity; and foretold, as
was thought, the destruction of the monasterys by Henry VIII. The passage is
certainly curious:

> '—ther shal come a king and confesse you religious.
> And beat you as the byble telleth for breaking of your rule.
> And amend monials, monkes and chanons,
> And put hem to her penaunce, *ad pristinum statum ire...*
> And than shall the abot of Abington and all his issue for ever
> Have a knocke of a kynge, and incurable the wounde'.[49]

Manuscript copys of this work are by no means uncommon in publick
librarys, but it requires a thorough and attentive investigation to decide upon
the comparative merits of the printed copy, respecting the faultyness and
imperfection whereof Mr. Tyrwhitt may have been somewhat too hastey in his
judgement.[50] After all, it is probable that the information which Crowley, the

---

[48] See Hickes, *Thesaurus*, I, 217; Percy, *RAEP*, II, 270.

[49] Cf note 159 and *Piers Plowman* B X, 316-26; ellipses are Ritson's.

[50] [*CTC*, IV, 74 n.57. Ritson could see that substantial variations existed in both printed
and manuscript versions of *Piers*, and quoted the first few lines of the poem from three versions
to demonstrate this. He continues:] The subsequent variations, throughout the poem, are still
more considerable; so that it appears highly probable that the author had revised his original
work, and given, as it were, a new edition; and it may be possible for a good judge of ancient
poetry, possessed of a sufficient stock of critical acumen, to determine which was the first, and
which the second. No MS. however, of this celebrated and really excellent composition
examined by the present annotator, has been found deserving, either for accuracy or antiquity,
to be prefered to that or those whence the printed copy appears to be taken. [It was left to
Richard Price, editor of the 1824 revision of Warton's *HEP*, to distinguish the third version of
the poem, and to Walter Skeat to edit all three as the A-, B-, and C-texts (1867-77). See
Charlotte Brewer, *Editing 'Piers Plowman': The Evolution of the Text* (Cambridge: Cambridge

original editor, says he had received from some men, more exercised than himself in the study of antiquitys, whom he had consulted, as to the authors being 'Robert Langeland, a Shropshire man, borne in Cleybirie; &c.' and which, in fact, he might have had from the printed book of Bales *Scriptores Britanniæ*, was not altogether accurate;[51] since, from numerous instances in the poem itself, there is every reason to conclude that he was a Londoner, by residence, at least, if not by birth. Where Selden had red 'that the authors name was John Malverne, a fellow of Oriel-College, who finished it 16 Ed. III.' does not appear; but the latter part of his information, though adopted by Wood, who calls him *Wigorniensis*, is manifestly erroneous.[52]

[...]

LYDGATE JOHN, a monk of Bury-St. Edmunds, in Suffolk, and a most prolix and voluminous poetaster [...] [There follows a very long bibliography of Lydgate's works.]

This is believed to be the completest list of this voluminous, prosaick, and driveling monk, that can be formed, without access, at least, to every manuscript library in the kingdom, which would be very difficult, if not impossible, to obtain. It is, at the same time, highly probable that some of these pieces, mostly anonymous in the MS. copys, are not by Lydgate; and that, on the other hand, he may be the author of many others in the same predicament. In the library of Trinity-college, Cambridge (Num. 377), is *Lidgati Opera*, 3 volumes. But, in truth, and fact, these stupid and fatigueing

---

University Press, 1996), pp. 47, 110.]

[51] As Ritson notes here, Crowley claimed to have 'consult[ed] such me*n* as I knew to be more exercised in the studie of antiquities, then I my self haue ben'; ('The Printer to the Reader', *Vision of Pierce Plowman*, p. ii'). John Bale's information concerning 'Robert' Langland in his *Index Britanniae Scriptorum*, written after 1546, is so similarly worded to Crowley's as to suggest it was his source, as Brewer maintains (*Editing 'Piers'*, p. 11). The index existed only in manuscript but this is consistent with Crowley's statement that he had the information direct from other antiquarians. Ritson is wrong to refer the reader to a printed source; Bale's two printings of his catalogue, *Illustrium Maioris Britanniae Scriptorum* ([Wesel], 1548, 1549) contain no references to Langland; the enlarged version printed as *Scriptorum Illustrium Maioris Brytannie*, 2 vols (Basle, 1557-59) does have an entry for Langland — seven years too late for Crowley. See also note 17 (in Percy extract).

[52] The antiquarian and legal historian John Selden had commented of *Piers Plowman* that he preferred it 'before many more seemingly serious invectives, as well for invention as judgment. But I have read that the author's name was *John Malverne*, a fellow of *Oriel* college in Oxford, who finished it in 16 Ed. III'. *Illustrations on the First Eighteen Songs of Drayton's Polyolbion*, in David Wilkins, ed. *Joannis Seldeni Jurisconsulti Opera Omnia*, 3 vols (London, 1725), III part 2, col. 1780. The historian of the University of Oxford, Anthony à Wood, repeated the information in his *Historia et Antiquitates Universitatis Oxoniensis*, [trans into Latin by Richard Peers and Richard Reeve.], 2 vols. (Oxford: Sheldonian Theatre, 1674), II, 106.

productions, which by no means deserve the name of poetry, and their still more stupid and disgusting author, who disgraces the name and patronage of his master Chaucer, are neither worth collecting, unless it be as typographical curiositys, or on account of the beautiful illuminations in some of his presentation-copys), nor even worthy of preservation: being only suitablely adapted '*ad ficum & piperem*', and other more base and servile uses. How little he profited by the correction, or instructions of his great patron is manifest in almost every part of his elaborate drawlings, in which there are scarcely three lines together of pure and acurate metre. Wel, therefor, and necessaryly did it behove him to address his readers:

> 'Because, i know the verse therein is wrong,
> As being some too short, and some too long'.[53]

He dyed, at a very advanced age, after 1446; no one, it is believed, having hitherto ascertained the precise year of his death.

Joseph Ritson, ed. *Ancient Engleish Metrical Romancees*, 3 vols (London: Nicol, 1802).

From: 'Dissertation on Romance and Minstrelsy', lv-cvii.

[This long and rambling dissertation actually has relatively little to say about Middle English literature as such; its literary-historical material focuses in particular on the still-vexed question of the origins of romance, which had by then been investigated by several scholars whose work Ritson opposed, Warton and Percy amongst them. Some of Ritson's reflections on the Middle English period are excerpted here.]

2: Saxon and Engleish Language

'At more than a century after the conquest', it is supposed, 'both the Norman and English languages would be heard in the houses of the great; so that, probably, about this æra, or soon after, we are to date that remarkable intercommunity of and exchange of each others compositions, which we discover to have taken place at some early period between the French and English minstrels: the same set of phrases, the same species of characters, incidents, and adventures, and often the same identical stories being found in the old metrical romances of both nations'.[54] This, though it could not,

---

[53] Apparently a remembering of Lydgate's lines, 'For wel wot I moche þing is wrong, / Falsly metrid, boþe of short & long'. *Troy Book* 3. v. 3481-82, in *Lydgate's Troy Book, A.D. 1412-1420*, ed. by Henry Bergen, 4 vols (London: EETS, 1906-35), III (1910), 872.

[54] Ritson is here quoting Percy once more, from the essay on ancient minstrels; cf the

possiblely, take place at so early a period, nor more than a century after, is, by no means, to be wonder'd at, as the Engleish minstrels, being far inferior, in genius and invention, to the French or Norman *trouveres*, were oblige'd to content themselves with translateing what had allready become celebrateëd, and they were unable to emulate. It is, at the same time, a gross misrepresentation and imposition, however confidently, or plausiblely, asserted or insinuateëd, that any one Engleish minstrel-romance was ever translateëd into French.

That William the bastard, his son Rufus, his daughter Maud, or his nephew Stephen, did, or could, speak the Anglo-Saxon or Engleish language we have no information. The Saxon chronicle ended in the last of these reigns, but, being imperfect toward the conclusion, it is not certainly known how low it was actually brought; and still less at what age it commence'd. King Henry the second, in his progress to Wales, was address'd by a singular character '*in Teutonica lingua*', very good Engleish, it would seem, and, it may be allso, very good German, at least for the time: the three first words of the speech deliver'd (all that is giveën in that language) being 'Gode olde kinge!' The king himself speaks French.

In this reign, it is most probable, Layamon, the priest, made his translation, in the stile of Saxon poetry without rime, from the *Brut* of *maistre* Wace; which affords a strange and singular mixture of the Saxon and Norman idioms, both apparently much corrupted. This curious work exhibits the progress of the Engleish language, properly so call'd, as we now have it, in its dawn or infancy, if one may use such an expression.

The change of Saxon into Engleish, however, was, probablely, still more rapid, as the Saxon chronicle terminateëd in the reign of king Stephen, who dye'd in 1154, and, in FIFTEEN years after, we have Engleish rimes by St. Godric, a hermit at Finchal, who dye'd in 1170; though, it must be confess'd, there are specimens, of a lateër period, in prose.

According to William of Malmesbury, in the time of King Henry the first, the whole language of the Northhumbrians, and most of all in York, creek'd so rudely, that they of the south could understand nothing of it: which hapen'd on account of the vicinity of barbarous nations, and the remoteness of the kings, formerly Engleish, then Norman, 'who are known' he says, 'to sojourn more to the south than to the north'.[55]

[...]

Percy extract, p. 71.

[55] *De Gestis Pontificum Anglorum*, prologue to book III; see *Willelmi Malmesbiriensis Monachi De Gestis Pontificum Anglorum*, ed. by N. E. S. A. Hamilton, RS 52 (London: Longman, 1870), p. 209.

'Our nation', say king Johns embassadours, to king Admiral of Morocco, 'is learn'd in three idioms, that is to say, *Latin, French*, and *Engleish*'.[56] There is no specimen of the Engleish language in this reign. It must, however, have been makeing its progress, as in the reign of his son and successour, Henry the third, we find it, to a certain degree, mature and perfect. This, if we take the year 1188, the penultimate year of Henry the second, when the work of Layamon may be thought to have been finish'd (the manuscript itself being of a not much late date), and the year 1278, when Robert of Gloucester completeëd his rimeing chronicle, no more than a single century, you find an entirely different appearance, with a considerable degree of rough energy, and a tolerablely smooth, and accurate, metre, for the time, though it is generally thought to be conceive'd in a provincial dialect, and, in that case, may afford a far from favourable specimen of the Engleish, even at that time.

The king of Engleland still adhere'd to the Norman French, as far as one may rely upon Robert of Brunne, a good evidence in general, and who had the opportunity, in this instance, of knowing his authours precise meaning, they resideing onely at a short distance from each other:

'The kyng said on hie, "*Symon, jeo vous defie!*"[']'.[57] We never know him to speak a word of Engleish. The last long expireing efforts of the Saxon language were made in the forty-third year of this reign (1258-9), in the shape of a writ to his subjects in Huntingdonshire, and, as it is there say'd, to every other in the kingdom, in support of the Oxford provisions.[58] Certain it is, that this once famous language had allready become obsolete, and utterly incapable of dischargeing its functions, being no longer either writen or spokeën: and 'There', as the worthy lord Balcarras express'd himself, at the close of his final speech, on the dissolution of the Scottish parliament, 'is the end of an auld sang'.

[Ritson further discusses the tri-lingual character of medieval England.]

Gower wrote much more in French and Latin than in Engleish; his *Speculum meditantis* is in the first of those languageës; his *Vox clamantis* in the second, and his *Confessio amantis*, though in the third, a manifest version from both. He even inserts pure French words in his Engleish poetry; for

---

[56] *Matthaei Parisiensis Monachi Sancti Albani Chronica Majora*, ed. by Henry Richards Luard, 7 vols (London: Longman; Trübner, 1872-83), II (1874), 560-61. Ritson used the edition of William Watts, 2 vols (1684-83). The Moroccan 'king' was in fact called Mohammed al Nassir, vulgarly Miramumelin; Ritson mistakes the title given him in the Latin for his name.

[57] Cf Idelle Sullens, ed. *Robert Mannyng of Brunne: Chronicle*, MRTS 153 (Binghamton, N.Y.: Binghamton University, 1996), p. 621, l. 5321.

[58] The proclamation is edited and discussed in Bruce Dickins and R. M. Wilson, eds., *Early Middle English Texts* (London: Bowes & Bowes, 1951), pp. 7-9.

instance:

> To ben upon his *bien venu*,
> The first, whiche shall him *salu*.
>
> > Fo. 35, b.
>
> The dare not drede *tant ne quant*:
>
> > Fo. 41, &c. &c.[59]

This, too, was the case with Chaucer, though disputeëd by mister Tyrwhitt,[60] who, however, allows, in another place that 'our poets (who have, generally, the principal share in modeling a language) found it there [*sic*] interest to borrow as many words as they, conveniently, could from France, &c. &c'.:[61] which is, certainly, as true of Chaucer, as of Gower, or any other poet; more especially in their translations, where, from a want of words, they take the French as they find it. A strikeing proof of this fact, in the case of both Gower and Chaucer, is, that they adopted the mode of French poetry, which ends one subject, or sentence, with half the rime, and, begins a new one with the other half; which few, if any other Engleish poets are, at least constantly, known to do. Nothing is more plausible than Wartons opinion that Chaucer imitateëd the Provençal poets; *his dreme, The flower and the leaf, The assemblé of ladies, The house of Fame*, and, it may be, others, are very much in the manner of the *troubadours*; even the *Roman de la rose* is, apparently, an imitation of this kind; which, peradventure, might rather set him upon the translation.[62] At any rate, the Engleish language, such as it is, or is esteem'd to be, was by these means greatly enlarge'd, as wel as improve'd, in this reign, particularly by those two poets, not forgetting Robert of Brunne, to whom Warton has done great injustice, and Lawrence Minot, whose merit he was a

---

[59] *Confessio Amantis*, II, ll. 1503-4; 2430; cf G. C. Macaulay, ed. *The Complete Works of John Gower*, 4 vols (Oxford: Clarendon Press, 1899-1902), II (1901), 170-71, 196.

[60] *CTC*, IV, 1-3, 45-46. – R.

[61] *CTC*, IV, 45; (the error is Ritson's). Note in Tyrwhitt's words the prevalent opinion, implicitly espoused by Ritson, that great poets are renovators of a corrupted language.

[62] See *HEP*, I, 458-60. Of the poems named several are among the Chaucerian apocrypha, though still accepted as genuine in the eighteenth century: *The Flower and the Leaf* and *Assembly of Ladies* are both fifteenth-century poems, the former first attributed to Chaucer in Speght's 1598 edition, the latter in the edition of Thynne in 1532; *Chaucer's Dream* is a title wrongly given by Speght to *The Isle of Ladies*, which is presumably what Ritson is referring to here, although the title was also used to refer to the *Book of the Duchess*. These attributions would be overturned in the later nineteenth century, as would Chaucer's exclusive claim to the translation of the *Roman de la Rose*.

stranger to.[63]

[...]

There is every reason, indeed, to believe that the Engleish language, before the invention of printing, was held, by learned, or literary men, in very little esteem. In the library of Glastonbury-abbey, which bids fair to have been one of the most extensive in the kingdom, in 1248, there were but four books in Engleish, and those upon religious subjects, all, beside, 'vetusta & inutilia'.[64] We have not a single historian, in Engleish prose, before the reign of Richard the second, when John Treviza translateëd the *Polychronicon* of Randal Higden. Boston of Bury, who seems to have consulted all the monasterys of Engleland, does not mention one authour who had writen in Engleish; and Bale, at a lateër period, has, comparatively, but an insignificant number: nor was Leland so fortunate as to find above two or three Engleish books, in the monastick and other librarys, which he rummage'd, and explore'd, under the kings commission. Gower, indeed, wrote wel, in all three languageës: *Latin, French,* and Engleish; and there is sufficient reason to think that Chaucer, though he prefer'd his native tongue, was wel acquainted not onely with the other two, but with the *Italian,* allso, which was, at that time, little cultivateëd in his mother-country.

3: Romanceës

No romanceës are to be expected among the Britons, at the time they posses'd the whole, or the greater part, of Britain, of which æra the present Welsh are unable to produce the slightest literary vestige. They pretend, indeed, to have the poems of several bards of the sixth century; but they have no fabulous adventures, or tales, in verse, of any age; and onely a few, chiefly translations, heretofore specify'd, none of which can be prove'd anteriour to the thirteenth century.

The Saxons, of whose learning or literature some account has been, allready, giveën, as wel as some idea of their poetry, being, for the most part, an ignorant and illiterate people, it wil be in vain to hope for proofs, among them, of genius, or original composition, at least, in their native tongue. In consequence, no romance has been yet discover'd in Saxon, but a prose translation allready noticed.[65] So that if, as Warton pretends, the flourishing of

---

[63] Warton had a low opinion of Robert Mannyng as a poet; see *HEP*, I, 59, 72-73, 77. He gives a selection of Laurence Minot's verse without making evaluative comment (III, 146-51).

[64] Ritson is referring to a catalogue of the books at Glastonbury printed by Hearne, in which four books of sermons and saints' lives in English are recorded. Only two of these are in fact described as 'vetust. & inutil.'. Thomas Hearne, ed. *Johannis Confratris & Monachi Glastoniensis Chronica sive Historia de Rebus Glastoniensibus*, 2 vols (Oxford: Sheldonian Theatre, 1726), II, 436.

[65] The Old English version of the story of Apollonius of Tyre, translated from Latin; the

'the tales of Scandinavian scalds among the Saxons', may be justly presume'd, it is certain they had been soon lost, as neither vestige nor notice is preserve'd of them in any ancient writeër; nor, in fact, would any but a stupid fool, or rank impostor, imagine that any of these supposititious Scandinavian tales existed in the middle of the fifth century, when the Saxons first establish'd themselves in Britain. He pretends, likewise, that 'they imported with them into Engleland the old Runick language and letters':[66] but whatever vestigeës of either exist in the northern parts of the kingdom are by more learned writeërs attributeëd to the Danes.

The most ancient romance now extant in the English language, if it may be so call'd, being a strange, and apparently corrupt, mixture of Saxon and Norman, in the stile of the Saxon poetry, without rime, is a sort of licentious version, by one Layamon, a priest, at Ernlye upon Severne, with great probability about the time of Henry II. or Richard I. the manuscript itself being not lateër than the commencement, or, at least, the earlyer part of the thirteenth century; chiefly, it seems, from the *Brut* of *maistre* Wace, Gace, or Gasse, which was itself, in some measure, a translation from Geoffrey of Monmouths *British history*, and was finish'd in 1155. A curious specimen of this singular production may be red to great advantage in the elegant 'Specimens of early English poetry', publish'd by George Ellis esquire. The original is in the Cotton-library (Claudius, A. IX): in which invaluable collection was formerly a lateër, and modernise'd, copy (Otho, C. XIII); unfortunately destroy'd in the dreadful fire which hapen'd, in that invaluable repository, 1731.[67] [...]

   [...]

No romance, in English rime, has been hitherto discover'd, or mention'd to exist, before the reign of Edward the first, toward the end of which, as we may fairly conjecture, that of *Horn child* [ie, *King Horn*], a very concise and licentious translation, or imitation, and abridgement, rather, of the French original, nearly two centurys older, made its first appearance. There is every reason to conclude that the other romanceës mention'd by Chaucer *Ypotys*, *Bevis*, *Sir Guy*, *Sir Lybeaus*, *Pleindamour*, and, possiblely, *Sire Percivell*, were in English verse, and, in all probability, much the same with those of which copys have been preserve'd; except the last, which no one but Chaucer ever

---

story was well known in several versions, particularly Gower's retelling in book VIII of *Confessio Amantis*, where it was one of the sources for Shakespeare's *Pericles*.

[66] *HEP*, I, E2ᵛ. – R.

[67] George Ellis, *Specimens of the Early English Poets*, 3 vols (London, 1801); see below. Laȝamon's *Brut* had also been excerpted by Warton in his *HEP*. The Otho manuscript was partially retrieved in the restoration program of the Cotton collection led by Frederic Madden.

noticeës.[68] This sort of translation continue'd til at least the time of king Henry the sixth; in which reign *The St. Graal* was translateëd into Engleish by Henry Lonelich, skynner, at the instance of one Harry Barton,[69] and contains, though imperfect both at begining and end, not less, according to mister Nasmith, than 40,000 lines; Thomas Chestre gave a free and enlarge'd version of the *Lai de Lanval* of Mary of France; and Robert de Thornton produce'd *Morte Arthure* and *Percyvell of Galles*. *Ywain and Gawain* seems to have been written at an earlyer period, and very probablely, in the reign of king Richard the second.[70] There are not above two or three originally Engleish, among which we may safely reckon *The squyr of low degree*; unless *Sir Eglamour*, and *Sir Tryamour*, may, likewise, have that honour, til the originals be discover'd.

It appears highly probable that the 'rime' mention'd by Robert of Brunne,[71] concerning Gryme the fisher, the founder of Grymesby, Hanelok the Dane, and his wife Goldeburgh, daughter to a king Athelwold; 'who all now', exclaims the learned Tyrwhitt, 'together with their bard,

> —illacrymabiles
> Urgentur ignotique longâ
> Nocte,—'[72]

was an English romance, extant not onely in the time of Henry de Knyghton, the historian, who wrote about the year 1400, but, allso, in that of Camden,[73] and even made use of by Warner, who, in the twentyeth chapter of his *Albions England*, has told the same story, in effect, though in a different manner,

---

[68] i.e. *Pleyndamour*, of which no version is extant, not *Sir Perceval of Galles*.

[69] i.e., the *Merlin* of Henry Lovelich, of the London Company of Skinners, undertaken as a translation from the French for Harry Barton, twice Lord Mayor of London; preserved in Corpus Christi College Cambridge 80 (*MWME*, I, 49). Edited again, under the title *Seynt Graal*, by Frederick Furnivall for the Roxburghe Club, 1861-63.

[70] i.e. *Launfal* and the alliterative *Morte Arthure*; neither the latter nor *Sir Perceval* are now thought to have been written by Robert Thornton, who was probably the scribe. *Ywain and Gawain* is of the first half of the fourteenth century.

[71] Thomas Hearne, ed. *Peter Langtoft's Chronicle (as illustrated and improv'd by Robert of Brunne)*, 2 vols (Oxford: Sheldonian Theatre, 1725), pp. 25-26. – R. [Cf Sullens, ed. *Robert Mannyng of Brunne: Chronicle*, p. 499-500, ll. 520-38.]

[72] *CTC*, IV, 63.

[73] The antiquary William Camden (1551-1623) first issued his *Britannia* in 1586. It was translated several times from Latin into English; Ritson used *Camden's Britannia, Newly Translated into English*, trans. by Edmund Gibson (London, 1695). Camden professed little interest in the story of Havelok: 'He performed I know not what great exploits, which for certain are fitter for tattling gossips in a winter night, than a grave Historian' (col. 471).

under the names *Argentile* and *Curan*, in exquisite poetry.[74] Whether this poem were originally compose'd in Engleish, or were no more than a translation from the French, cannot be now ascertain'd, as it seems to be utterly destroy'd:[75] but in a part of a French metrical romance, upon the history of Engleland, by Geoffrey Gaimar, a poet anterior to *maistre* Wace, to whose poem of *Le Brut* (though unfortunately mutilateëd) it serves as a continuation, in a manuscript of the kings library, in the British museum, ([Royal MS] 13 A XXI), the story itself is certainly preserve'd, though whether writen originally by Geoffrey, or takeën from some one of the '*liveres Engleis, en romanz e en Latin*', of which he had purchase'd many a copy, before he could draw his work to the end; particularly a book, which, at the instance of the gentle dame Constance Fitz-Gilbert, Robert earl of Gloucester, who dyed in 1147, and was sent for it to Helmsley, brought it away for him from Walter Espec, who was ded in 1140; or the Engleish book of Washingburgh, in Lincolnshire, or how otherwise, does not appear.[76] It is, however, a great curiosity, though too imperfect, as wel as too prolix, to insert here. In the mean time the paraphrase may be peruse'd, with great pleasure, and equal delicacy, in Warners book allready mention'd.

[...]

The two most famous, if not the most ancient, Engleish metrical romanceës, now existing, are those of *Guy of Warwick*, and *Bevis of Southampton*. Walter of Exeter, according to Bale (*Ex bibliothecis*, from the bookselers shops), a native of Devonshire, and professor of a sect of beging friers (a Dominican, as he thinks), at the instance of one Baldwin, a citizen of Exeter, in the year 1301, resideing at St. Carrock in Cornwall, wrote the life of Guy, formerly a famous earl of Warwick, in one book: but Bale is a very dubious authority.[77] At any rate no such work is now extant; though Carew, as

---

[74] *Albions England*, by William Warner (1558-1609) was a retelling (largely in rhyming couplets of fourteen-syllable lines which few would now call exquisite) of British history mixed in with classical myth. It first appeared in 1586 and in several enlarged versions in the late sixteenth and early seventeenth centuries. Sidney Lee described the loose retelling of the Havelok story as 'The finest passage' in the work (*DNB* LIX, 407).

[75] The romance of *Havelok the Dane* was rediscovered in the Bodleian library in 1826 by Frederic Madden and edited by him in 1828.

[76] Ritson refers to the Anglo-Norman version of the Havelok story by Geoffrey Gaimar, which appears at the beginning of his *L'Estoire des Engleis* (c. 1135-40); Gaimar's patron was Constance, wife of Ralph Fitzgilbert, whom Ritson mentions here. Fitzgilbert owned lands in Lincolnshire, which leads G. V. Smithers to speculate that Gaimar learnt the Havelok story (with its Lincolnshire affiliations) through Constance (G. V. Smithers, ed. *Havelok* [Oxford: Clarendon Press, 1987.], p. xvii).

[77] See *Index Britanniae Scriptorum [...] John Bale's Index of British and Other Writers*, ed. by Reginald Lane Poole (Oxford: Clarendon Press, 1902), p. 104.

if he had had it in his library, says, that this Walter '(de-)formed the historie of Guy of Warwick'. Hearne, in his appendix to the *Annales de Dunstaple*, has inserted '*Girardi Cornubiensis Historia Guidonis de Warwyke*' from an old MS. in the library of Magdalen-college Oxford. n.147.[78] This authour, however, is supposititious, and the MS. in all probability, no older than the fourteenth or fifteenth century: Lydgate translateëd from him. Guy of Warwick is mention'd by no Engleish historian before Robert of Brunne, or Peter de Langtoft, about 1340.[79] His story, at the same time, is relateëd in the *Gesta Romanorum*, C.172;[80] 'and, probably', as warton thinks, 'this is the early outline of the life of that renowned [but ideal] champion' (*HEP*, III, lxxi [Warton's square brackets]); and, in the Harley MSS. (Num 525) is an old Engleish poem entitle'd '*Speculum Gy de Warewyke* per Alquinum '*heremitam*', begining 'Herkenethe alle unto my speche'.[81] [...] But, in fact and truth, famous as his [Guy's] name is, the man himself never existed. This, likewise, is the case with sir Bevis, of whom Camden, with singular puerility, says, 'At the comeing-in of the Normans, one *Bogo*, or *Beavose*, a Saxon, had this title [of earl of Winchester]; who, in the battel at Cardiff in Wales, fought against the Normans'.[82] For this, however, in a way too usual with him, he cites no authority; nor does any ancient or veracious historian mention either *Bogo*, *Beavose*, or the battle of *Cardiff*; which, by the way, was not, as we learn from honest Carádoc of Llancarvan, contemporary with Geoffrey of Monmouth, in 1138, built before 1079. His *roman*, in French, however, is of the 13th century, and was extant in the magnificent library of the duke de la Valliere, as it is at present in the late royal library at Turin: an Engleish translation was printed by Pynson, Copland, East, and another; and three MS. copys are extant in the Publick-library, and that of Caius-college, Cambridge, and in the Auchinleck collection, Edinburgh; all three different from the printed copy, and, at least, two of them from each other.[83]

Neither Bevis nor Guy is mention'd by Dugdale in his *Baronage*, and he

---

[78] Thomas Hearne, ed. *Chronicon sive Annales Prioratus de Dunstaple [...]*, 2 vols (Oxford: Sheldonian Theatre, 1733), II, 825-32.

[79] Sullens, ed. *Robert Mannyng of Brunne: Chronicle*, p. 506, l. 697.

[80] i.e. chapter 172 of the Latin story collection, *Gesta Romanorum* (widely available in Ritson's time in various versions, many of them black-letter); the story of Guy is not in the Middle English redaction of the collection.

[81] The homiletic *Speculum* represents Guy as seeking the spiritual advice of Alcuin and is partly based on the latter's *De Virtutibus et Vitiis Liber*.

[82] Gibson, *Camden's Britannia*, col. 128. Square brackets are Ritson's.

[83] Cambridge University Ff. 2.38; Caius Cambridge 175; Advocates 19.2.1 (Auchinleck); Richard Pynson (London, c. 1503, *STC* 1988); William Copland (c. 1565, *STC* 1989). *MWME* (I, 215, art. [6.]) also records fragments of a Wynkyn de Worde print (Westminster 1500, *STC* 1987) but no print by East.

must have been conscious that the latters story was alltogether fabulous when he introduce'd it into his *History of Warwickshire*.[84]

'Bevis', as we are gravely told by the historian of Engleish poetry, 'was a Saxon chieftain, who seems to have extended his dominion along the southern coasts of England, which he is said [by whom?] to have defended against the Norman invaders. He lived at Downton in Wiltshire'.[85] This is highly ridiculous: Bevis and Guy were no more 'English heroes' than Amadis de Gaule or Perceforest: they are mere creatures of the imagination, and onely obtain an establishment in history because (like mister Wartons) it was usually writen upon the authority of romance. He accounts very ingeniously, however, for the fable of Dugdale, that the Saracens had the story of Guy 'in books of their own language' [*HEP*, I, 145 n.y.].

Chaucer, who mentions these two romanceës, noticeës, likewise, *Horn-child*, *Ypotis*, *Sire Lyb*, and *Pleindamour*; none of which can, of course, be so late as the year 1380, when *The Canterbury tales* are generally suppose'd to have been publish'd; and one of them, at least, wil be prove'd, in another place, to be near a century older. The last is unknown. 'That of sir ISEMBRAS', likewise, according to Warton, 'was familiar in the time of CHAUCER, and occurs in THE RIME OF SIR THOPAS': actually refering in a note to 'V.6'. It is, however, a monstrous lye.[86]

'The stories of Guy and Bevis, with some others, were probably the invention of English minstrels' [*RAEP* III, vii]. There are, doubtless, metrical romanceës, such as *Eglamour*, *Triamour*, *the Squyr of lowe degree*, and, it may be, one or two more, of which no French originals are known, and, therfor, may be fairly concluded to be of Engleish invention; but it is absolutely impossible that this can be the case with *Guy*, *Bevis*, or the rest, of which these originals are extant, and no one, who will take the trouble to compare them, could have the slightest doubt upon the subject. The MS. French metrical romanceës are mostly of the 12th or 13th century, the Engleish of the 14th

---

[84] *The Antiquities of Warwickshire* by the antiquary William Dugdale (1605-86) first appeared in 1656; Ritson probably read it in the reprint by John Jones (Coventry, 1765), pp. 262-64; Dugdale's *The Baronage of England* (1675-76) was the first major account of the English peerage.

[85] *HEP*, I, 142; square brackets are Ritson's.

[86] *HEP*, II, 173; Percy repeats Warton's contention, *RAEP*, III, xix. *Sir Isumbras* is one of around a dozen romances from which, Laura Hibbard Loomis suggests, Chaucer 'may have taken hints and phrases' for *Thopas*, but it is difficult to be certain because of 'the brevity of *Thopas* and the conventionality of the romances alike [...]'. 'Sir Thopas', in *Sources and Analogues of Chaucer's Canterbury Tales*, ed. by W. F. Bryan and Germaine Dempster (Chicago: University of Chicago Press, 1941), pp. 486-559 (p. 488). Ritson's accusation of a 'monstrous lye' is therefore not warranted, but typical of his excessive critiques of contemporaries, especially late in his life.

and 15th; obviously, therefor, they do not stand upon the same footing, and the originals are allways superior, and, sometimes, to a very extraordinary degree.

Mister Tyrwhitt thinks it extremely probable that these romanceës [*Horn child*, *sir Guy*, and *Bevis*], though, originally, writen in French, were compose'd in Engleland, and, perhap, by Engleishmen; for, says he, 'we find that the general currency of the French language here engage'd several of our own countrymen to use it in their compositions['].[87] He instanceës (doubtfully) Peter of Langtoft, as he is say'd 'by some to have been a Frenchman'; Robert Grosseteste, bishop of Lincoln, in the time of Henry III. a native of Suffolk, *Helis de Guincestre*, *i.e.* Winchester, and a romance, allso, in French verse, which he suppose'd to be the original of the Engleish *Ipomedon*, by *Hue de Rotelande*; and Gower. This, indeed, may be so, but it, likewise, may be otherwise: Andrew of *Wyntown*, which, equally, implys *Winchester*, was not, therefor, an Engleishman, nor ever in Engleland.[88]

In the year 1361 appear'd a singular allegorical and satyrical romance in alliterative metre without rime, by one Robert Langeland, as it is alledge'd, by some, without sufficient authority. It is, at any rate, however, a poem of great merit.

Geoffrey Chaucer, the famous poet, who pass'd his youth, and, the greater part of his life, in the reign of Edward III. was a writeër of romanceës, though in his *Rime of sire Thopas*, he attempts to burlesque and ridicule those of his predecessours and contemporarys, on account of what he calls their 'drafty riming'.[89] The specimen, however, completely proves how successful he would have been in a more serious exertion of his lyrical and inventive powers. His *Troilus and Cresside* was intended to be either red, or sung, probablely, in publick, or, even, in the latter case, to the harp:

'And *redde* where so thou be, or ellis *songe*'.[90]

A learned and judicious gentleman is incline'd to believe that we have no Engleish romance, prior to the age of Chaucer, which is not a translation of some earlyer French one.[91]

[...]

---

[87] *CTC*, IV, 69 n.55; square brackets are Ritson's.

[88] In this paragraph Ritson backs away from a notion of 'Anglo-Norman' language and literature as tentatively proposed by Tyrwhitt. In Britain the concept of Anglo-Norman literature would come into more general use in the early nineteenth century; see Frederic Madden extract, note 181.

[89] Cf *CT*, VII, l. 930; Ritson follows Tyrwhitt's reading 'drafty' for 'drasty', *CTC*, II, 240, l. 13858.

[90] Cf *Troilus and Criseyde*, V. 1797. – R.

[91] Tyrwhitt: *CTC*, IV, 68 n.55. – R.

That the Engleish acquire'd the art of romance-writeing from the French seems clear and certain, as most of the specimens of that art, in the former language, are palpable and manifest translations of those in the other, and this, too, may serve to account for the origin of romance in Italy, Spain, Germany, and Scandinavia: but the French romanceës are too ancient to be indebted for their existence to more barbarous nations. It is, therefor, a vain and futile endeavour to seek for the origin of romance: in all ageës and all countrys, where literature has been cultivateëd, and genius and taste have inspire'd, whether in India, Persia, Greece, Italy, or France, the earlyest product of that cultivation, and that genius and taste, has been poetry and romance, with reciprocal obligations, perhap, between one country and another. The Arabians, the Persians, the Turks, and, in short, almost every nation in the globe, abound in romanceës of their own invention. [...]

[...]

The fragment of a metrical romance, intitle'd *Le mort Arthure*, preserve'd in the Harleian MSS. Num. 2252, and of which Humphrey Wanley has say'd that the writeër 'useth many Saxon or obsolete words'; and doctor Percy, fancyfully and absurdly, that 'it *seems* to be quoted in *Syr Bevis*', is, in fact, nothing more than part of the *Morte Arthur* of Caxton turn'd into easey alternate verse, a very unusual circumstance, no doubt, in the time of Henry the seventh, to which Wanley properly allots it.[92] The antiquateëd words use'd by this versifyer are manifestly affected. Caxtons book is the onely one known by the name of *La mort D'Arthur*, which he took as he found it.

It is no proof, because any metrical romanceës in Engleish may not hapen to mention reading, they were not actually compose'd by writeërs at their desk. The minstrels were too ignorant, and too vulgar, to translate pieceës of several thousand lines; though such pieceës may have been translateëd or writen for them; as many a minstrel, no doubt, could sing and play, what he had not the genius to compose, nor even the capacity to write or read.

The 'lytell geste of Robyn Hode', could not, it is true have been compose'd by any *monk*, in his *cel*; but there can be no reason for supposeing it not to have been compose'd by a *priest* in his *closet*: and, in

---

[92] [Humphrey Wanley et al.], *A Catalogue of the Harleian Collection of Manuscripts*, 2 vols (London, 1759), II, no. 2252, art. 49; Percy, *RAEP*, III, xix. Humphrey Wanley (1672-1726) compiled the manuscript catalogue found in the second volume of Hickes's *Thesaurus* (1705); he was librarian to both Robert and Edward Harley, the father and son who established the great collection, and he began the catalogue of their collection. See further Milton McC. Gatch, 'Humphrey Wanley (1572-1726)', in Helen Damico, ed., *MSBS2*, 45-57. The stickler for accuracy trips himself up here; the stanzaic *Morte Arthur* influenced Malory, not the other way around. Ritson originally perpetrated this error in his *Observations on the Three First Volumes of The History of English Poetry* (London, 1782), p. 10.

fact, to an authour of that description, this identical legend, or one of the same kind, hath been expressly ascribe'd.

Sir Launfal is, certainly, a translation, the French original being extant in many librarys. It is not, however, by any means, 'the only piece of this sort, in which is inserted the name of the author'.[93]

There is not, however, one single metrical romance in Engleish known to exist, which appears to have been writen by a minstrel.

[The remainder of the dissertation, 117 pages, is devoted to attacks on Thomas Percy and his notion of the minstrels. Ritson first turns to Percy and his folio manuscript, accepting the existence of the manuscript but savagely criticising the use Percy made of it. Then in the fourth and concluding section of the essay, Ritson again turns to Minstrels and Minstrelsy', essentially expanding earlier arguments against Percy's vision of these figures.]

---

[93] The half-veiled criticisms here and in the previous paragraph are directed at Percy and points made in the fourth and final version of the essay on ancient minstrels: *Reliques*, 4th edn, 3 vols (London, 1794), I, lxxxi.

5. George Ellis (1753-1815)

George Ellis was an occasional poet, historian, diplomat, member of parliament, and co-founder of the *Anti-Jacobin*, who turned to early English literature in 1790 with the publication of *Specimens of the Early English Poets*; this was followed by a more highly detailed version in three volumes in 1801, discussed and excerpted below. He was from 1801 a friend and frequent correspondent of Scott's, and the two influenced one another on the topic of early romances. Like Scott, and doubtless as a consequence of knowing him, Ellis was influenced by the Auchinleck manuscript. The poems of the manuscript form the structural core of the *Metrical Romances*.

Arthur Johnston sees Ellis, along with Scott, as being in the second generation of British romance scholars, and both are in the school of Percy.[94] This is evident in the long introduction (126 pages) to *Specimens of Metrical Romances*, in which Ellis provides his own contribution to the debates on the nature of chivalric society, feudalism, the minstrels, and their relation to literature. This accessible work was successful, far more so than actual editions of romances. It was republished in a revised edition as part of Bohn's Antiquarian Library in 1848 by James Orchard Halliwell, who wrote: 'It is, indeed, difficult to estimate too highly the services which Ellis rendered to literature by the publication of this work. The interminable ballad romances of the middle ages had daunted all but the few initiated; but then, as if by magic, they became the friends and companions of thousands. Ellis, in fact, did for ancient romance what Percy had previously accomplished for early poetry [...] Our country almost ceases to be merry England without its ballads and its romances'.[95]

See further *EG*, ch. 6; Ellis's letters in H. J. C. Grierson, ed. *The Letters of Sir Walter Scott*, 12 vols (London: Constable, 1932-37); *MME*, ch. 3.

George Ellis, *Specimens of the Early English Poets, to which is prefixed an Historical Sketch of the Rise and Progress of the English Poetry and Language*, 3 vols (London, 1801).

Ellis on early Middle English language and literature (I, 60-83).
Chapter III

While Norman literature was making a rapid progress in this country, under the fostering influence of royal patronage; and the Latin compositions of John of Salisbury, Peter of Blois, Joseph of Exeter, and others, bore

---

[94] *EG*, p. 121.
[95] *Specimens of Early English Metrical Romances*, new edn rev. by J. O. Halliwell (London: Bohn, 1848), pp. iii-iv.

testimony to the no less powerful encouragement of the church; the Saxon language, however degraded, still continued to maintain its ground; was generally spoken, and even employed in works of information and amusement, for at least a century after the Norman conquest. This is incontestably proved, not only by the Saxon Chronicle, which, as it relates the death of King Stephen, must have been written after that event, but by a much more curious composition, a poetical translation of Wace's Brut, written by one Layamon, 'a priest of Ernleye upon Severn', (as he calls himself,) a copy of which is preserved in the British Museum, MSS. Cot. Calig. A. ix.

As this very curious work never was, and probably never will be printed, it appeared necessary to depart, in this instance, from the practice usually adopted in the present sketch, and to give the following extract in the spelling of the original MSS.
[Ellis quotes extensively from Laȝamon's *Brut*.]

The reader is certainly aware that a large proportion of the French words which have found their way into our language, were introduced through the medium of translations from Norman literature; and it is evident that such terms are particularly to be expected in descriptions of dress, of feasts, and of amusements; it is therefore presumed that the foregoing extract, both on account of its subject and its length, may be received as a tolerably fair specimen of Layamon's phraseology. And as it does not contain any word which we are under the necessity of referring to a French origin, we cannot but consider it as simple and unmixed, though very barbarous Saxon. At the same time, the orthography of this MS. in which we see, for the first time, the admission of the soft *g* together with the Saxon *ȝ*, as well as some other peculiarities, seem to prove that the pronunciation of our language had already undergone a considerable change. Indeed the whole style of this composition, which is broken into a series of short, unconnected sentences, and in which the construction is as plain and artless as possible, and perfectly free from inversions, seems to indicate that little more than the substitution of a few French for the present Saxon words, was now necessary, to produce an exact resemblance with that Anglo-Norman, or English, of which we possess a few specimens, supposed to have been written in the early part of the thirteenth century.

Layamon's versification also, is no less remarkable than his language. Sometimes he seems anxious to imitate the rhymes, and to adopt the regular number of syllables which he had observed in his original; at other times he disregards both; either because he did not consider the laws of metre, or the consonance of final sounds as essential to the gratification of his readers, or because he was unable to adopt them, throughout so long a work, from the want of models in his native language on which to form his style. The latter is, perhaps, the most probable supposition; but at all events, it is apparent that the recurrence of his rhymes is much too frequent to be the result of chance; so that upon the whole it seems reasonable to infer, that Layamon's work was composed at, or very near the period, when the Saxons and Normans in this country began to unite into one nation, and to adopt a common language. As this is a most curious epocha in our literary as well as political history, it is worth while to inquire how far it is capable of being ascertained; if not with precision, at least within some definite limits.

[...]

It is apparently impossible to establish, with any degree of certainty, a chronological series of those English poems which we still possess in manuscript, or to determine the year in which that series ought to commence; but if any conclusion can be drawn from internal evidence, arising from a comparison of the many pieces ascribed to the middle of the thirteenth century, it may be presumed, from the facility of rhyming evinced in many of them, and even in the very dull history of Robert of Gloucester, which contains more than thirteen thousand rhymes, that much poetry had been written before this period, and some probably as early as the accession of Henry III. in 1216. Perhaps, therefore, we may fairly infer, that the Saxon language and literature began to be mixed with the Norman about 1185; and that in 1216 the change may be considered as complete.

[...]

It is evident that nothing less than the most minute enquiry into all the circumstances of our history under the first Norman kings, would be sufficient for the full investigation of this subject; but the preceding observations will perhaps authorize us to assume, that the formation of the English language took its rise, and was probably far advanced, during the interval of about thirty years which preceded the accession of Henry III.

After quitting Layamon, we shall waste little time on the compositions of his immediate successors. The earliest of these, according to Mr. Tyrwhitt, is a paraphrase of the Gospel histories, called *Ormulum*, composed by one Orme or Ormin, which seems to have been considered as mere prose by Hickes and Wanley, who have given extracts from it, but is really written in verse of fifteen syllables, without rhyme, in imitation of the most common form of the Latin tetrameter iambick.[96] The next is a moral poem on old age, written in rhyme, and extracted by Hickes, part of which is to be found in the introduction to Dr. Johnson's Dictionary. Another poem, also transcribed from Hickes's extract, by Dr. Johnson, is a life of St. Margaret, which, as Mr. Warton tells us, forms part of a voluminous MS. in the Bodleian library, containing various lives of the saints, translated, perhaps, from some earlier Latin or French

---

[96] *CTC*, IV, 64 n.52. Hickes printed sections of the *Ormulum* as prose; *Thesaurus*, chap. 22, I, 165-66.

original.[97]

But the most entertaining and curious specimen preserved in Hickes's Thesaurus, is one which that learned editor has characterised as a *most malevolent satire* on the religious orders.[98] It, however, by no means deserves this disgraceful appellation, because it does not contain one of those opprobrious expressions which are so liberally employed, as a substitute for wit, by the early satirists. The author, whoever he was, takes advantage of a popular tradition respecting the existence of an imaginary terrestrial paradise, in some unknown quarter of the globe, which he calls the Land of *Cokaine*; in which his Houris are nuns, and their happy companions white and grey monks; and his object is to insinuate, that the ease and luxury enjoyed in the monasteries, had scarcely less effect in peopling the monastic orders, than the inducements more usually assigned by the proselytes of zeal and devotion. [...] The word *cokaine* seems to be Frenchified Latin; and our poem bears the strongest mark of being a translation; because the elegance of the sketch, and the refined irony of the general composition, are strongly contrasted with the rudeness of the language. As the poem is not excessively long, it is here printed entire [...]

Ellis on Robert of Gloucester (I, 97-106).
Chapter IV

We are now arrived at the poet whom his editor, Mr. Hearne, emphatically calls 'the British Ennius', but concerning whom we know little more, than that he was a monk of the abbey of Gloucester; that his christian name was Robert; that he lived during the reigns of Henry III. and Edward I.; and that he wrote, in English rhymes, an history of England from the days of the imaginary Brutus, to his own time. His work seems to have been completed about the year 1280 [...]

It would be quite hopeless to attempt a defence of Robert of Gloucester's poetry: perhaps his own wish was merely to render more intelligible a body of history which he considered as curious, and certainly believed to be authentic, because it was written in Latin, the language of truth and religion. Addressing himself to his illiterate countrymen, he employed the vulgar language as he found it, without any attempt at embellishment or refinement; and perhaps wrote in rhyme, only because it was found to be an useful help to the

---

[97] Here and in the next paragraph Ellis is simply summarising what is found in chapter twenty-four of the first part of Hickes's *Thesaurus* (pp. 222-35). His phrasing might be interpreted to imply that Hickes edited a Bodleian manuscript of the Life of St. Margaret (either from MS Bodley 2567 (779), presumably, at 308 leaves, the 'voluminous MS', or 14528 (Rawl. poet. 34), but this is not the case, as Hickes used MS Trinity College Cambridge 323.

[98] Hickes, *Thesaurus*, chap. 24, I, 231.

memory, and gave his work a chance of being recited in companies, where it could not be read. The latter part of his poem, in which he relates the events of his own time, will not appear quite uninteresting to those, who prefer the simple and desultory narratives of contemporary writers, to the philosophical abridgments of the moderns; and a great part of his obscurity will be found to result from that unnecessary mixture of the German or black letter with the Saxon characters, in which Mr. Hearne, from his inordinate appetite for antiquity, has thought proper to dress this ancient English author.

Robert of Gloucester, though cold and prosaic, is not quite deficient in the valuable talent of arresting the attention; and the orations with which he occasionally diversifies the thread of his story, are in general appropriate and dramatic, and not only prove his good sense, but exhibit no unfavourable specimens of his eloquence. In his description of the first crusade he seems to change his usual character, and becomes not only entertaining, but even animated; and the vision, in which a 'holy man' is ordered to reproach the Christians with their departure from their duty, and at the same time to promise them the divine intervention, to extricate them from a situation in which the exertions of human valour were apparently fruitless, would not, perhaps, to contemporary readers, appear less poetical, nor less sublime and impressive, than the introduction of the heathen mythology into the works of the early classics. The expectations awakened by this grand incident are, indeed, miserably disappointed by the strange morality which our monk ascribes to the Supreme Being, who declares himself offended, not by the unnecessary cruelties of the crusaders, nor by the general profligacy of their manners, so much as by the reflection, that they

> With women of *Paynim* did their foul kind,
> Whereof the stench came into heaven on high.[99]

But these absurdities and inconsistencies present, perhaps, a more lively picture of the reigning manners and opinions, than could have been intentionally delineated by a writer of much superior abilities to Robert of Gloucester [...]

It is, however, very probable, that a few of those compositions which we now call metrical romances, and which, by older writers, are termed *gests* (from the Latin word *gesta*, which was become the fashionable appellation of

---

[99] Cf *The Metrical Chronicle of Robert of Gloucester*, ed. by William Aldis Wright, 2 vols, RS 86 (London: HMSO, 1887), II, 597, ll. 8353-54. The displeasure of God with an army previously favoured is a common trope in medieval writing; there is nothing either absurd or inconsistent here, as Ellis goes on to claim. Ellis's characteristically mocking tone is evident, the tone he would elevate into an artform in the later *Specimens of Metrical Romances*.

every learned story-book) were written about this time; because Robert de Brunne expressly mentions two poets, *Thomas* and *Kendale*, as excelling in this mode of writing, and says, of the story of Sir Tristram, that

> Over *gestes* it has th'esteem:
> *Over all that is or was,*
> If men it said, as made *Thomás*.[100]

The bard who is thus distinguished from a crowd of competitors, is supposed to be Thomas Leinmouth of Erceldoun, or Ersilton, in the shire of Mersh, generally known by the honourable appellation of Thomas the Rymer, who lived in the reign of Edward I. and was reputed (though it seems falsely) to be the author of some metrical prophecies not yet forgotten in Scotland.[101] His contemporary Kendal is only known by the accidental mention of Robert de Brunne. There is, however, an unclaimed metrical Romance apparently belonging to this period, which the generosity of future critics may possibly assign to him. This is the Gest of King Horn, which is preserved in a very curious miscellany in the British Museum, (Harl. MSS. No. 2253) and mentioned by Chaucer as one of the *romances of price*. Mr. Warton has given an excellent abridgment of it, together with a considerable extract, in the first volume of his [History of English] Poetry, p. 39.[102]

Ellis on the minstrels (I, 124-34).
Chapter V

During the first period of our poetry, comprehending the greater part of the thirteenth, and about half of the fourteenth, century, our English versifiers are divided into two classes, the ecclesiastics, and lay-minstrels, who are generally distinguished from each other by a very different choice of subjects; the former exhibiting their talents in metrical lives of the saints, or in rhyming chronicles; the latter in satirical pieces, and love-songs. Tales of chivalry, being equally the favourites of all descriptions of men, were, to a certain degree, the common property of both.

There is reason to believe, that a marked difference of style and language, was apparent in the compositions of these rival poets, because the inferior

---

[100] Cf Idelle Sullens, ed. *Robert Mannyng of Brunne: The Chronicle*, MRTS 153 (Binghamton, N.Y.: Binghamton University, 1996), p. 93, ll. 98-100.

[101] More properly, Thomas Learmouth or Leirmouth. From early 1801, Ellis was engaged in correspondence with Walter Scott about Thomas the Rhymer and his supposed work, the romance of *Sir Tristrem* (Auchinleck manuscript) which Scott was editing, though it was not to appear until 1804. See *Letters*, ed. by Grierson, XII, 175-212.

[102] The generosity of Walter Scott would shortly credit *King Horn* to 'Thomas'. See below, p.146.

orders of the priesthood, and the several monastic societies, being chiefly conversant with the inhabitants of the country of the villages, were likely to retain more of the Saxon phraseology, and to resist the influx of French innovations much longer than their competitors: and it is principally to this circumstance that it seems reasonable to attribute those peculiarities of style, which Mr. Warton thought he discovered in Robert of Gloucester, and which he has ascribed to the provincial situation of the writer. The northern provinces, it is true, on account, perhaps, of their long subjection to the Danes, are represented by John de Trevisa (in a passage often quoted)[103] as differing materially in their pronunciation from those of the south: but Gloucester is not a northern county. The charge of provincial barbarism might, with more justice, be imputed to Robert de Brunne, as being a native of Yorkshire; but he has taken care to assure us, that his simple and unadorned diction was the result of care and design; that he considers his 'fellows' as the depositaries of pure and true English; that he

> —made nought for no *disours*,
> Ne for no *seggers*, no *harpours*,
> But *for the love of simple men*
> That *strange English* cannot ken.[104]

These *disours* or *seggers*, he tells us, took the most unwarrantable liberties with the diction of the works they recited; and he omits no opportunity of protesting against their licentious innovations in our language.

The reader who shall take the pains of comparing a few pages of the glossary annexed by Mr. Tyrwhitt to his edition of Chaucer, with that which Mr. Hearne has compiled, for the illustration of Robert de Brunne, will probably think that our author's complaints were just, and that the language of the city and inns of court, was much more infected with Gallicisms, than that of the monasteries; although a rapid change in both, appears to have taken place during the reign of Edward III. Many of the Norman words then introduced, have, indeed, long since become obsolete, and the Saxon has recovered its superiority; because the gradual dissemination of wealth, and liberty, and learning, among the common people, has, in some measure, blended in our language all the provincial dialects; but the torrent of fashion, at the period of which we are now treating, was irresistible. It was, perhaps, in some degree assisted by the practice of the dignified ecclesiastics, who, when

---

[103] Cf *Polychronicon Ranulphi Higden, Monachi Cestrensis; together with the English translations of John Trevisa [...]*, ed. by Churchill Babington and J. Rawson Lumby, 9 vols (London: HMSO, 1865-86), II (1869), 159, 161-63.

[104] Cf Sullens, ed. *Chronicle*, p. 92, ll. 75-78.

they did not write in Latin, universally affected to use the French language; but it is principally to be ascribed to the numerous translations, which were made at this time, from the French writers of those fabulous histories which we now call *Romances*. Such translations were hastily written, because eagerly called for; and their authors took the liberty (in which they were imitated by the disours or reciters) of admitting without scruple such '*strange*' words as happened to suit their rhyme, as well as those for which they could not immediately recollect the correspondent term in English.

As the public reciters here mentioned by Robert de Brunne, may possibly be unknown to many readers, it will perhaps be proper in this place to take some notice of them, as well as of the minstrels, with whom they were nearly connected.

It appears, that during the reign of our Norman kings, a poet, who was also expected to unite with the talent of versifying, those of music and recitation, was a regular officer in the royal household, as well as in those of the more wealthy nobles, whose courts were composed upon the same model. This practice seems to have originated in the admiration, which all the northern nations entertained for their ancient *Scalds*; and it gave rise to the appellation of *Minstrel* (ministrellus, an officer or servant), which, therefore (as Dr. Percy has observed in his learned Dissertation on this subject), was not strictly synonymous with those of *jougleur*, or *jongleur* (joculator), called, in old English, a *glee-man*, *juggler*, or *jangler*; because the latter might or might not be attached to a particular patron, and frequently travelled from castle to castle, for the purpose of reciting his compositions during the principal festivals. But as it is very difficult for the same person to attain equal excellence in all the sister arts, the professions of the poet, the harper, and the reciter, were afterwards undertaken by several associates, all of whom, on account of the privileges attached to the official minstrels, thought fit to assume the same honourable but equivocal title.

That these purveyors of poetry and music to the king and principal barons were, during the eleventh, twelfth, and thirteenth centuries, a privileged class, is perfectly certain from the universal testimony of contemporary writers. Indeed they were essential, not only to their amusement, but, in a great measure, to their education; because even the use of arms, and the management of a horse, were scarcely more necessary to a courteous knight, than the talent of playing on the harp, and composing a song in praise of his mistress. But in the course of the fourteenth century the minstrels, in France at least, had greatly declined in talents and reputation. There was a street at Paris, called *la Rue St. Julien des Menétriers*, peculiarly appropriated to their habitation; and they had a fraternity, or *confrérie* in the church of that saint, the well-known patron of hospitality: but these minstrels are described as a set of pantomimical fidlers, accompanied by monkies or bears, who were hired at weddings for the amusement of the guests: so much had they degenerated from the ingenious inventors of the fabliaux.

The history of this order of men in England is, for various reasons, very obscure and embarrassed. On the one hand it is evident, that if English began to be introduced at court as a colloquial language, about the beginning of the fourteenth century, it was not yet considered, either by our kings, or by the nobles, or by the dignitaries of the church, as fitted for literary purposes: and as our native minstrels, not having yet attempted any original poetry, could only have offered to their courtly audience, translations much more barbarous, and at the same time less familiar to their ears, than the compositions of the French trouveurs, it is not likely that such rivals could have displaced the Norman minstrels, already established in the post for which they were candidates. On the other hand, the testimony of Robert de Brunne to the existence of a body of *disours*, or *seggers*, accustomed to recite English metrical compositions in public, who were listened to with applause, and habituated to make arbitrary alterations in the language or metre of such compositions, is direct and positive. The most obvious solution of this difficulty would be to suppose, that the more opulent inhabitants of the towns, in imitation of their superiors, had adopted the mode of introducing at their banquets the amusements of music and recitation, and thus laid the foundation of a native minstrelsy on the French model; and this order of men being once established, might, on the decline of the rival language, find their way to the castles of our nobility; to which they would be recommended, by their previous exhibitions at the neighbouring fairs, where they never failed to appear as attendants on the merchants.

Indeed we have numerous proofs of their increasing popularity; for Chaucer, in his address to his Troilus and Cressida, tells us that it was intended to be 'read or elles *sung*',[105] which must relate to the chanting recitation of the minstrels; and a considerable part of our old poetry is simply addressed to an *audience*, without any mention of readers.

That our English minstrels at any time united all the talents of the profession, and were at once poets, and reciters, and musicians, is extremely doubtful: but that they excited and directed the efforts of their contemporary poets to a particular species of composition, is as evident, as that a body of actors must influence the exertions of theatrical writers.[106] They were, at a time when reading and writing were rare accomplishments, the principal medium

---

[105] Troilus and Criseyde, v, 1797.

[106] In this and the preceding two paragraphs Ellis offers a more cautious assessment of the possibility of a class of English minstrels than Percy had put forward. It is evident here and elsewhere that Ellis had read Ritson sympathetically; however, unlike Ritson, he is not ready entirely to jettison the exalted vision of the minstrel created in the *Reliques*.

of communication between authors and the public; and their memory in some measure supplied the deficiency of manuscripts, and probably preserved much of our early literature till the invention of printing: so that their history, if it could be collected, would be by no means uninteresting. But our materials for this purpose are too scanty, to enable us to ascertain the date of their formation, their progress, or their disappearance. Judging from external evidence, we should be disposed to place the period of their greatest celebrity, a little before the middle of the fifteenth century; because at that time our language had been successively improved by the writings of Gower, Chaucer, and Lydgate. Much wealth and luxury had been introduced by the two victorious reigns of Edward III. and Henry V.; and the country had not yet suffered any distress either from internal revolution, or from the length and disastrous termination of the war with France. The general poverty and discontent that prevailed during the subsequent period, the declension of chivalry, and the almost utter extirpation of our principal nobles, during the contest between the houses of York and Lancaster, must have been fatal to the prosperity of the minstrels; and two causes of a different nature, viz. the invention of printing in A.D. 1474, and the taste for religious disputation introduced by Henry VIII. may have tended to complete their ruin.

Though the minstrel character be now lost both in England and France, the traces of it are not universally effaced. In Wales, the modern harper is occasionally found to possess the accomplishments of the ancient bard: and among the Italians, the *improvisatori* of Rome and Florence, who are usually ready to attend the table of a traveller, and greet him with an extemporary poem on any subject which he shall prescribe, and protracted to a length which is only measured by his patience, are no bad representations of the antique minstrels; particularly when they are accompanied (as frequently happens) by an attendant musician, who gives the tone to their recitative, and fills up the pauses between the stanzas by a few notes on his instrument. The third character, or *disour*, is also to be found in many parts of Italy, but particularly at Venice; where, mounted on a temporary scaffolding, or sometimes on a stool or barrel, he recites, from memory, whole cantos of Ariosto.

The situation of a minstrel prescribed to him the choice of his subject. Addressing himself to an audience who lived only for the purpose of fighting, and who considered their time as of little value when otherwise employed, he was sure of being listened to with patience and credulity, so long as he could tell of heroes and enchanters: and he could be at no loss for either, because the histories of all the heroes and enchanters that the world had produced, were to be found in a few volumes of easy access.

As vanity is not easily subdued, a people who are not quite satisfied with their present insignificance, will often be tempted to indemnify themselves by a retrospective warfare on their enemies; and will be the more prodigal in assigning triumphs to their heroic ancestors, because those who in former ages contested the battle, can no longer be brought forward to dispute the claim of victory. This will explain the numerous triumphs of King Arthur: we have already seen, that a book containing the relation of his exploits, and of those of his knights of the round table, and of his faithful enchanter, Merlin, together with the antecedent history of the British kings, from the destruction of Troy, was purchased in Brittany, about the year 1100, by Walter, archdeacon of Oxford, a learned antiquary of those days, and confided to Geoffrey of Monmouth, a Welch Benedictine monk, who translated it into Latin, with some additions and interpolations. The French translations of Wace and Rusticien de Pise, and the Saxon and English versions of Layamon and Robert de Brunne, laid open this mass of history, to readers of every description.

Ellis on the poetry of the reign of Edward III (I, 146-212).
Chapter VI

The first English poet that occurs in the reign of Edward III. is Richard Rolle, hermit of the order of St. Augustine, and doctor of divinity, who lived a life of solitude near the nuns of Hampole, four miles from Doncaster, in Yorkshire. He was a very popular and learned, though inelegant writer in Latin, on theological subjects, and his pretensions to the character of an English poet are founded on a metrical paraphrase of the book of Job, another of the Lord's Prayer, seven penitential psalms, and a piece in seven parts, called 'the Prick of Conscience', all of which are usually attributed to him.

[...]

The next poet in succession is Laurence Minot, whose name was unknown to our antiquaries, till Mr. Tyrwhitt, in searching after the manuscripts of Chaucer, accidentally discovered a copy of his works, consisting of a collection of poems upon the events of the former part of this reign. It is sufficient in this place to have mentioned his name, as a very elegant edition of his works, accompanied with all the illustrations that could be drawn from contemporary history, has, within these very few years, been published by Mr. Ritson.[107]

Laurence Minot appears to have flourished about the year 1350, a few years after which was written the very curious poem called the 'The Vision of Pierce Ploughman'. Its reputed author is Robert Langland, a secular priest,

---

[107] This praise for Ritson's fine 1795 edition of the poems of Minot is significant in that it signals a shift away from the implacable opposition of most antiquarians to Ritson at the end of the eighteenth century. After Ritson's death in 1803 a slow rehabilitation of his scholarly reputation began.

born at Mortimer's Cleobury, in Shropshire, and fellow of Oriel College, Oxford.[108] His work is divided into twenty distinct passus, or breaks, forming a series of visions, which he supposes to have appeared to him while he was asleep, after a fatiguing walk amongst the Malvern Hills, in Worcestershire.

A dream is certainly the best excuse that can be offered, for the introduction of allegorical personages, and for any incoherences that may result from the conduct of a dialogue, carried on between such fanciful actors: and it must be confessed, that this writer has taken every advantage of a plan so comprehensive and convenient, and has dramatized his subject with great ingenuity. His work may be considered as a long moral and religious discourse, and as such, is full of good sense and piety; but it is farther rendered interesting, by a succession of incidents, enlivened sometimes by strong satire, and sometimes by the keenest ridicule on the vices of all orders of men, and particularly of the religious. It is ornamented also by many specimens of descriptive poetry, in which the genius of the author appears to great advantage.

But his most striking peculiarity is the structure of his versification, which is the subject of a very learned and ingenious essay in the second volume of the 'Reliques of Ancient English Poetry'.[109] His verses are not distinguished from prose, either by a determinate number of syllables, or by rhyme, or indeed by any other apparent test, except the studied recurrence of the same letter three times in each line; a contrivance which we should not suspect of producing much harmony, but to which (as Crowley, the original editor of the poem, justly observes) even a modern ear will gradually become accustomed.[110] This measure is referred by Dr. Percy to one of the 136 different kinds of metre which Wormius has discovered amongst the works of the Islandic poets; but the principal difficulty, is to account for its adoption in Pierce Ploughman's Vision.

Perhaps this alliterative metre having become a favourite with the northern Scalds, during the interval which elapsed between the departure of the Anglo-Saxons from Scandinavia, and the subsequent migration of the Danes, may have been introduced by the latter into those provinces of England, where they established themselves; and, being adopted by the numerous body of

---

[108] The standard biographical information about Langland goes back through Ritson, Warton, and Percy ultimately to John Bale; see Percy extract, note 17.

[109] In his Essay on Langland's metre, Percy opened with a discussion (not represented in the extract) of the metres of Icelandic poetry, drawing on the influential work of Wormius (the Danish scholar Ole Worm), in his *Literatura Runica* (1636, reissued 1651).

[110] Crowley, the sixteenth-century printer of the poem, briefly explained the alliteration and added: 'This thinge noted, the miter shall be very pleasaunt to read'. Crowley, 'The Printer to the Reader', *The Vision of Pierce Plowman*, prefatory material, p. ii[v].

minstrels, for which those provinces were always distinguished, may have maintained a successful struggle against the Norman ornament of rhyme, which was universally cultivated by the poets of the south. This at least seems to be suggested by Mr. Tyrwhitt who observes, that Giraldus Cambrensis describes by the name of 'Annomination', what we now call *alliteration*, and informs us that it was highly fashionable amongst the English, and even the Welsh poets of his time.[111] That it effectually stood its ground in some parts of the kingdom during the reign of Edward III. and even long after, appears from the numerous imitations of Langland's style, which are still preserved; and it is evident, that a sensible and zealous writer in the cause of religion and morality, was not likely to sacrifice those great objects, together with his own reputation, to the capricious wish of inventing a new, or of giving currency to an obsolete, mode of versification.

Mr. Warton is of opinion, that 'this imposed constraint of seeking identical initials, and the affectation of obsolete English, by demanding a constant and necessary departure from the natural and obvious forms of expression, while it circumscribed the powers of our author's genius, contributed also to render his manner extremely perplexed, and to disgust the reader with obscurity'.[112] But it may be doubted whether a work apparently addressed to the plain sense of common readers was written with an affectation of obsolete English; and much of its obscurity may perhaps be ascribed to the negligence of the transcriber of the MSS. from which the printed copy is taken. Neither is it certain that the 'imposed constraint of seeking identical initials' is at all more embarrassing to those, whose ear is accustomed to such a scheme of poetry, than the imposed constraint of identical final sounds; a constraint which, by exacting from the author, greater attention to the mode of expressing his thoughts, is rather likely to increase than to diminish, the precision and clearness of his language.

[Ellis presents some passages of *Piers Plowman*.]

Langland's work, whatever may be thought of its poetical merit, cannot fail of being considered as an entertaining and useful commentary on the general histories of the fourteenth century, not only from its almost innumerable pictures of contemporary manners, but also from its connection with the particular feelings and opinions of the time. The reader will recollect, that the minds of men were greatly incensed by the glaring contradictions that appeared between the professions and actions of the two great orders of the state.

The clergy of a religion founded on humility and self-denial, united the

---

[111] *CTC*, IV, 49 n.40.
[112] *HEP*, I, 267.

most shameless profligacy of manners with the most inordinate magnificence. An armed aristocracy, who, by their oath of knighthood, were bound to the maintenance of order, and to the protection of the helpless and unfortunate, were not satisfied with exercising, in their own persons, the most intolerable oppression on their vassals, but were the avowed protectors of the subordinate robbers and assassins who infested the roads, and almost annihilated the internal intercourse of every country in Europe. The people were driven to despair, flew to arms, and took a most frightful revenge on their oppressors. Various insurrections in Flanders; those of the Jacquerie in France, and those of Wat Tyler and others in England, were the immediate consequences of this despair; but the popular discontents had been in a great degree prepared and fomented by a set of itinerant preachers, who inveighed against the luxury and crimes of the great, and maintained the inalienable rights and natural equality of man.

Langland's poem, addressed to popular readers, written in simple, but energetic language, and admirably adapted, by its dramatic form, and by the employment of allegorical personages to suit the popular taste, though it is free from these extravagant doctrines, breathes only the pure spirit of the Christian religion, and inculcates the principles of rational liberty: this may possibly have prepared the minds of men, for those bolder tenets which, for a series of years, were productive only of national restlessness and misery, but which ultimately terminated in a free government, and a reformed religion. [...]

Chapter VII
    [...]
    To return to the Confessio Amantis. This poem is a long dialogue between a lover and his *confessor*, who is a priest of Venus, and is called GENIUS. As every vice is in its nature unamiable, it ought to follow, that immorality is unavoidably punished by the indignation of the fair sex; and that every fortunate lover must, of necessity, be a good man, and a good Christian; and upon this presumption, which, perhaps, is not strictly warranted by experience, the confessor passes in review, all the defects of the human character, and carefully scrutinizes the heart of his penitent with respect to each, before he will consent to give him absolution.

Because example is more impressive than precept, he illustrates his injunctions by a series of apposite tales, with the morality of which our lover professes to be highly edified; and, being of a more inquisitive turn than lovers usually are, or perhaps hoping to subdue his mistress, by directing against her the whole artillery of science, he gives his confessor an opportunity of incidentally instructing him in chemistry, and in the Aristotelian philosophy. At length, all the interest that he has endeavoured to excite, by the long and minute details of his sufferings, and by manifold proofs of his patience, is rather abruptly and unexpectedly extinguished: for he tells us, not that his mistress is inflexible or faithless, but that he is arrived at such a good old age that the submission of his fair enemy, would not have been sufficient for insuring his triumph.

[...]

[Gower] is wise, impressive, and sometimes almost sublime. The good sense and benevolence of his precepts, the solemnity with which they are enforced, and the variety of learning by which they are illustrated, make us forget that he is preaching in masquerade, and that our excellent instructor is a priest of Venus. But his narrative is often quite petrifying; and when we read in his work the tales with which we had been familiarized in the poems of Ovid, we feel a mixture of surprise and despair, at the perverse industry employed in removing every detail, on which the imagination had been accustomed to fasten. The author of the Metamorphosis was a poet, and at least sufficiently fond of ornament; Gower considers him as a mere annalist; scrupulously preserves his facts; relates them with great perspicuity; and is fully satisfied when he has extracted from them as much morality, as they can be reasonably expected to furnish.

The popularity of this writer is, perhaps, not very likely to revive: but although few modern readers will be tempted to peruse a poem of more than thirty thousand verses, written in obsolete English, without being allured by the hopes of more entertainment than can easily be derived from the Confessio Amantis, there are parts of the work which might very probably be reprinted with advantage. [...]

Chapter VIII

[Ellis opens his section on Chaucer with a sketch of the poet's life.]

All Chaucer's immediate successors, those who studied him as their model, Occleve, Lydgate, King James I. & c. speak with rapture of the elegance and splendor of his diction. He is 'the flower of eloquence'—'superlative in eloquence'; his words are 'the gold dew-drops of speech'. Such exaggerated praises certainly imply an enthusiastic, though perhaps absurd, admiration; and as these poets would probably attempt to imitate, what they considered as eminently beautiful, it seems likely, that an examination of their style, must enable us to discover what they considered, as the improvements introduced by Chaucer.

Now the characteristics of our poetry, during the fifteenth and sixteenth centuries, are, an exuberance of ornament, and an affectation of Latinity, neither of which peculiarities are to be found in Robert of Gloucester, Robert de Brunne, Laurence Minot, Langland, or indeed in any of the poets anterior to Chaucer. This, therefore, may be supposed to be what Chaucer himself, and his successors, meant by what they called an *ornate style*, of which the following stanza, extracted from the 'Court of Love', is a curious specimen.

Honour to thee, celestial and clear,

Goddess of Love, and *to thy celsitude*,
That givest life us light so far down from thy sphere,
Piercing our heartis *with thy pulchritude*;
Comparison none of similitude
May to thy grace be made in no degre,
That hast us set with love in unity.[113]

It is not meant that this is an example of Chaucer's usual style; indeed no poet is, in general, more free from pedantry: but the attentive reader will find that in the use of words of Latin derivation, most of which are common to the French and Italian languages, he very generally prefers the inflections of the latter, either as thinking them more sonorous, or because they are nearer to the original; and that in his descriptive poetry he is very fond of multiplying his epithets, and of copying all the other peculiarities of the Italian poetry, (from which his favourite metre is unquestionably derived) with the view of 'refining our numbers, and improving our language, by words borrowed from the more polished languages of the Continent'.[114]

[...]

[...] On the whole it may be doubted, whether he thought himself sufficiently qualified to undertake an original composition till he was sixty years of age, at which time it is conjectured that he formed, and began to execute, the plan of his Canterbury Tales.[115]

This elaborate work was apparently intended to contain a delineation of all the prominent characters in society; these were to be sketched out in an introductory prologue; to be contrasted by characteristic dialogues, and probably to be engaged in incidents which should farther develope their peculiarities of disposition: and as stories were absolutely necessary in every popular work, an appropriate tale was to be assigned to each of the pilgrims. It is not extraordinary, that the remainder of Chaucer's life, should have been insufficient for the completion of such a plan. What is actually executed can only be considered as a fragment; but, imperfect as it is, it contains more information respecting the manners and customs of the fourteenth century, than could be gleaned from the whole mass of contemporary writers, English or Foreign; and the poetical beauties with which it abounds have insured to its

---

[113] *Court of Love*, ll. 610-16, in *The Complete Works of Geoffrey Chaucer*, ed. by W. W. Skeat, 7 vols (Oxford: Clarendon Press, 1894-97), VII (1897), 27-28. Not finally expelled from the Chaucer canon until Skeat placed it in the apocrypha, this poem, probably of the sixteenth century, was attributed to Chaucer by Stow in 1561.

[114] Unreferenced quotation, untraced; the notion that Chaucer refined the English language in this way is a commonplace of critical opinion.

[115] Bearing in mind that like everyone else, Ellis thought Chaucer was born in 1328.

author, the first rank among the English poets, anterior to Shakspeare. [...]

Ellis on Lydgate (I, 273-76)
Chapter XI

Among the immediate successors of Chaucer, in England, John Lydgate, the celebrated monk of Bury, is confessedly the most tolerable. The time of his birth is not exactly known; but the documents extracted by Mr. Warton, from a register of the church of Bury, in the Cotton library, will ascertain it, with sufficient precision. It appears that he was ordained a subdeacon A.D. 1389; a deacon in 1393; and a priest in 1397: so that, even if we suppose him to have received the first ordination at fourteen years of age, he cannot have been born later than 1375; that is to say, twenty-five years before the death of Chaucer. This date naturally assigns him to the reign of Henry V. at whose command, he undertook his metrical history of the siege of Troy, the best and most popular of his almost innumerable productions.

Few writers have been more admired by their cotemporaries; yet none have been treated with more severity by modern critics. The learned Editor of the 'Reliques of Ancient Poetry', mentions him with compassionate contempt; Mr. Ritson ridicules his 'cart-loads' of poetical rubbish; and Mr. Pinkerton considers him as positively stupid. Mr. Warton alone has thought it worth while to study him with much attention, or to attempt a general discussion of his literary character [...]

[...] Lydgate's style, though natural, and sometimes rich, does not possess that strength and conciseness which is observable in the works of his master. It is dangerous for a mere versifier to attempt the completion of a plan [i.e. the *Canterbury Tales*], which has been begun by a poet. Lydgate's poem is not long; but it is possible to be tedious in a very small compass. [...]

George Ellis, *Specimens of Early English Metrical Romances, chiefly written during the early part of the fourteenth century*, 3 vols (London: Longman, Hurst, Rees; Edinburgh: Constable, 1805).

From: Section I, Introduction (I, 22-23).

[In the introduction to this work, Ellis opens with an augmented account of minstrelsy and the minstrels, developing the ideas of the 1801 *Specimens of Early English Poets* seen above. It is essentially a more subtle — and somewhat more plausible — version of Percy's theory of minstrelsy. It concludes:]

The next step was easy. Being compelled to a frequent exercise of their talent in extemporaneous compositions, the minstrels were probably, like the *improvisatori* of Italy, at least equal, if not superior, to more learned writers, in the merely mechanical parts of poetry; they were also better judges of the public taste. By the progress of translation they became the depositaries of nearly all the knowledge of the age, which was committed to their memory: it was natural, therefore, that they should form a variety of new combinations from the numerous materials in their possession; and it will be shown hereafter, that many of our most popular romances were most probably brought by their efforts to the state in which we now see them. This was the most splendid æra of their history, and seems to have comprehended the latter part of the twelfth and perhaps the whole of the thirteenth century. After that time, from the general progress of instruction, the number of readers began to increase; and the metrical romances were insensibly supplanted by romances in prose, whose monotony neither required nor could derive much assistance from the art of declamation. The visits of the minstrels had been only periodical, and generally confined to the great festivals of the year; but the resources, such as they were, of the ponderous prose-legend were always accessible. Thus began the decline of a body of men, whose complete degradation seems to have been the subsequent result of their own vices. During the period of their success they had most impudently abused the credulity of the public; but it is a whimsical fact, that the same fables which were discredited while in verse, were again, on their transfusion into prose, received without suspicion. It should seem that falsehood is generally safe from detection, when concealed under a sufficient cloak of dulness.

[Ellis's abstract of *Bevis of Hampton* is a typical example of his method in this work. In a two-page introduction to *Bevis*, he notes the manuscripts and prints of the texts. He bases his abstract on a conflation of the version in the manuscript in Caius College (Caius Cambridge 175), with its considerable gaps filled in from the print of Richard Pynson (c. 1503; *STC* no 1988), a copy of which was then owned by Francis Douce. The retelling of Bevis occupies 73 octavo pages. Ellis in effect has translated the medieval romance into an amusing, ironic novella, complete with poetic interludes which, with glosses supplied by Ellis (and retained here) would have provided some easily comprehensible light reading.]

From: II, 95-113.

The Earls of Southampton, being possessed of territories which it was frequently necessary to defend against foreign invasion, were always disinguished by superior valour and intrepidity; but the most illustrious champion of this warlike house was Sir Guy, father of Sir Bevis whose adventures we are preparing to relate. Sir Guy, constantly occupied during his youth in enterprises undertaken for the security or enlargement of his dominions, had unfortunately never thought of matrimony, till he was past the prime of life, when he chose a wife many years younger than himself, distinguished by her high birth and unrivalled beauty. Our author remarks that such a choice was very imprudent; and as his remarks are not always equally just, we take great pleasure in recording this instance of his sagacity.

In fact, this haughty fair one, who was daughter to the King of Scotland, had long since bestowed her affections on a younger lover, Sir Murdour, brother to the *Emperor of Almayne*: it was therefore with a very bad grace that she submitted to the positive commands of her father, who preferred to this illustrious son-in-law an alliance with the sturdy earl of Southampton. She submitted however: she became the mother of Bevis, for whom she never felt a mother's affection; and continued, during eight years, to share the bed of a husband whom she hated, and whose confidence she studied to acquire for the sole purpose of insuring his destruction.

Having matured her project, and gained over to her interest a number of her husband's vassals, she selected a trusty messenger whom she directed to salute her lover on her part,

> And bid him, on the first day,
> That cometh in the month of May,
>   Howso that it be,
> That he be with his *ferde*[116] *prest*[117]
> For to fight in that forèst
>   Upon the sea:
> Thider I wol my lord send,
> For his love, for to *schende*[118],
>   With little meyné.
> And say, that *it be nought bileved*,[119]
> That he ne smyte off his heved,
>   And send it me.[120]

Sir Murdour returned an answer expressive of the warmest gratitude and joyfully undertook his share in this atrocious project. He assembled a small troop of armed knights, embarked with them, landed near Southampton, and, taking his station in the forest, patiently waited for his victim. In the mean time the lady appeared to be suddenly indisposed; and, sending for her lord, informed him, that 'an evil on her was fall', and that she longed to eat of the flesh of a wild boar from his forest, such food being a sovereign remedy for her disease. Sir Guy, without hesitation, undertook to procure the object of her wishes; and, riding in to the forest with his hounds, was soon encompassed by the troops of his treacherous rival, who after bidding him defiance, and

---

[116] army. – E.
[117] ready. – E.
[118] to ruin or destroy him. – E.
[119] that no delay take place. *Byleve*, Sax. is to *stay*. – E.
[120] Cf Eugen Kölbing, ed. *The Romance of Sir Beues of Hamtoun*, 3 vols, EETS, e.s. 46, 48, 65 (London: EETS, 1885-94), I, 6, ll. 91-102 (Auchinleck).

avowing his purpose of murder, magnanimously assaulted the defenceless veteran. A few attendants, who had followed their master to the chace, instantly fled in confusion; but the earl himself, though provided only with a simple boar spear, evaded the lance of his antagonist, threw him from his horse upon the ground, and, drawing his trusty sword, defended himself with such skill and courage that a hundred of his assailants successively fell beneath his blows. The victory was long doubtful; but, his horse being killed under him, the knight was at length overpowered by numbers, and kneeling to Sir Murdour, who was now replaced on his horse, earnestly prayed that he might be permitted to seek a more glorious death, and not perish by assassination. His base antagonist replied by a blow which severed the head of the suppliant from his shoulders; and, having fixed it on a spear, sent it to his mistress as the stipulated price of her affection.

[As a result of his father's murder, Bevis is ultimately sold into slavery and comes to the court of Ermyn, a Saracen king. Bevis falls in love with the king's daughter Josyan. Ellis relates an adventure of Bevis's later career as follows:]

There was in the royal forest a wild boar, who had long been the terror of Ermyn's court. His size was enormous, his hide so thick as to be invulnerable, and his tusks so sharp that no common armour could withstand them; besides which, he was distinguished from other boars by a contemptuous disregard for beech-mast and acorns, and by an unnatural predilection for human flesh, which he gratified at the expense of all those who ventured to attack him. Bevis, finding his strength restored, began to consider of the best modes of employing it; and one night, whilst he lay in bed, luckily bethought himself of the boar. In the morning he saddled his horse; took a good shield and spear, together with an excellent sword; spurred across the plain with a grace which further captivated the fair Josyan, who beheld him from her window; and, when arrived at the forest, dismounted, tied his horse to a tree, and began to blow his horn. The boar, whether from sleepiness, or from a natural indifference to such music, took no notice of the defiance; and Sir Bevis, constantly advancing, blowing his horn, and searching every thicket, began to despair of meeting his enemy, when he was directed to the animal's den by the human bones with which the road was almost wholly covered. [...]

The hunting-spear which our hero had chosen for this occasion was of unusual strength, but it was shivered at the very first onset. The sword was, fortunately, so well tempered that it did not break in his hand; but he soon perceived that it made no more impression on the boar than it would have done on a rock of marble. But his ineffectual exertions were very fatiguing; his situation became every moment more discouraging; and in a short prayer, which he uttered with great devotion, the fainting hero confessed that he had no hopes of success but from the merciful interposition of heaven. During this time his antagonist, whose temper was naturally choleric, and perhaps rendered more so by the inflammatory nature of his favourite food, began to be in his turn much distressed by the effects of his own impetuosity; and, being unable to reach his too nimble enemy, became almost blind with fury, and breathless from exhaustion. Bevis, perceiving that the panting animal was unable to close his jaws without risk of suffocation, instantly seized this advantage; and, when the boar attempted to regain his den, met him in his full career and plunged the sword down his throat. This blow was decisive. The hero, who from his long education in a royal court was an adept in carving, now severed the head from the body; and, placing it on the truncheon of his spear, bore it off in triumph.

During the life of this boar, the keepers of the royal forest never ventured to go their rounds except in complete armour, and in numerous companies. Twelve of these happening to meet Bevis on his return, and perceiving that he was quite unarmed (his sword having been accidentally left with the body of the animal), resolved to wrest from him the fruits of his victory. He had just emerged from the forest, and arrived within sight of the tender Josyan, who from her tower had been anxiously watching for his return, when he was suddenly assailed by the company of twelve armed foresters. But, though armed, they were not invulnerable; and the truncheon of a spear was by no means an inefficient weapon in the hands of Bevis. At the first blow it came into contact with the helmets of three of these assailants, and scattered their brains to some distance. A second stroke and a third were repeated with equal success; and the three survivors having made a timely retreat, Bevis quietly resumed the boar's head, and pursued his journey to the palace; where Ermyn, who had already learned from his daughter the news of this astonishing adventure, received him with open arms, and recommended him to all his courtiers as a perfect model of courtesy and valour.

6. Sir Walter Scott (1771-1832)

Sir Walter Scott is well known as perhaps the most broadly influential figure in the revival of romance and medievalism generally through such works as his ballad anthology, *Minstrelsy of the Scottish Border* (1802-3), his long poem *The Lay of the Last Minstrel* (1805) and his famous novel, *Ivanhoe* (1819). *Sir Tristrem*, by contrast, is a largely forgotten edition of an awkwardly composed poem, incomplete in the manuscript and little read either then or now. Yet it was originally a key part of the phase of Scott's work represented by the *Minstrelsy* and the *Lay*. For a time it was a highly influential text in British medieval romance, and generated discussion long after Scott's death. Unlike earlier editions of romances, which tended to be in the form of anthologies, *Sir Tristrem* devoted an entire book to a single poem in a manner commonplace now but innovative at the time. Arthur Johnston thought that Scott's *Sir Tristrem*, 'even with its wild conjectures, still stands as the first great edition of a medieval romance', pointing 'the way to the scholars who produced the Early English Text Society editions later in the century' (*EG*, p. 187).

The fame of *Sir Tristrem* was disproportionate to the interest excited by the actual text. Scott made some extravagant claims about the romance, ascribing to it an author, the semi-legendary Thomas the Rhymer of Erceldoune, arguing that it was a Scottish poem, and arguing that this version of the Tristram story was the source of the continental versions, rather than the other way around. All of these central propositions were soon attacked, but Scott's vision of a Scottish (rather than Middle English) *Sir Tristrem* was an extraordinarily persistent one.

On Scott's medievalism, see Alice Chandler, *A Dream of Order: The Medieval Ideal in Nineteenth-Century English Literature* (London: Routledge & Kegan Paul, 1971), chapter 1, and Mark Girouard, *The Return to Camelot: Chivalry and the English Gentleman* (New Haven: Yale University Press, 1981), chapter 3. On Scott and romance see *EG*, ch. 7. Of the many biographies, see John Sutherland, *The Life of Walter Scott: A Critical Biography* (Oxford: Blackwell, 1995), esp. pp. 91-3 for *Sir Tristrem*; see also Cedric E. Pickford, 'Sir Tristrem, Sir Walter Scott and Thomas', in *Studies in Medieval Literature and Languages in Memory of Frederick Whitehead*, ed. by W. Rothwell, W. R. J. Barron, David Blamires and Lewis Thorpe (Manchester: Manchester University Press, 1973), pp. 219-28, and *MME*, ch. 3.

Walter Scott, ed. *Sir Tristrem; a Metrical Romance of the Thirteenth Century; by Thomas of Ercildoune, called The Rhymer* (Edinburgh: Constable; London: Longman and Rees, 1804).

Scott published three further editions, in 1806, 1811, and 1819; John Gibson Lockhart published it again in *The Poetical Works of Sir Walter Scott, Bart.*, 12 vols. (Edinburgh, 1833), V; it was edited for the Scottish Text Society by George P. McNeill in 1886 and again by George Eyre-Todd in his Abbotsford Series of the Scottish Poets in 1891. It has recently been re-edited by Alan Lupack in *Lancelot of the Laik and Sir Tristrem* (Kalamazoo: Medieval Institute Publications, 1994).

From: Introduction (pp. xxii-lxxxix).

[Several medieval Scottish accounts record Thomas of Erceldoune as the supposed author of prophecies; none of them states that he was a poet. A passage early in Robert Mannyng's *Chronicle* does appear to say that Thomas of Erceldoune was author of a tale of Sir Tristram, though it is not straightforward and could equally well be referring to an otherwise unknown 'Thomas Kendal'.[121] Scott links all the references in giving an account of Thomas the Rhymer of Erceldoune, to state that he was a poet; that he flourished in the second half of the thirteenth century; that he was the author of *Sir Tristrem* (Auchinleck manuscript), which he composed around 1250; that he was a landowner in Erceldoune, and 'that Thomas of Erceldoune was a man of considerable rank, and honoured with the acquaintance of the great and gallant of the time in which he lived'. He then turns to his poet's supposed creation.]

II. THE TALE OF TRISTREM was not invented by Thomas of Erceldoune. It lays claim to a much higher antiquity; and, if we may trust the Welch authorities, is founded upon authentic history.

---

[121] The relevant passage runs:
> I see in song, in sedgeyng tale
> of Erceldoun & of Kendale:
> Non þam says as þai þam wroght,
> & in þer sayng it semes noght.
> Þat may þou here in sir Tristrem,
> ouer gestes it has þe steem,
> ouer alle þat is or was,
> if men it sayd as made Thomas.
> Bot I here it no man so say
> Þat of some copple som is away.

Idelle Sullens, ed. *Robert Mannyng of Brunne: The Chronicle*, MRTS 153 (Binghamton, N.Y.: Binghamton University, 1996), p. 93, ll. 93-102.

[Scott then gives the outlines of the Tristram story, and notes the way in which stories originally from Welsh tradition are drawn into the expanded Arthurian tradition created by Geoffrey of Monmouth (whom he wrongly dates to the ninth century). He proposes that Cornwall held out until well into the tenth century against the invading Saxons and concludes that Tristram was a real figure who lived there. After some further consideration of Arthurian literature, Scott discusses the apparent presence of the Tristram story in French literature of the twelfth and thirteenth centuries; Chrétien de Troyes, he says, possibly composed a Tristram poem, and the story seems otherwise to have been current.]

Thus, the story of Tristrem appears to have been popular in France, at least thirty years before the probable date of Thomas of Erceldoune's work. A singular subject of enquiry is thus introduced. Did Thomas translate his poem from some of those which were current in the Romance language? Or did he refer to the original British authorities, from which his story had been versified by the French minstrels? The state of Scotland, at the period when he flourished, may probably throw some light on this curious point.

Although the Saxons, immediately on their landing on the eastern coast of England, obtained settlements, from which they were never finally dislodged, yet the want of union among the invaders, the comparative smallness of their numbers, and a variety of other circumstances, rendered the progress of their conquest long and uncertain. For ages after the arrival of Hengist and Horsa, the whole western coast of Britain was possessed by the aboriginal inhabitants, engaged in constant wars with the Saxons; the slow, but still increasing tide of whose victories still pressed onward from the east. These western Britons were, unfortunately for themselves, split into innumerable petty sovereignties; but we can distinguish four grand and general divisions. 1st, The county of Cornwal, and part of Devonshire, retained its independence, in the south-west extremity of the island. 2dly, Modern Wales was often united under one king. 3dly, Lancashire and Cumberland formed the kingdom of the Cumraig Britons, which extended northward, to Solway firth, which is now the borders of Scotland. 4thly, Beyond the Scottish border lay the kingdom of Strathclwyd, including, probably, all the western part of Scotland, betwixt the Solway Firth and Firth of Clyde. With the inhabitants of the Highlands, we have, at present, no concern. This western division of the island being peopled by tribes of a kindred origin and language, it is natural to conceive, even were the fact dubious, that the same traditions and histories were current among their tribes. Accordingly, the modern Welch are as well versed in the poetry of the Cumraig and the Strathclwyd Britons, as in that of their native bards; and it is chiefly from them that we learn the obscure contentions which these north-western Britons maintained against the Saxon invaders. The disputed frontier, instead of extending across the island, as the more modern division of England and Scotland, appears to have run longitudinally, from north to south, in an irregular line, beginning at the mountains of Cumberland, including the high grounds of Liddesdale and Teviotdale, together with Ettrick forest and Tweeddale; thus connecting a long tract of mountainous country with the head of Clydesdale, the district which gave name to the petty kingdom. In this strong and defensible country, the natives were long able to maintain their ground. About 850 the union of the Scots and Picts enabled Kenneth and his successors to attack, and, by degrees, totally to subdue the hitherto independent kingdoms of Strathclwyd and Cumbria. But, although they were thus made to constitute an integral part of what has since been called Scotland, it is reasonable to conclude, that their manners and customs continued, for a long time, to announce their British descent. In these districts had flourished some of the most distinguished British bards; and they had witnessed many of the memorable events which decided the fate of the island. It must be supposed that the favourite traditions of Arthur and his knights retained their ground for a length of time, among a people thus descended. Accordingly, the scene of many of their exploits is laid in this frontier country; Bamborough castle being pointed out as the Castle Orgeillous of romance, and Berwick as the Joyeuse Garde, the stronghold of the renowned Sir Lancelot. In the days of Froissart, the mountains of Cumberland were still called *Wales*; and he mentions Carlisle (so famous in romantic song) as a 'city beloved of King Arthur'. Even at this day, the Celtic traditions of the Border are not entirely obliterated, and we may therefore reasonably conclude, that in the middle of the 13th century they flourished in full vigour.

If the reader casts his eye upon the map, he will see that Erceldoune is situated on the borders of the ancient British kingdom of Strathclwyd; and I think we may be authorized to conclude, that in that country Thomas the Rhymer collected the materials for his impressive tale of *Sir Tristrem*. The story, although it had already penetrated into France, must have been preserved in a more pure and authentic state by a people, who, perhaps, had hardly ceased to speak the language of the hero. There are some considerations which strongly tend to confirm this supposition.

In the first place, we have, by a very fortunate coincidence, satisfactory proof, that the romance of *Sir Tristrem*, as composed by Thomas of Erceldoune, was known upon the continent, and referred to by the French minstrels, as the most authentic mode of telling the story. This is fortunately established by two metrical fragments of a French romance, preserved in the valuable library of Francis Douce, Esq. F. A. S. of which the reader will find a copious abstract, beginning on p. 203.[122] The story, told in those fragments,

---

[122] Francis Douce (1757-1834), antiquarian and collector, owned two manuscript fragments containing about 1,800 lines of the *Tristan* of Thomas of Britain (or Thomas

will be found to correspond most accurately with the tale of *Sir Tristrem*, as narrated by Thomas of Erceldoune, while both differ essentially from the French prose romance, afterwards published. There seems room to believe, that these fragments were part of a poem, composed (as is believed) by Raoul de Beauvais, who flourished in 1257, about the same time with Thomas of Erceldoune, and shortly after we suppose the latter to have composed his grand work.[123] As many Normans had settled in Scotland about this period, it is probable that Thomas's tale was early translated, or rather imitated, in the Romance language. The ground for believing that this task was performed by Raoul de Beauvais, is his being the supposed author of a romance on the subject of *Sir Perceval*, preserved in the library of Foucault.

[The argument now takes a convoluted turn, and relies on misreadings of texts with which Scott is clearly not closely acquainted. Ritson had earlier quoted the opening of the *Cligés* of Chrétien de Troyes, in which Chrétien lists his own works, erroneously saying it was from *Perceval* (*AEMR*, I, xlii-xliii). Scott perpetuates the error and, furthermore, states that the romance is not by Chrétien but Raoul de Beauvais (Chrétien says his source for *Cligés* was a book in the library at Beauvais).[124] In the *Cligés* prologue, Chrétien claims to have written the story of King Mark and Iseult the Blonde; this is no longer extant, but Scott argues that this work of 'Raoul' is probably represented in the Douce fragments (in fact by Thomas of Britain). He now quotes a digressive passage from these fragments in which the narrator discusses the different versions of the story of Tristram.[125] The narrator here refers to

---

d'Angleterre). They probably date, as Douce knew himself, from the late twelfth century while Thomas's poem is usually placed 1170-80. It is this Thomas rather than Thomas of Erceldoune who was the source for succeeding continental writers of Tristan narratives.

[123] Raoul de Beauvais was a troubadour of the mid-thirteenth-century to whom are attributed around five lyrics; he has no association with Tristan stories, and Scott's attribution is based on the flimsiest evidence (see the linking note, following). There is perhaps some association in Scott's mind with Raoul de Houdenc, an early imitator of Chrétien who wrote the romance *Meraugis de Portlesguez*.

[124] Why neither Ritson nor Scott could see that Chrétien was the author of *Perceval* (*Le Conte du Graal*) or *Cligés*, and why both compounded the two, is not clear, given that Chrétien names himself in the opening lines of both romances. The likelihood is that both were working with the texts at second or third hand, given that neither text had been edited and the manuscripts were mostly to be found in Paris — not always easy for a Briton to visit in this period. Neither antiquarian seems to have been aware of the Anglo-Norman version of *Perceval* in College of Arms MS Arundel XIV. See Keith Busby, et al, eds. *Les Manuscrits de Chrétien de Troyes*, 2 vols. (Amsterdam and Atlanta: Rodopi, 1993), 2:81.

[125] See *Tristan et Yseut: Les Tristan en Vers*, ed. and trans. by Jean Charles Payen (Paris: Editions Garnier Frères, 1974), pp. 212-14, ll. 2107-56. In this passage Thomas of Britain refers to himself in the third person (in the characteristic fashion of the romancers) in such a way that it could be imagined the passage was the work of another writer *referring* to Thomas.

'Thomas' — i.e., himself. But Scott maintains that this must be a reference to Thomas of Erceldoune. He admits that the language of the passage looks more like that of the twelfth century than the thirteenth, but explains this away by proposing that it was actually written in Britain, where the written French preserved an earlier state of the language. In short: 'Raoul' tells us in his 'Perceval' that he is the author of a Tristan story; that story must be the one in the Douce fragments; Raoul de Beauvais worked after 1250, therefore the Douce fragments must date from after that time, and the Thomas referred to in the fragments must be the 'earlier' Thomas of Erceldoune.]

The reference to stile [of language] being thus uncertain, the evidence on the other side must be allowed to countervail it. For, that Thomas of Erceldoune wrote the romance of *Sir Tristrem*, a work of most extended reputation, is ascertained by Robert de Brunne: That he flourished in the 13th century, is proved by written evidence: That the tale, as told in the *Fragments*, corresponds exactly with the edition now published, while they both differ widely from every other work upon the same subject, is indisputable. As the one, therefore is affirmed to be the work of Thomas, and the other refers to a Thomas who composed such a work, the connection betwixt them is completely proved, and the ascertained period of Thomas's existence may be safely held as a landmark for fixing the date of the fragments, notwithstanding the obsolete language in which they are written.

Assuming, therefore, that Thomas of Erceldoune is the person referred to by the contemporary French author, it will be difficult to give any other reason for the high authority which the minstrel assigns to him, than his having had immediate access to the Celtic traditions concerning *Sir Tristrem*, with which the Anglo-Norman romancers were unacquainted. The author of the fragments quotes the authority of Breri, apparently an Armorican, to whom were known all the tales of the kings and earls of Brittany; and with equal propriety he might refer to Thomas of Erceldoune, as living in the vicinity of what had been a British kingdom, where, perhaps, was still spoken the language in which the feats of *Sir Tristrem* were first sung. But it is plain, that, had Thomas translated from the French, the Anglo-Norman minstrel would have had no occasion to refer to a translator, when the original was in his own language, and within his immediate reach. What attached authenticity

---

Scott needs this to be the case so that he can say 'Raoul' is referring to Thomas of Erceldoune. In addition, later in this introduction he will deny that poets of this era referred to themselves in the third person, as Ritson had suggested might be the case with Thomas of Erceldoune and the Auchinleck *Sir Tristrem*; he does so because he wants to argue for a greater distance between original composition and the writing down of the poem. As he has made the *Tristan* of the Douce fragments contemporary with Thomas of Erceldoune, it would be inconvenient to discover in the fragments a poet referring to himself in the third person.

to Thomas's work seems, therefore, to have been the purity of his British materials, by which he brought back, to its original simplicity, a story, which had been altered and perverted into a thousand forms, by the *diseurs* of Normandy.

In the second place, if Thomas of Erceldoune did not translate from the French, but composed an original poem, founded upon Celtic tradition, it will follow, that the first classical English romance was written in part of what is now called Scotland; and the attentive reader will find some reason to believe, that our language received the first rudiments of improvement in the very corner, where it now exists in its most debased state.

In England, it is now generally admitted, that, after the Norman conquest, while the Saxon language was abandoned to the lowest of the people, and while the conquerors only deigned to employ their native French, the mixed language, now called English, only existed as a kind of *lingua franca*, to conduct the necessary intercourse between the victors and the vanquished. It was not till the reign of Henry III. that this dialect had assumed a shape fit for the purposes of the poet; and even then, it is most probable that English poetry, if any such existed, was abandoned to the peasants and menials, while all, who aspired above the vulgar, listened to the *lais* of Marie, the *romances* of Chretien de Troyes, or the interesting *fabliaux* of the Anglo-Norman *trouveurs*. The only persons, who ventured to use the native language of the country in literary composition, were certain Monkish annalists, who usually think it necessary to inform us, that they condescended to so degrading a task out of pure charity, lowliness of spirit, and love to the 'lewd men' who could not understand the Latin of the cloister, or the Anglo-Norman of the court. Even when the language was gradually polished, and became fit for the purposes of the minstrels, the indolence or taste of that race of poets induced them, and those who wrote for their use, to prefer translating the Anglo-Norman and French romances, which had stood the test of years, to the more precarious and laborious task of original composition. It is the united opinion of Warton, Tyrwhytt, and Ritson, that there exists no English Romance, prior to the days of Chaucer, which is not a translation of some earlier French one.

While these circumstances operated to retard the improvement of the English language in England itself, there is great reason to believe, that in the Lowlands of Scotland its advances were more rapid. The Saxon kingdom of Bernicia was not limited by the Tweed, but extended, at least occasionally, as far northward as the Frith of Forth. The fertile plains of Berwickshire, and the Lothians, were inhabited by a race of Anglo-Saxons, whose language resembled that of the Belgic tribes whom they had conquered, and this blended speech contained, as it were, the original materials of the English tongue. Beyond the Friths of Forth and of Tay, was the principal seat of the Picts, a Gothic tribe, if we can trust the best authorities, who spoke a dialect of the Teutonic, different from the Anglo-Saxon, and apparently more allied to

the Belgic.
[Scott develops this argument, suggesting that English developed separately at the Scottish court, largely uninfluenced by French; Scottish English is supposedly a development separate from and parallel with English in the south.[126]]

Thus, the language, now called English, was formed under very different circumstances in England and Scotland; and, in the latter country, the Teutonic, its principal component part, was never banished from court, or confined to the use of the vulgar, as was unquestionably the case in the former.

[The outcome of the argument is that a vernacular literature developed in Scotland before it did in England. Moreover, because of the decline of Scottish Gaelic, it was minstrels working in English who came to be revered.]

From this short statement it follows, that, while the kings and nobles of England were amused by tales of chivalry, composed in the French or Romance language, those which were chaunted in the court of Scotland must have been written originally in Inglis. The English did not begin to translate these French poems till about 1300, nor to compose original romances in their own language, until near a century later. But Thomas of Erceldoune, Kendal (whose name seems to infer a Cumbrian descent), Hutcheon of the Awle Royal, and probably many other poets, whose names and works have now perished, had already flourished in the court of Scotland. Besides *Sir Tristrem*, there still exist at least two Scottish romances, which, in all probability, were composed long before the conclusion of the 13th century. These are entitled *Gawan and Gologras*, and *Galoran of Galoway*.[127] This opinion is not founded merely upon their extreme rudeness and unintelligibility, for that may be in some degree owing to the superabundant use of alliteration, which required many words to be used in a remote and oblique sense, if indeed they were not invented 'for the nonce'. But the comparative absence of French words, and French phraseology, so fashionable in Scotland after the time of Robert Bruce, when the intercourse of the countries became more intimate, and, above all, evident allusions to the possession of part of Scotland by the British tribes, seem to indicate

---

[126] This was an argument Scott derived from John Pinkerton (1758-1826). In his *Ancient Scotish Poems*, 2 vols (London, 1786), Pinkerton argued that the Picts spoke a 'Gothic' language from which modern Scots was descended, much as modern English was descended from Saxon (I, lxii, lxvi). But the notion that Scottish was derived from Anglo-Saxon or was simply a dialect of English was, Pinkerton said, a 'vulgar error' (I, lxx).

[127] *Golagrus and Gawain* is a Scottish poem of the late fifteenth century; *Galoran of Galloway* is the late fourteenth-century Northern English poem now better known as *The Awntyrs of Arthur*.

sufficiently their remote antiquity. Even the alliteration is a proof of the country in which they are composed. Chaucer tells us, that the composition of gestes, or romances, and the use of alliteration, was in his time peculiar attributes of the northern poets. His Persone says,

> But trusteth wel, I am a sotherne man,
> I cannot *gest, rem, ram, ruf*, by my letter,
> And God wote, rime hold I but litel better.[128]

In these romances there does not appear the least trace of a French original; and it seems probable that, like *Sir Tristrem*, they were compiled by Scottish authors from the Celtic traditions, which still floated among their countrymen. To this list, we might perhaps be authorized in adding the *History of Sir Edgar and Sir Grime*; for, although only a modernized copy is now known to exist, the language is unquestionably Scottish, and the scene is laid in Carrick, in Ayrshire.[129]

The very early and well known romance of *Hornchild* seems also to be of border origin; nay, there is some room to conjecture, that it may have been the composition of Thomas of Erceldoune himself.[130] The French MS. of the romance, in the Museum, begins thus:

> Seignurs oi avez le vers del parchemin,
> Cum le Bers Aaluf est venuz a la fin;
> Mestre Thomas ne volt qu'il seit mis a declin,
> K'il ne die de Stern le vaillant orphalin.

And it ends with the following odd couplet:

> Tomas n'en dirrat plus; *tu autem* chanterat,
> *Tu autem, domine, miserere nostri.*[131]

A poet, named Thomas, being thus referred to as the author of a tale, the scene of which is laid in Northumberland, and in which every name, whether of place or person, attests an origin purely Saxon, there seems no reason why

---

[128] Cf *CT*, x, ll. 42-44.

[129] *Eger and Grime* is a Scottish poem, but has been dated to the mid-fifteenth century. It exists in the Percy Folio (BL Add MS 27,879, c. 1650) and some late prints.

[130] Scott refers to *King Horn*, as it is now known, rather than the later *Horn Child* in the Auchinleck manuscript. However, as the ensuing remarks suggest, Scott appears to regard the later poem simply as another version of *King Horn* rather than a separate poem.

[131] Cf Mildred K. Pope, ed. *The Romance of Horn by Thomas*, ANTS 9, 10, 12, 13, 2 vols (Oxford: Blackwell, 1955-57), I, 1, ll. 1-4; 174, ll. 5239-40.

he may not be identified with Thomas of Erceldoune, a celebrated border poet, to whom every tradition respecting Deiria and Bernicia must have been intimately familiar.[132] If the apparent antiquity of the language of the French *King Horn* be alledged against this opinion, we may oppose the difficulty and apparent impossibility of ascertaining the chronology of French poetry, considering how widely it was extended, and into how many dialects it must necessarily have been divided. Even in our own literature, did we not know the age of Gawain Douglas, we should certainly esteem his language older than that of Chaucer, when, in fact, it is nearly two centuries later. It is impossible, where other evidence fails, to distinguish, from the circumstance of the style alone, that which is *provincial* from that which is really *ancient*. But whatever may be thought of Thomas of Erceldoune's claim to be held the author of this romance,[133] it does not appear less certain, that it has originally been written in or near the country, which is described with so much accuracy. It is not sufficient to answer, with a late ingenious antiquary, that the names and references are all northern, because the story is predicated of the Saxons and Danes in England and Ireland.[134] We know how totally indifferent the

---

[132] The connections here become highly tenuous. As the lines quoted show, the AN *Romance of Horn* appears to have been composed by a Mestre Thomas. However, it was probably written c. 1170-80, and was certainly much earlier than Scott's 1250 date for *Sir Tristrem* (leaving aside that poem's more probable late thirteenth-century date). Neither is the AN romance set in Northumberland: Horn is from 'Suddene', and whether or not this is to be identified as the coast of South Devon, as Pope argues (II, 4), it clearly implies a *southern* location. In the ME *King Horn*, Horn is heir to the island of Sudene and only in *Horn Child* is Northumberland important: it is the kingdom of Horn's father Hatheolf. As *Horn Child* appears in the Auchinleck manuscript, which Scott had in his possession for months at a time when editing *Sir Tristrem*, he has perhaps let it dominate his thinking. He seems not to have read the Anglo-Norman poem, then unedited, very closely.

[133] The editor's opinion is only stated hypothetically; nor will he be surprised at any one inclining to believe that the Thomas of the French *Horn-Child* is, in fact, the *rimeur* himself, and not the bard of Erceldoune: but he cannot allow that such Anglo-Norman Thomas, supposing him to exist (which, after all, is matter of supposition), shall be identified with the Tomas in the Fragments of *Sir Tristrem*. In that point, the ground taken in these remarks seems much stronger; for we know certainly the existence of Thomas of Erceldoune, who did write a romance of *Sir Tristrem*, highly esteemed by his contemporaries; we have also seen reasons why his authority should be referred to by a French *rimeur*, who, at the same time, and probably for the same reasons, quotes that of an Armorican minstrel. But, granting the French *rimeur*, Thomas, to have existed, we can see no natural connection betwixt him and the tale of *Sir Tristrem*, and no reason why, supposing him to have written such a tale (which, again, is a matter of gratuitous supposition), his authority should have been referred to as irrefragable by posterior narrators of the same history. In the one view of the case, we have indisputable fact, in the other mere hypothesis. Above all, the reference seems conclusive to the correspondence betwixt the poems. – S.

[134] Ritson, *AEMR*, I, xcix. – S.

minstrels and their hearers were to every thing allied to *costume*, which their ignorance would have disabled them from preserving, had their carelessness permitted them to strive after such an excellence. When, therefore, we find a romance, like that of *Horn*, without the least allusion to Norman names and manners, we may, I think, safely conclude, that, although it exists in both languages, it must have been originally composed in that of the country where the scene is laid, and from which the actors are brought. [...] It may finally be remarked, that, although the more modern romance of *Hornchild* in the Auchinleck MSS. has some phrases, as 'in boke we read', 'in rime, as we are told', generally supposed to imply a translation from the French, yet nothing of the kind occurs in the older tale, published by Mr Ritson, which bears every mark of originality.

The romance of *Wade*, twice alluded to by Chaucer, but now lost, was probably a border composition.[135] The castle of his hero stood near the Roman Wall, which he is supposed to have surmounted; and it was long inhabited by his real or fancied descendants. It is absurd to suppose that Norman minstrels came into these remote corners of the kingdom, to collect or celebrate the obscure traditions of their inhabitants; although, finding them already versified, they might readily translate them into their own language.

These general observations, on the progress of romantic fiction in the border counties, lead us to consider the evidence given by Robert de Brunne, concerning the poetry of Thomas of Erceldoune, which is thus expressed in the introduction to his annals:

[Scott quotes a long passage from Robert Mannyng, including the lines about Erceldoune and Kendal (see note 121). He argues that 'quaint Inglis' has been read mistakenly, and in fact refers to a high and ambitious style used by Thomas of Erceldoune and Kendale.]

[...] Thus, the testimony of this ancient historian, who was a contemporary of Thomas of Erceldoune, establishes at once the high reputation of his work, and the particular circumstances under which it was written. While the English minstrels had hardly ventured on the drudgery of translating the French romances, or, if they did so, were only listened to by the lowest of the people, our northern poets were writing original *gests* 'for pride and nobleye', in a high stile and complicated stanza, which the southern harpers marred in repeating, and which their plebeian audience were unable to comprehend. In one word, the early romances of England were written in French, those of Scotland were written in English.

If the editor has been successful in his statement, two points have been established; 1st, that the minstrels of the south of Scotland, living in or near

---

[135] This romance remains lost; for speculations on its possible nature see *MEL*, p. 125.

the British tribes of Reged and Strathclwyd, became the natural depositaries of the treasures of Celtic tradition, esteemed so precious in the middle ages; 2dly, That, from the peculiar circumstances under which the English language was formed in the Lowlands of Scotland, and north of England, it probably was more early fitted for the use of the poet in that country, than in the more southern parts of the sister kingdom, where it was so long confined to the use of the populace. Whoever shall be tempted to pursue this curious subject, will find that this system, if confirmed upon more minute investigation, may account for many anomalous peculiarities in the history of English romance and minstrelsy. In particular, it will shew why the Northumbrians cultivated a species of music not known to the rest of England, and why the harpers and minstrels of the 'North Countree' are universally celebrated, by our ancient ballads, as of unrivalled excellence. If English, or a mixture of Saxon, Pictish, and Norman, became early the language of the Scottish court, to which great part of Northumberland was subjected, the minstrels, who crowded their camps, must have used it in their songs. Thus, when the language began to gain ground in England, the northern minstrels, by whom it had already been long cultivated, were the best rehearsers of the poems already written, and the most apt and ready composers of new tales and songs. It is probably owing to this circumstance, that almost all the ancient English minstrel ballads bear marks of a northern origin, and are, in general, common to the borderers of both kingdoms. By this system we may also account for the superiority of the early Scottish over the early English poets, excepting always the unrivalled Chaucer. And, finally, to this we may ascribe the flow of romantic and poetical tradition, which has distinguished the borders of Scotland almost down to the present day.

[Scott continues with a description of various continental versions of the Tristram story, and concludes the section by warning against Malory's telling in the two Tristram books, the only other English version of the story:]

Those, unaccustomed to the study of romance, should beware of trusting to this work, which misrepresents the adventures, and traduces the character of Sir Gawain, and other renowned Knights of the Round Table.

III. THE PRESENT EDITION of the romance of *Sir Tristrem* is published from the Auchinleck MSS., a large and curious collection of such pieces, of which the reader will find an account in the Appendix to these observations. The date of the MS. cannot possibly be earlier, and does not seem to be much later, than 1330, at least eighty years after the romance of *Sir Tristrem* had been composed. The immediate narrator does not assume the person of Thomas of Erceldoune, but only pretends to tell the tale upon his authority.

> I was at Erceldoune,
>   With Tomas spak Y thare,
> There herd Y read in roune,
>   Who Tristrem gat and bare, &c.
>
> ....
>
> Thomas telles in toun
> The auentors as thei were.[136]

A late eminent antiquary suggested, that Thomas of Erceldoune might himself assume the character of a third person, to add a greater appearance of weight to his own authority: it must be owned, however, that this finesse is not suitable to the period in which he lived.[137] It seems more reasonable to conclude, that some minstrel, having access to the person of Thomas the Rhymer, had learned, as nearly as he could, the history of *Sir Tristrem*, and, from his recitation, or perhaps after it had passed through several hands, the compiler of the Auchinleck MSS. committed it to writing. As Thomas certainly survived 1284, betwixt thirty and forty years will, in the supposed case, have elapsed betwixt the time, when the minstrel might have learned the romance, and the date of its being committed to writing; a long interval, doubtless, and in which many corruptions must have been introduced, as well as a material change in the style, which, in poetry preserved by oral tradition, always fluctuates, in some degree, with the alterations in language. Accordingly, those who examine attentively the style of *Sir Tristrem*, as now published, will not find that it differs essentially from that of Barbour, who wrote a century after the Rhymer, although some traces of antiquity may still be observed. On the other hand, if this romance be really the production of Erceldoune, we must expect to distinguish the peculiarities pointed out by Robert de Brunne; that quaint English, which was difficult to compose; and that peculiarity of stanza, which no minstrel could recite without omitting some part of the couplet: For, although we may allow for the introduction of more modern words, and for corruptions introduced by frequent recitation, these general characteristics of the original composition of Thomas must still

---

[136] Scott's ellipsis; see Derek Pearsall and I. C. Cunningham, intro. *The Auchinleck Manuscript: National Library of Advocates' MS.19.2.1* (London: Scolar Press, 1977), fol. 281r.

[137] Joseph Ritson had made this suggestion in a private letter in 1801; see Henry Alfred Burd, *Joseph Ritson: A Critical Biography* (Urbana: University of Illinois, 1916), p. 128. He may well also have suggested it directly to Scott when he visited him in August 1801. See Scott to Ellis, 24 September 1801, in *The Letters of Sir Walter Scott*, ed. by H. J. C. Grierson, 12 vols (London: Constable, 1932-37), XII, 194-95. As the next sentence suggests, Scott requires the intervening minstrel or minstrels to account for the manifest imperfections in the work of 'Thomas'.

be visible, or the romance which we read is none of his. Accordingly, the construction of the poem, now given to the public, bears a very peculiar character. The words are chiefly those of the fourteenth century, but the turn of phrase is, either from antiquity or the affectation of the time when it was originally written, close, nervous, and concise even to obscurity. In every composition of the later age, but more especially in the popular romances, a tedious circumlocutory style is perhaps the most general feature. Circumstantial to a degree of extreme minuteness, and diffuse beyond the limits of patience, the minstrels never touch upon an incident without introducing a prolix description.[138] This was a natural consequence of the multiplication of romantic fictions. It was impossible for the imagination of the minstrels to introduce the variety demanded by their audience, by the invention of new facts, for every story turned on the same feats of chivalry; and the discomfiture of a gigantic champion, a lion, or a dragon, with the acquisition of his mistress's love, continued to be the ever-recurring subject of romance, from the days of Thomas the Rhymer till the metrical tales of chivalry altogether lost ground. The later minstrels, therefore, prolonged and varied the description of events, which were no longer new in themselves; and it is no small token of the antiquity and originality of the present work, that the author seems to rely upon the simple and short narration of incidents, afterwards so hackneyed, as sufficient in his time to secure the attention of the hearers. We have only to compare this mode of narration with the circuitous and diffuse flourishes of the Anglo-Norman Rimeur, to decide the question already agitated, which of these poems was the model of the other.

It is not alone in the brevity of the narrative, but also in the occasional obscurity of the construction, that the style of an age, much older than that of Barbour, may be easily recognized. There is an elliptical mode of narration adopted, which rather hints at than details the story, and which, to make my meaning plain by a modern comparison, is the *Gibbonism* of romance. Whoever attempts to make a prose translation of this poem will find, that it is possible to paraphrase, but not literally to translate it. In this peculiar structure of style consisted, we may suppose, the *quaint Inglis*, complained of by Robert de Brunne, which nobles and gentry alone could comprehend, and which had that annalist adopted, the poor and ignorant, whom in charity he

---

[138] Even Chaucer was infected by the fault of his age, and, with all his unrivalled capacity of touching the real point of description, he does not always content himself with stopping when he has attained it: It has been long since remarked, that when he gets into a wood, he usually bewilders both himself and his reader. But such a work as *Sir Guy*, or *The Squire of Low Degree*, will best illustrate the diffuse style which characterizes the later metrical romances. – S.

laboured to instruct, could not have comprehended his history.

To answer the description of Robert de Brunne, in every respect, it is farther necessary that the romance of *Sir Tristrem* should be written in a strange and peculiar stanza. Accordingly, a stanza so complicated, and requiring so many rhimes as that of the following poem, is perhaps no where employed in a long narrative, at least it has not been the fortune of the editor to meet any romance, written in any which nearly approaches it in difficulty. The common romances are either in short rhiming couplets, or in verse similar to that adopted in *Sir Thopas*, both stanzas of a simple structure. But in *Sir Tristrem* the 1st, 3d, 5th, and 7th lines of each stanza must rhime together, as must the 2d, 4th, 6th, 8th, and 10th; and, finally, the 9th and 11th must also correspond in sound. It may be impossible to determine whether this be the *rime coweé*, or *strangere*, or *baston*, or *entrelaceé*, mentioned by Robert de Brunne;[139] but every dabbler in verses will agree, that the formation of the stanza is very intricate, and such as could only be undertaken by one who held himself master of the language, and who wrote for persons of rank, capable of understanding the merits of the complicated rules to which he had subjected himself.[140] In truth, the present copy bears a closer resemblance to those which Robert de Brunne heard recited, than could have been desired by the editor. For, as the historian says, he never heard it repeated but what of some *copple* (i.e. stanza) part was omitted; so there are at least two instances of breaches in the following poem, flowing, in all probability, from the same cause.[141] To conclude, the rules which the poet has prescribed to himself are observed with strict accuracy, and his rhimes, though multiplied and complicated, correspond with rigid exactness. Since, therefore, this more

---

[139] Sullens, ed. *Chronicle*, p. 93, ll. 85-86, 89.

[140] Scott's more private utterances are far less complimentary to this 'high style': 'I shall certainly at least attempt something of a conclusion in poetry altho' the villainous cramp stanza of our Thomas almost scares me', he wrote to Ellis in 1801; 'With the assistance of "Bidene" "Of yore" "In lede" "I wot & nou3t at werre" and all the other legitimate crutches which prop the hobbling stanza of the Minstrels it would be no difficult task to compleat the poem somewhat in Thomas' own stile but if it is expected that any thing like the graces of modern poetry can be introduced into such a sketch I fear it might be as well required that a modern dancing Master should open his Ball dressd cap-a-pie in Sir Tristrems armour'. Scott to [Ellis.], 21 August 1801, in *Letters*, ed. Grierson, XII, 186-87. In the sentence following, Scott does excuse this by contrasting what he believes to be the version of the poem mangled by the scribe with the imagined purer, authorial original. As he has just argued that the poem in the manuscript could be several retellings away from its original composer, he is in effect stating both that it is hopelessly corrupted and that in it he can see the high literary style of a 'master of the language'.

[141] See Fytte I. st. 80, Fytte III. st. 1, each of which stanzas wants two lines, though there is no *hiatus* in the MS. – S.

modern edition of *Tristrem* agrees in diction and structure to the detailed description of Robert de Brunne, we may safely admit, that, though the language may have been softened into that of the fourteenth century, the general texture and form of the poem must closely resemble that of Thomas of Erceldoune.

[At the end of the poem — and clearly marked off from it — Scott provided his own conclusion to the poem in pastiche medieval language, taking the events from the French story. As he wrote to Ellis, 'I agree perfectly that everything of this sort should be above board — I mean an avowed imitation' (Scott to [Ellis], 21 Aug 1801, *Letters*, ed. by Grierson, XII, 187). This signals a change; in the wake of the work of Ritson, it was no longer acceptable to be seen as inventing rather than editing, as Percy had done.]

From: pp. 193-200.

I

The companyons fiftene,
    To death did thai thringe;
And sterveth bidene,
    Tho Tristrem the yinge;
Ac Tristrem hath tene,
    His wounde gan him wring,
To hostel he hath gene,
    On bedde gan him flinge
        In ure;
    Fele salven thai bringe,
His paine to recure.

II

But never thai no might,
    With coste, nor with payn,
Bring Tristrem the wight,
    To heildom ogayn:
His wounde brast aplight,
    And blake was the bane;
Non help may that knight,
    The sothe for to sayne,
        Bidene,
    Save Ysonde the bright,
Of Cornwal was quene.

III

Tristrem clepeth aye,
    On Ganhardin trewe fere;
—'Holp me, brother, thou may,

And bring me out of care;
To Ysonde the gaye,
    Of Cornwail do thou fare;
In tokening I say,
    Mi ring with the thou bare,
        In dern;
    Bot help me sche dare,
Sterven wol ich gern.

IV

'Mi schip do thou take,
    With godes that bethe new;
Tuo seyles do thou make,
    Beth different in hew;
That tone schall be blake,
    That tother white so snewe;
And tho thou comest bake
    That tokening schal schew
        The end,
    Gif Ysonde me forsake,
The blake schalt thou bende'.—

V

Ysonde of Britanye,
    With the white honde,
In dern can sche be,
    And wele understonde,
That Ysonde the fre,
    Was sent for from Inglonde,
—'Y-wroken wol Y be
    Of mi fals husbonde
        Saunfayle,
    Bringeth he haggards to honde,
And maketh me his stale?'—

VI

Ganhardin to Inglonde fares,
    Als merchaunt, Y you saye;
He bringeth riche wares
    And garmentes were gaye;
Mark he giftes bares,
    Als man that miche maye,
A cup he prepares,
    The ring tharein can laye,
        Bidene;

Brengwain the gaye,
Y-raught it the quene.

VII

Ysonde the ring knewe,
That rich was of gold,
As tokening trewe,
That Tristrem her yold;
Ganhardin gan schewe,
And priviliche hir told,
That Tristrem hurt was newe,
In his wounde that was old,
Al right:
Holp him gif sche nold
Sterven most that knight.

VIII

Wo was Ysonde than,
The tale tho sche hard thare,
Sche schope hir as a man,
With Ganhardin to fare;
O bord are thai gan,
A wind at wil thame bare;
Ysonde was sad woman,
And wepeth bitter tare,
With eighe:
The seyls that white ware,
Ganhardin lete fleighe.

IX

Ysonde of Britanye,
With the white honde,
The schip sche can se,
Seyling to londe;
The white seyl tho marked sche,
—'Yonder cometh Ysonde,
For to reve from me,
Miin fals husbonde;
Ich sware,
For il tho it schal be,
That sche hir hider bare'.—

X

To Tristrem sche gan hye,
O bed thare he layne,

—'Tristrem, so mot Ich thye,
    Heled schalt thou bene,
Thi schippe I can espye
    The soth for to sain,
Ganhardin is comen neighe,
    To curen thi paine,
        Aplight'.—
    —'What seyl doth thare flain,
Dame, for God almight?'—

XI

Sche weneth to ben awrake,
    Of Tristrem the trewe,
Sche seyth—'thai ben blake,
    As piche is thare hewe'.—
Tristrem threw hym bake,
    Trewd Ysonde untrewe,
His kind hert it brake,
    And sindrid in tuo;
        Above,
    Cristes merci him take!
He dyed for true love.

XII

Murneth olde and yinge,
    Murneth lowe and heighe,
For Tristrem, swete thinge,
    Was mani wate eighe;
Maidens thare hondes wringe,
    Wives iammeren and crii;
The belle con thai ring,
    And masses con thai seye,
        For dole;
    Prestes praied aye,
For Tristremes sole.

XIII

Ysonde to land wan,
    With seyl and with ore;
Sche mete an old man,
    Of berd that was hore:
Fast the teres ran,
    And siked he sore,
—'Gone is he than,
    Of Inglond the flore,

                    In lede;
              We se him no more:
          Schir Tristrem is ded!'—

                       XIV

          When Ysonde herd that,
                Fast sche gan to gonne,
          At the castel gate
                Stop hir might none:
          Sche passed in thereat,
                The chaumbre sche won;
          Tristrem in cloth of stat
                Lay stretched thare as ston
                      So cold—
                Ysonde loked him on,
          And faste gan bihold.

                       XV

          Fairer ladye ere
                Did Britannye never spye,
          Swiche murning chere,
                Making on heighe:
          On Tristremes bere,
                Doun con sche lye;
          Rise ogayn did sche nere,
                But thare con sche dye
                      For woe:—
                Swiche lovers als thei
          Never schal be moe.

7. Henry Weber (1783-1818)

Henry Weber was born Heinrich Weber into the Moravian Community in St. Petersburg in 1783, to a German father and an English mother. He grew up in England but took some of his schooling in Germany, before studying medicine from 1803-4 at Edinburgh and later in Germany. Weber returned to Edinburgh from Jena when the university there was closed after Napoleon's defeat of the Prussian army. In Edinburgh he met Sir Walter Scott in 1806 or 1807. Weber's true interests were in literature; he eventually became Scott's amanuensis and edited various works under his auspices, his edition of metrical romances being his sole venture in Middle English. It was a commercial failure, the market perhaps glutted by Ritson's *Ancient Engleish Metrical Romanceës*, Scott's *Sir Tristrem*, and Ellis's *Specimens*, and Weber was no more accurate an editor than his contemporaries, making many errors of transcription. But he was a serious scholar, better-read in Continental literature than his contemporaries and well equipped by his German education to read Middle English. Weber also edited the plays of John Ford and Beaumont and Fletcher, and, with Robert Jamieson and Walter Scott, produced *Illustrations of Northern Antiquities* (1814), in which his abstract of *Das Nibelungenlied* appeared.

Alongside the customary appreciation of the historical value of medieval texts as illustrations of customs and manners, Weber brings a vocabulary of aesthetic appreciation to the verse, unusual in the context of the criticism of the time. Despite this, his work is very much part of the Scott-Ellis school, and so by extension in the lineage going back to Percy. Like Scott and Ellis, he is greatly influenced by the Auchinleck manuscript (Advocates 19.2.1), access to which Scott would have secured for him. Texts in the Auchinleck manuscript form the structural core of *Metrical Romances*, just as they did for Ellis's *Specimens of Metrical Romances*.

Under the rubric of 'romances' Weber collected *The Lyfe of Alisaunder*, *Sir Cleges*, *Lay le Freine*, *Richard Coer de Lyon*, *The Lyfe of Ipomydon*, *Amis and Amiloun*, *Seven Sages of Rome*, *Octavian*, *Sir Amadace*, and *The Hunting of the Hare*.

For biography see Kurt Gamerschlag, 'Henry Weber: Medieval Scholar, Poet, and Secretary to Walter Scott', *Studies in Scottish Literature* 25 (1990), 202-17.

Henry Weber, *Metrical Romances of the Thirteenth, Fourteenth, and Fifteenth Centuries: Published from Ancient Manuscripts [...]*, 3 vols (Edinburgh: Constable, 1810).

From: Introduction (I, ix-xix).

The study of ancient English poetry in general, having very rapidly increased within these few years, and given occasion to a great number of publications and selections, it was thought that a second collection of metrical romances of the thirteenth, fourteenth, and fifteenth centuries, excluding all those which have already been published by modern editors, would be highly acceptable to the lovers of ancient literature. With all their imperfections, they are certainly to the full as amusing as the prolix and wire-drawn moralities and second-hand narrations of Gower, Occleve, and Lydgate, though the works of these poets are generally spoken of with far greater respect. It is undoubtedly an evidence, that these tales, though dressed in the most homely garb, contain something very attractive, when we consider that they formed the favourite study of Warton, and that they have been collected and illustrated by some of the most polite scholars of the present day. Nor should their less disputed utility, in throwing great light upon the manners, customs, and vernacular language of their age, which, without elucidations derived from their source, would be involved in inexplicable obscurity, be forgotten. Several of the romances, at present submitted to the public in their original entire state, have been already analyzed by Mr Ellis, in a manner which has made them accessible to those readers, who have not been initiated into the delightful sensations which the antiquary experiences, in labouring through the greatest difficulties, occasioned by the combination of ancient spelling and antiquated words, nor can join in the superior applauses bestowed on that editor, who copies and illustrates the ancient text with the greatest fidelity and diligence.

It was originally the wish of the editor to rescue all the ancient English romances, or, at least, all those which merit preservation for any reason whatever, from their present precarious existence in manuscript, and difficult accessibility in public libraries, and thus contribute his share to what is so very desirable for the study of the language, a regular series of English metrical compositions, and to collect materials for some future compiler of that great desideratum, a dictionary of the ancient English tongue after the conquest. To his great mortification, however, he was obliged to give up his original plan, and to print a select portion only of the collections he had made and intended for publication.[142] In selecting the poems, the principal object of preference was their intrinsic merit, and the popularity they were likely to obtain; but regard was also had to exhibit specimens of the difference of language, style, and versification, which obtained in the three centuries during which English

---

[142] The unachieved project Weber announces here is, prophetically, almost that of the Early English Text Society and the *New English Dictionary* (later the *OED*), in the 1860s. At the time, about 56 romances were known, making the project highly ambitious, and probably not undertaken for financial reasons.

romances were produced.

It has been usual with the different editors and illustrators of ancient English poetry, to prefix dissertations on the origin of that favourite species of fiction, called the romantic. But it is only necessary to consider the different ideas of writers who have formed hypotheses of their own, and the fallacies which they have reciprocally detected in their several systems, to see the impropriety of deducing from one source, what in fact originated in the universal propensity of all nations for poetry in general, and that species in particular which calls in the aid of marvellous fictions. The deities, nymphs, satyrs, and mythological metamorphoses of the Greeks and Romans, and the genii and peries of the Oriental nations, are not less boldly imagined and hardily brought forward, than the most extravagant wonders of Bojardo, Ariosto, the French trouveurs, and the Spanish prose romances; nor are the anachronisms, of which the poets of the middle ages have been guilty, much greater than some committed by the classical writers of *epic poetry*. Poetical chronicles, often accurate to absurdity, were composed in both the great æras of the world, though those of the middle ages can certainly not be compared with the productions of Lucan and Statius in point of poetical excellence. The giants of the Odyssey, and those of Turpin's Chronicle, of Sir Bevis, and of the Teutonic romances; the pygmies of Pliny, and those of the Scandinavians and Germans; the dragons of Medea, and those of romance; the enchantments of Calypso, Medea, Circe, Alcina, and Armida; in short, the occurrence of fairies, monsters, and wonders of all kinds in the poetry of every nation—renders their derivation from any one particular source not only very uncertain, but almost preposterous. They undoubtedly came originally from Asia, the cradle of mankind; but all nations, in every age, manifestly had a strong inclination to receive from their neighbours any popular and successful fiction which obtained among them, and to communicate to them their own in return.

While the origin of romance has engaged the attention of such numerous writers, the no less singular history of its decline has been scarcely touched upon. For an elaborate dissertation on the causes which gradually abstracted the attention of all classes from these fascinating productions, the editor is not prepared. But the following short enumeration of some of the means by which they were gradually supplanted, thrown together without much regularity, may assist in forming an opinion on the subject, and lead to a more complete and elaborate investigation. The principal reasons were, no doubt, the more general diffusion of science among all classes, shortly before the reformation; the unclosing [of] those treasures of classic lore which had been confined in the monasteries; the substitution of other models of imitation; and, above all, the invention of printing. The nobles began to read, instead of listening to the recitation of strolling minstrels. A middle rank was formed, raised by the extension of commerce and manufactures, owing to the sudden discoveries of other regions, and of new sources for employing human industry. Every thing began to assume a more regular and systematical appearance. System was again introduced in poetry, after having been banished for many centuries: and the public and private utility of each class of poems, which the knights and ladies of the feudal age had never inquired after, began to be investigated. Instead of being only amused, it began to be the fashion to ask after instruction also. Those poems of the earlier centuries, which conveyed some concealed signification, were sought after and read with avidity, and none with greater relish than Reynard the Fox; because the whole science of government was supposed to be conveyed in the wiles of Reynard, and the cunning with which he over-reached his opponents. But the introduction of these refinements required a considerable struggle. The higher ranks would still leave the new systematical writers, for the works of mere imagination; and those of the lower classes, for a length of time, listened with unabated delight to their old romances reduced into the shape of ballads. The long admired heroes of romance were besides destined to sustain another signal defeat from a class whom they had treated with sovereign disdain. These were no other than illustrious robbers, rogues, and vagabonds. Arthur, Charlemagne, Guy of Warwick, Theodoric of Bern, and Orlando, gave way to Robinhood and Little-John, the imaginary Dr Faustus, and Eulenspiegel; and the illustrious Amadis and Cid were laid on the shelf, while Don Juan, Gusman d'Alfarache, and Lazarillo, usurped their popularity. At length, the whole fabric of romance gave way. Though the poets still introduced dragons, and giants, and horrid monsters, the mind of the reader was not long kept in terror, when he discovered them to be no other than Antichrist, or some one of the vices personified. The reformers went so far, as to endeavour to persuade the public, that the light-minded Ariosto had shadowed forth the virtues and vices under the names and attributes of his heroes and heroines. Even the truly romantic mind of Spencer was not able to withstand the torrent of these conceits; and, instead of producing a romance which would have paralleled that of his favourite Ariosto, he has left us a poem, the perusal of which is even rendered painful, wherever we find ourselves unable to keep his mask of mystery out of sight. In short, romance was not immediately abandoned, but very injudiciously made the vehicle of allegory, which, in its turn, was banished, and followed by many successive systems of poetry, which this is not the proper place to enumerate. Fortunately, romance has at length regained a great share of its ancient popularity, and has been revived by several living poets, with a degree of success, not inferior to that which encouraged the humble minstrels of the middle ages in France, England, and Germany, and the more dignified poets of Italy.

The inventive powers of the *trouveurs* of the different European nations were pretty equally distributed, with the exception of those of Italy; but it was unfortunate for the English language, that the best poets, born in the island soon after the conquest, chose to write in French, at that time the language of the court. This will in some measure account for the curious circumstance, that all the English romances, with the exception of the St Graal, Percival, and Launfal, are anonymous. On the contrary, we have the names of many Englishmen, who chose to write French poetry for the English court, transmitted down to our days. The real existence of some of them has been doubted, while that of the *romanciers* born in France, Provence, Germany, and Spain, has never been called in question.

For the reason just assigned, the English romances are generally (perhaps, in every case) translations from the French, and the æra of their production is at least a century later than that of their Gallic prototypes. It would require a longer disquisition, than the limited space allotted for this preface offers, to decide whether these tales have suffered, or been improved by their transfusion into the English language. In general, they have been shortened to at least one half of their original length, partly owing to the greater number of monosyllables, and perhaps also occasioned by the superior difficulty of rhyming, in a language so little cultivated as that of this island had been at the time. We must also regret that the choice of subjects for translation was not always the most judicious. But too unlimited a judgment on this head should not be formed, as we have evidence that some of the most romantic productions of the kind once existed in translations, and were lost, while the dull wire-drawn history of Guy of Warwick, and the mystic lucubrations of such poets as Hampole and Occleve were carefully preserved.

Another instance of strange want of judgment in the old poets, is their unaccountable neglect of the short entertaining fabliaux and lays of the trouveurs, which exist in such numbers in the Imperial Library at Paris. The few ancient translations of them which we possess may be easily enumerated. Four will be found in the present collection, and a few more (as Sir Orfeo, Lanval, How the Merchant did his Wife betray, &c.) have been published by Ritson. To these may be added the comical tales of The Wife lapped in a Morrel's skin, the Friar and the Boy, and a few others still extant in black letter. The Germans, according to their innate rage for translating, made versions of many of the French fabliaux, and have, besides, innumerable others, founded upon native tales, mostly of the ludicrous kind. In the works of the honest and diligent shoemaker and poet Hans Sachs, several hundreds of the latter sort occur.

The public are now in possession of a sufficient number of these romantic poems to appreciate their value; and should more be required, they are ready to be communicated. The most valuable of them are no doubt King Alexander, Ywaine and Gawaine, and Sir Tristrem. But most of them have something attractive; and few, even of those which remain unpublished, are entirely worthless. In some of them the general cloud of dulness is now and then dissipated by a few brilliant lines. This is the case even in the ponderous gests of Guy of Warwick, Sir Bevis, and Merlin. Others, though their poetry and versification are generally very mean, are rendered attractive by the romantic wildness of the tale, such as Sir Launfal, Le Beaus Desconus, Ipomidon, and Amis and Amiloun. All of them demand the attention of those who would form a true judgment of the manners, amusements, and modes of thinking which obtained in the darker ages, and of that, perhaps most wonderful of all human institutions, the chivalrous and feudal system.

I proceed to give an account of the several romances included in the present selection, together with an enumeration of those written upon the same subjects in other languages. The account may be considered by many too detailed; but it was thought that the reader, by seeing at one view the different, and frequently very numerous, romances, founded on one original story, would be better enabled to judge of their very extensive popularity. A particular account of the manuscripts of the several romances now published, particularly of those from which the text was formed, was of course indispensible.

On *The Lyfe of Alisaunder* (I, xx-xxxix).

[The section opens with a long description of the sources of the Alexander story and detailed summaries of examples of the story in various literatures before Weber turns to the English poem:]

There is no doubt, that few English romances can boast of a greater share of good poetry. The lines are less burdened with expletives, and exhibit far better versification, than those of other poems of the time, and frequently possess an energy which we little expect. The descriptions of battles and processions, in particular, is often animated to a degree, which would not disgrace the pages of Chaucer, and for which we look in vain in those of Gower, Lydgate, and their contemporaries; and the short descriptions of nature, interspersed without reference to the subject, are frequently very delicate and beautiful. In order not to burden the present introductory pages with quotations from the work itself, I will confine myself to the two following short passages, which will prove that the opinion of the old minstrels poetical powers just given does not want proofs. The first gives an excellent account of the preparations before battle:

> Mony stede ther proudly leop:
> Stilliche mony on weop.
> The recheles and the proude song:
> The cowardis heore hondis wrong.
> There thou myghtest heore bere:
> Mony faire pencel on spere,
> Mony knyght with helm of steil.
> Mony scheld y-gult ful wel,
> Mony trappe, mony croper,

> Mony queyntise on armes clere.
> The eorthe quakid heom undur;
> No scholde mon have herd the thondur,
> For the noise of the taboures,
> And the trumpours and jangelours. (v. 3411-24.)[143]

For lines equally spirited with the four last of this extract, we might search volumes of ancient poetry in vain. Alexander's camp in the night is thus splendidly described:

> Before the kyng honge a charbokel-ston,
> And two thousande laumpes of gold and on,
> That casten also mychel lighth,
> As by day the sonne brighth.
> The gleymen useden her tunge;
> The wode aqueightte so hy sunge.
> To a twenty milen aboute
> Of barouns and knighttes lasted the route. (v. 5252-59.)[144]

A singular circumstance in this poem is the great irregularity of the rhymes in many instances. The author frequently thinks it sufficient when the first syllable of a feminine termination rhymes to the correspondent male termination of the other line. For instance, v. 2761:

> Tho of Thebes fast *foughte*;
> And tho of Grece as knyghtis *doughty*.

And again, v. 2813:

> He hette quyk his fotemen *alle*
> To brynge of Thebes doun the *wallis*.[145]

In other instances, he is still more licentious, often substituting mere assonance for legitimate rhyme.

Notwithstanding the great merit of this romance, it was not printed at the time when Wynkyn de Worde, Pynson, Chapman, and others, gave to the

---

[143] Cf G. V. Smithers, ed. *Kyng Alisaunder*, EETS 227, 237, 2 vols (London: EETS, 1952-57), I, 190, ll. 3392-3405.

[144] Cf Smithers, ed. *Kyng Alisaunder*, I, 280, ll. 5243-50.

[145] This is a tendency of the Lincoln's Inn text, which Smithers thought so corrupt as to be not worth editing (I, xi), rather than the Bodleian; cf Smithers, ed. *Kyng Alisaunder*, I, 154, ll. 2745-46; 156, ll. 2795-96 (Lincoln's Inn); cp. 155, ll. 2757-58; 157, ll. 2809-10 (Bodleian).

world Richard Cœur de Lion, Guy of Warwick, Bevis, Degare, and even the wretched Eglamour of Artoys. [...]

The romance is unquestionably a free translation from the French. Indeed, in one passage, (v. 2199), the poet professes that he had supplied the description of a battle, which was wanting in the French, from the Latin. Who the author was we have no evidence to determine. The following lines making it somewhat probable that he was of the clerical profession:

> N'is so fair a thyng, so Crist me blesse,
> So knyght in queyntise,
> *Bote the prest in Godes servyse!*[146]

Tanner has attributed the work to one Adam Davie.[147] Mr Warton, and even Ritson himself, precipitately followed Tanner's opinion, which rests on the following very slender evidence.[148] In the same MS., in the Bodleian Library, which contains a copy of this romance, besides other, chiefly religious, legends, a kind of mystical poem occurs, professedly written by 'Adam Davie, the marchal of Stratford atte Bowe'. It contains seven separate visions in about 250 lines, and begins thus:

> To oure lord Jesu Crist in heuene
> Ich to-day shewe myne sweuene,
> That ich mette in one nighth
> Of a knighth of mychel mighth,
> His name is y-hote Sir Edward the kyng,
> Prince of Wales Engelonde the faire thyng, &c.

This is undoubtedly Edward II. But we are certainly not warranted to attribute all the various poems, collected by the monks into one folio volume, to one poet who happens to have written a single one of them, but whose name does not occur in any other. We must, therefore, discard the opinion of Tanner and Warton, and content ourselves with admiring the work of an anonymous author.

Only two copies of 'the Lyfe of Alisaunder' are in our public libraries, besides a fragment, containing about 200 lines of the conclusion, in the

---

[146] Cf Smithers, ed. *Kyng Alisaunder*, I, 200, ll. 3562-64.

[147] Thomas Tanner, *Bibliotheca Britannico-Hibernica* (London, 1748), p. 221. The attribution, which Weber is right to argue against, is an example of the antiquarian desire to attach author-names to works wherever possible.

[148] Cf Warton, *HEP*, I, 214; Joseph Ritson, *Bibliographia Poetica* (London: Nicol, 1802), p. 23.

Auchinleck MS., agreeing very nearly with the other MSS. One of them is in the Bodleian MS. Laud, I. 74. fol.[149] It is evidently of the fourteenth century, and written upon vellum, in a hand generally very plain. There are many parts, however, which have greatly suffered, and some passages are become entirely illegible. Others, for what reason I know not, have been completely erazed. Fortunately they are supplied by the second copy, which exists in a MS., preserved in the library of Lincoln's Inn (No. 150), which, from the language, appears to be of an age not much, if at all, posterior to the former. It was copied, and intended for publication by Mr Park, but he was deterred from proceeding in the work, by discovering that a large portion, of above 1200 lines (v. 4772-5989), was entirely wanting, besides a great number of verses dispersed in different parts of the romance.[150] These have been supplied from the Bodleian MS. by the editor, so that the present edition is as perfect as the two existing MSS. could make it. Mr Park's transcript, for the accuracy of which his well-known character as an antiquarian will be a sufficient warrant, had been enriched by numerous and valuable, chiefly glossarial, notes, by Mr Ellis and Mr Douce. The very curious illustrative annotations of the latter will be found in the third volume. The explanatory and etymological notes of these gentlemen have been incorporated with the glossary.

In order to facilitate the perusal of so long a romance, subdivisions were rendered highly necessary; and fortunately, the poem itself furnished them. It very evidently consists of two parts, one containing the early life of the hero, and the other the adventures of his latter days, with the manner of his death, in the same manner as the MS. No 2702, in the library of the Duke of La Valliere, above described.[151] The subdivision into chapters is also very evident, each of them being prefaced with a few descriptive or moral lines. For the sake of illustrating the progress of the tale, contents have been prefixed to each chapter, which the editor found ready drawn up by Mr Ellis, excepting those which occur in the part supplied from the Bodleian MS.

To have given all the various readings of the two MSS. would have been a needless and useless task. For this reason, those only have been noticed, where the text of the Lincoln's Inn MS. has been abandoned, and that of the Bodleian substituted.

---

[149] Now Bodl 1414 (Laud Misc. 622).

[150] The sometime poet and antiquary Thomas Park (1759-1834) assisted George Ellis, the Shakespeare editor George Steevens, and Ritson in *Bibliographia Poetica*; he considered and abandoned a re-edition of Warton's *HEP* and his notes were incorporated in the revisions of the *HEP* by Richard Price (1824) and Richard Taylor (1840). He edited the fifth edition of Percy's *Reliques* (1812) and the second of Ritson's *Select Collection of English Songs* (1813).

[151] Containing the AN *Roman de toute chevalerie*, on which the English poem is loosely based.

[*The Lyfe of Alisaunder* is the centrepiece of Weber's collection, the substantial romance with which he begins his anthology, just as Ritson had opened his *Ancient Engleish Metrical Romanceës* with *Ywain and Gawain*. Other entries are briefer, such as the following:]

On *The Life of Ipomydon* (I, li-lii).

This highly romantic poem, which, owing to the comparatively modern language of the only MS. copy known to exist; the easy, and even fluent versification, the playful variety of the tale, and the very accurate idea which it conveys of the state of the later and more accomplished system of chivalry, might be recommended as a proper introduction to a perusal of the ancient metrical romances, was certainly translated from the French; and indeed Mr Tyrwhitt notices a poem in that language, written by Hue de Rotelande, (probably Rutland), which he supposes to be the original.[152] The translation probably existed at the time the romance of Richard Cœur de Lion was put forth, as it is mentioned in the second part of the latter poem, (v. 6660).[153]

On editorial principles (I, lxiv-lxvii).

In preparing these romances for the public, it was the wish of the editor, without in the least disturbing a single letter of the old text, to render their perusal as accessible to general readers as possible. For this reason, the longer ones were subdivided, as has been already mentioned, regular punctuation was introduced, capital letters were used to distinguish names of persons and places, the abbreviations were reduced to the peculiar standard of orthography, employed in each particular romance, and the Saxon letters for th, gh, and y, discarded. In all these points excepting the first, the accurate Ritson has given an example to the editor: who, however, judged it expedient, by going a little further, to facilitate the reader's progress still more. For this reason, the pronoun I or Y, is always spelt with a capital letter, and the very common Saxon prefix y, has been separated by a hyphen from the word it is attached to, as y-core, y-burnt, &c. Indeed, in many cases, there is an evident well-marked space left in the old MSS., particularly in the Auchinleck MS. The negative prefixed to verbs has, in most cases, also been separated by an inverted comma, as in n'as, n'is, n'il, &c. And finally, when a word terminated with a single e, which it was necessary to pronounce, as for instance, cete for city, an accent has been placed over the last letter. The same

---

[152] *CTC*, IV, pp. 69-70 n.55. The ME *Life of Ipomydon* is a translation from the AN romance *Ipomédon* by Hue de Rotelande (speculatively, Rhuddlan in Flintshire).

[153] *Richard Coer de Lyon* dates from the early fourteenth century, *Ipomydon* the early fifteenth.

course was adopted in cases where the accent, against the general rule, fell upon the last syllable. Where the pronoun *thee* is spelt, as it is generally in old poetry with a single e, it has been accented to distinguish it from the article. Without, in this manner, facilitating their perusal, it is in vain to expect that any but professed antiquarians should study the poems of the earliest centuries of English Literature. Every one in the least acquainted with ancient MSS., will at once discover where these variations have been introduced.

It would have been an easy task to have swelled the notes to double the space which they at present occupy: but the editor rather preferred retrenching many which he had collected, fearing to encroach upon the more immediate object of the work, the romances themselves. For the same reason, he was forced to be very concise in his explanations of the words introduced into the glossary, which he found to be numerous far beyond his expectation. With regard to this last, and perhaps most important branch of his task, the editor feels the peculiar necessity of appealing to the indulgence of etymological critics. Though he was so fortunate as to find the greatest number of words in the Lincoln's Inn MS. of Alexander ably explained by Mr Ellis and Mr Douce, yet his share of the labour, comprising the remainder of that romance, and all the others contained in the work, was no very easy one; and he often found himself compelled, for want of authority, to substitute conjecture. In such a case, however, he has always stated his diffidence of opinion by a mark of interrogation. The number of words left entirely without an explanation, or only with a mere conjecture, from the context annexed to them, will, however, be found not to exceed fifteen or twenty. Many of these will, no doubt, find a successful interpretation from some subsequent glossarist. An indifferent person frequently hits at once upon a happy conjecture, where a word has long puzzled the compiler of a glossary, whose mind is necessarily bewildered by searching for the signification of such a multiplicity of words. As to etymological researches, they are clearly, as the learned Tyrwhitt has remarked, not a necessary branch of the duty of a glossarist.[154] For this reason, the original language from which the word has been derived, has been merely mentioned; which, with very few exceptions, has been found to be one of those great fountains of the English tongue, the French, and the Saxon branch of the Teutonic. If that great and necessary work, a dictionary of old English, should ever be accomplished, several of the editor's explanations will, no doubt, be refuted; others may, perhaps, be cavilled at in reviews, or in the similar works of his antiquarian brethren, who labour in the same vineyard; but the editor has the consolation to reflect, that neither of those vehicles of abuse, though so liberally lavished

---

[154] *CTC*, v (1778), iii.

upon the works of Warton, Percy, and even Ritson himself, have been able from deterring that part of the public interested in the literature of our ancestors, from perusing them, and appreciating the pains and toil bestowed upon their illustration.

8. Thomas Dunham Whitaker (1759-1821)

The Lancashire vicar Thomas Dunham Whitaker made two ventures into Middle English with this edition and a far simpler edition of *Pierce the Ploughman's Crede* (1814), based on the 1553 print of Reynolde Wolfe (*STC* 19904). Apart from his work in Middle English, he was the author of several detailed local histories, topographies and surveys of antiquities of Yorkshire and Lancashire. His edition of *Piers Plowman* was based on the C-text in Huntington Library Hm 137; he also consulted Hm 114 and MS Oriel College Oxford 79. Whitaker's was the first new edition of the work since that of Robert Crowley two and a half centuries earlier.

For detailed analysis of Whitaker's edition see Charlotte Brewer, *Editing 'Piers Plowman': The Evolution of the Text* (Cambridge: Cambridge University Press, 1996), pp. 37-49.

Thomas Dunham Whitaker, ed. *Visio Willī de Petro Plouhman [...] Or the Vision of William concerning Peirs Plouhman, and the Visions of the same concerning the Origin, Progress, and Perfection of the Christian Life* (London: Murray, 1813).

From: Introductory Discourse (pp. i-xli).

To the reign of Edward the Third may be assigned the first general dawn of taste and genius in England, since the formation of the language. Before that period, whatever of invention, or of elegance may have been displayed by Englishmen in Latin poetry, their efforts at versification in their own tongue had been confined to rude romances, metrical chronicles, or to a few short compositions, chiefly satirical, which alone displayed much power either of feeling or imagination.

But in that reign, the spirit of the Monarch, and the splendor of his court, seem more or less to have pervaded and animated all ranks of men in the kingdom. The intellects of our countrymen awoke from their long repose. A spirit of inquiry was exerted. The more inquisitive and studious among the clergy began to feel the fetters of ignorance and spiritual tyranny, which they had hitherto borne without a murmur: and before the close of this period, Wickliff had taught the laity to think for themselves on religious, and, in some degree, on political subjects.

It was, indeed, high time to awake out of sleep. The conduct of the superior clergy called aloud for animadversion: the Bishops, a few only excepted, seemed to have lost all sense of their apostolical character: the more wealthy of the monastic orders were become indolent and luxurious; while the gross rapacity of the mendicants exposed them to the scorn of the lowest among the people.

Meanwhile great corruptions had crept into the ecclesiastical courts, and some into those of common law. The Nobility, whose business was war, and their amusements little less barbarous, paid no attention to the morals or the happiness of their dependants, who were merely considered as a breed of superior cattle, nourished for the lord's use; and the only protection or patronage which they experienced, consisted in countenancing their disorders, and protecting them from the hand of justice. Neither had the Nobility themselves the advantage of better examples: the Court itself, scarcely acquainted with any virtues but those prescribed by the code of chivalry, was in other respects a very indifferent school of morality or decorum.

Other established correctives of life and manners there were none, for penances, even then become contemptible to the rich, were too feebly and injudiciously applied to their inferiors, to oppose any barrier to the progress of vice: while the pulpit, considered as a national organ of instruction and reproof, may be affirmed to have been nearly silent.

While, however, the national *morals* had been gradually declining, the state of national *intelligence* had suddenly risen to that point of elevation, at which satire will always be attempted as an instrument of correction, and seldom without effect. It is never the growth of an age wholly barbarous, for even the licence of personal abuse in the Fescennine songs belonged to a later period: uncouth hymns chanted to the deities of uncivilized tribes, the brief but measured rudiments of legislation, the rude song of victory, and afterwards the metrical chronicle, are the only efforts of versification in the first and most simple period of society. Of this process the reason is obvious:—Perhaps the first movement of the human heart is spontaneously directed to some unknown but superior power; its next operation will be directed to embody certain fixed principles, by which infant societies are to be held together: next in order will be the first attempt to record interesting facts (and, to savages, what facts are so interesting as those of war?); but facts must be long studied, and a habit of abstracting and generalizing in some degree be formed, before men begin to contemplate *characters*, which are the proper and legitimate objects of satire. These first efforts have always been metrical. That there is something in the human ear naturally attuned to rhythm, may be proved from the spontaneous efforts of children to produce it; and the savage scarcely begins to speak, before he forms some jingle of sounds.

On the other hand, society may be too far advanced for satire, or satire may, by its frequency and licentiousness, have lost its effect. In a luxurious age it is possible for the wealthy and the great to be so deeply plunged in corruption, or sunk in indolence, that wit and sarcasm shall be no more able to arouse their feelings, than those of dissolute and brutal savages: and about that period it will generally happen, that the same correctives, which, if administered with decorum and reserve, might have been efficacious, by wantonly and indiscriminately attacking the best characters and the worst, by converting invective into a trade, and propagating calumny, instead of pursuing vice, will succeed only in depraving the public taste, and disgracing their authors. Thus legitimate satire at once reverts to its origin, and degenerates into its worst abuse, which is personal scurrility.

During the reign of Edward the Third, one of the most splendid, but not the most refined of our annals, yet equally removed from both these extremes, arose in this country two poets, the writings of one of whom contributed to enlarge the minds, and of the other to improve the moral feelings of their contemporaries in a degree unfelt since the æras of the great Roman satirists. The first of these, a man of the world and a courtier, at once informed and delighted the higher orders by his original and lively portraits of human nature in every rank, and almost under every modification, while he prevented or perverted the proper effect of satire by the most licentious and obscene exhibitions. The latter, an obscure country priest, much addicted to solitary contemplation, but at the same time a keen and severe observer of human nature; well read in the scriptures and schoolmen, and intimately acquainted with the old language and poetry of his country, in an uncouth dialect and rugged metre, by his sarcastic and ironical vein of wit, his knowledge of low life, his solemnity on some occasions, his gaiety on others, his striking personifications, dark allusions, and rapid transitions, has continued to support and animate an allegory (the most insipid for the most part and tedious of all vehicles of instruction) through a bulky volume. By what inducement he was led to prefer this vehicle, it is not difficult to conjecture. From his subordinate station in the church, this free reprover of the higher ranks was exposed to all the severities of ecclesiastical discipline: and from the aristocratical temper of the times he was liable to be crushed by the civil power. Every thing, therefore, of a personal nature was in common prudence to be avoided. The great were not then accustomed, as a licentious press has since disciplined them, to endure the freedoms of reprehension: — authority was, even when abused, sacred; and rank, when united with vice, was enabled to keep its partner in countenance. — Above all, the great ecclesiastics were as vindictive as they were corrupt: and hence the satirist was compelled to shelter himself under the distant generalities of personification.

But, unfortunately, by this means, whatever he gained in personal security, he lost in the point and distinctness of his satire. Mere personifications of virtues and vices, however skilfully and powerfully touched, are capable of few strokes: the quality is simple, but different individuals, who partake of it in a degree however pre-eminent, combine and modify it in such an infinite variety of ways, with other subordinate traits and features of character, that while the abstract property is one and the same, in its actual existence, as part of the moral nature of man, it is capable in skilful hands of infinite diversities of representation. It is indeed far from being necessary that the characters be real, but, for the purposes of satirical painting, they must be *persons*.

From this uniformity of appearance in his abstract qualities the author has been betrayed, by the necessity of combination in some way or other, into the fault of mixing his personifications with each other; as, *ex. gr.* avarice and fraud, qualities which, though nearly akin, have no necessary co-existence: and, for the same reason, wherever he deviates into personality, as in the coarse but striking scene of 'Gluttons'' Debauch, where the characters, though imaginary, are persons, not personifications, he paints with all the truth and distinctness of a Dutch master.

To the same necessity of reserve and concealment, which dictated the vehicle of allegory, is to be ascribed the uncertainty which must now for ever remain as to the name of the writer; for it is to tradition only that we are indebted for the name of Robert Langland, a secular priest, born at Mortimer's Cleobury, in Shropshire, and of Oriel College in Oxford, as the author of these Visions.[155]

The first writer, so far as I know, who mentions him, is Bale, in the next century but one; after whom, the numerous testimonies of writers concerning the author of Peirs Plouhman are reducible to his own single authority. This, however, is prima facie evidence, and must be allowed, till there is something to rebut it. But, wherever born or bred, and by whatever name distinguished, the author of these Visions was an observer and a reflector of no common powers. I can conceive him (like his own visionary William) to have been sometimes occupied in contemplative wanderings on the Malvern Hills, and dozing away a summer's noon among the bushes, while his waking thoughts were distorted into all the misshapen forms created by a dreaming fancy. Sometimes I can descry him taking his staff, and roaming far and wide in search of manners and characters; mingling with men of every accessible rank, and storing his memory with hints for future use. I next pursue him to his study, sedate and thoughtful, yet wildly inventive, digesting the first rude drafts of his Visions; and in successive transcriptions, as judgment matured, or invention declined, or as his observations were more extended, expanding or contracting, improving and sometimes perhaps debasing his original text. The time of our author's death, and the place of his interment, are equally unknown, with almost every circumstance relating to him. His contemporaries, Chaucer and Gower, repose beneath magnificent tombs, but Langland (if such were really his name) has no other monument than that which, having framed for himself, he left to posterity to appropriate. That the author of these Visions, however, was an inhabitant of some of the midland counties, the style

---

[155] While Tyrwhitt had noted that the name of the narrator of the poem — and therefore presumably of the poet — was Will, the tradition going back to Bale that Langland's name was Robert, along with the biographical information given here, was still persistent. See Percy extract, note 17.

of the work affords strong internal proof. I can detect it in many vestiges of the dialect, which was originally formed upon the Mercno-Saxon, and which prevails, to this day, under many subordinate modifications, from Lancashire to the counties of Warwick and Salop. Every one of that age, who wrote in his mother tongue at all, wrote it as he heard it spoken; and the language of Peirs Plouhman is as strongly tinctured with the dialect and idioms of these counties, as that of Robert of Gloucester is with the orthography of the west. The truth is, that, from the extinction of the pure Saxon, of which the latest specimen is perhaps to be found in the conclusion of the Saxon Chronicle, to the reign of Edward the Third, the language of our country, which, during that period, may be called Semi-Saxon, had scarcely been reduced to any standard, or undergone any radical change. Under the refining hand of Chaucer, indeed, it became almost a new language; but with those courtly improvements the author of these Visions was either unacquainted, or disdained to adopt them. Perhaps the last was our author's case; for, small as the circulation of manuscripts then was, we can scarcely suppose the fame of a contemporary genius like Chaucer not to have reached the centre of the kingdom. But Langland was too deeply enamoured of the old Saxon models, whose spirit he had early imbibed, to be much delighted with the uniform recurrence of rhyme, or the restraints imposed by regular versification.

This leads us to consider the *measure* of Peirs Plouhman, a subject which has already been treated with so much elegance and precision by the late Bishop of Dromore, that, as the Relics of Ancient English Poetry must be familiar to every reader of this work, we shall forbear to draw any thing from that well-known fountain; while we trace the subject somewhat higher, and open the original sources of alliterative verse.

[A detailed and learned discussion of metre follows, with examples drawn from Anglo-Saxon and Old Norse poetry, arguing 'that the Saxon metres, as well as that of Peirs Ploughman, are generally reducible to a kind of dactilics, or their opposite, anapæstics, accordingly as they are scanned; though some are too irregular to be included under either, and some are so exact, as to be incapable of any measurement, but one'.]

The Reformers of the sixteenth century claimed as their own the Author of these Visions; but surely on no good grounds. That he believed and taught almost all the fundamental doctrines of Christianity has no tendency to prove him a Wickliffite or Lollard. The best and soundest members of the Church of Rome have done the same. It is not defects but redundancies which we impute to them. Of the predestinarian principles afterwards professed by Wickliff, Langland seems to think with disapprobation; and when his visionary hero speaks of himself as belonging to the Lolleres, he evidently means, not the religious party distinguished by a similar name, but, in the usual strain of his irony, a company of idle wanderers. Yet in the midst of darkness and spiritual slavery, his acute and penetrating understanding enabled him to discover the multiplied superstitions of the public service, the licentious abuse of pilgrimages, the immoral tendency of indulgences, the bad effects upon the living of expiatory services for the dead, the inordinate wealth of the papacy, and the usurpations of the mendicant orders, both on the rights of the diocesans and of the parochial clergy. These abuses, Langland, with many other good men who could endure to remain in the communion of the church of Rome, saw and deplored; but though he finally conducted his pilgrim out of the particular communion of Rome into the universal church, he permitted him to carry along with him too many remnants of his old faith, such as satisfaction for sin to be made by the sinner, together with the merit of works, and especially of voluntary poverty; but, above all, the worship of the cross; incumbrances with which the Lollards of his own, or the Protestants of a later age, would not willingly have received him as a proselyte.

Neither was he an enemy to monastic institutions in themselves: on the contrary, he appears to have sighed for the quiet and contemplative life of the cloister, could it have been restored to its primitive purity and order.

On the nature and origin of civil society, as on most other subjects, he thought for himself; and, at a period when mankind had scarcely begun to speculate on such subjects at all, he boldly traced the source of kingly power to the will of the people, and considered government as instituted for the benefit of the governed. Indeed a strong democratic tendency may be discovered in many passages of his work.

[Whitaker concludes this section by saying that internal evidence dates the poem to the reign of Edward III; he concedes that 'The work is altogether the most obscure in the English language', and so proceeds to a lengthy summary of what takes place in *Piers*.]

The conclusion is singularly cold and comfortless, inasmuch as it leaves the enquirer, after a long peregrination, still remote from the object of his search, while Antichrist remains triumphant, and not a single hint is given at his final destruction, or the final and universal dominion of his great antagonist. Such, however, is the outline of this singular work, of which it has now, for the first time, been shewn that it was written after a regular and consistent plan.

A few miscellaneous observations are yet necessary, before the reader can be prepared for the perusal of the text itself.

It has long been understood by curious scholars, that the editions of this work by Crowley were printed from MSS. of later date and lower authority than others which were known to be extant. The discrepancies of these MSS. from others, and their respective agreement with a third and fourth class, have also been remarked, so that they have been considered as forming, in critical language, distinct schools. This phenomenon, though singular, may yet be accounted for. To the friendship of Mr. Heber the present Editor has been indebted for two MSS. of these Visions, severally marked in the notes A. and

B.; and to the kindness of Mr. Copleston for a third, belonging to Oriel College in Oxford.

Of the first of these, which, from a note in the conclusion, appears to have been transcribed by one Thomas Dankaster, there can be no doubt that it is a faithful representation of the work, as it came first from the Author, immediately after the year 1362. It abounds with Saxon words and idioms, which in succeeding transcriptions, at a period when the English language was undergoing a rapid change, were gradually removed, with many original passages, which the greater maturity of the author's judgment induced him to expunge; in short, it bears every mark of being the first but vigorous effort of a young poet.

To that text, as it was the Editor's purpose to represent so noble an effort of English genius in its nearest approximation to the Saxon language, he has rigidly adhered. For this prepossession, beside an habitual leaning to antiquity, as such, he has another excuse; namely, that the orthography and dialect in which this MS. is written approach very near to that Semi-saxon jargon, in the midst of which he was brought up, and which, notwithstanding some inroads within the last half century upon its archaisms, he continues to hear daily spoken on the confines of Lancashire, and the west riding of the county of York.

He has elsewhere shewn that this, the dialect of the author of these Visions, was, as far as it remained uncorrupted by additions since the conquest, the true Mercian language.

The second MS. which contains the Visions greatly enlarged and altered, is a thick octavo volume, bearing the autographs of Sir Henry Spelman, Dr. Taylor, the editor of Demosthenes, Mr. Gough, and Mr. Heber, its successive and distinguished owners.[156] From the hand-writing it may probably be assigned to the reign of Richard the Second: but, in addition to the present

---

[156] The historian and antiquary Sir Henry Spelman (1564?-1641) became interested in Anglo-Saxon when researching etymologies and origins of legal terms; one consequence was the short-lived Lectureship of Anglo-Saxon that he endowed at Cambridge, taken up by Abraham Wheelock in 1638. The fund was later diverted to William Somner to help with the completion of his Anglo-Saxon dictionary. Richard Gough (1735-1809), a Fellow of the Society of Antiquaries and its Director from 1771-97, produced a new and augmented edition of Camden's *Britannia* in three volumes in 1789. Richard Heber (1773-1833), founder-member of the Roxburghe Club and one of the founders of the Athenaeum Club, was a famous book collector whose huge library took three years to sell after his death. He was a generous lender of his treasures and is often credited with this kind of help by scholars. His manuscripts of *Piers* used by Whitaker are now in the Huntington Library. Edward Copleston (1776-1849) was a Fellow and later Provost of Oriel College, Oxford. Whitaker's use of 'A' and 'B' as manuscript sigla here has no relation to the distinction of A-, B- and C-texts of *Piers Plowman*, which was drawn later by W. W. Skeat.

work, it contains the 'Travels of Sir John Maundevyle', the poem of 'Susanna', already quoted; a short story in prose, entitled 'Joseph'; 'Troilus', in five books; and a strange satirical proclamation from 'Lucifer, Prince of the depe Dominion of Darknesse'.

The third MS. (that of Oriel College) from an allusion to a statute empowering the diocesan alone to commit heretics to the flames, which was enacted in the second of Henry Fourth, must be later, and from other internal proofs, can be but little later than that period.

This differs widely from both the former, and approaches considerably nearer to Crowley's text.

All these varieties, however, bear marks, not of the same spirit and genius only, but of the same peculiar and original manner, so that it is scarcely to be conceived that they are interpolations of successive transcribers. Whatever be the cause, however, it may confidently be affirmed, that the text of no ancient work whatever contains so many various readings, or differs so widely from itself.

To account for this phenomenon, however, in the penury, or rather in the absence of original information relating to the author, we are at liberty to suppose that the first edition of his work appeared when he was a young man, and that he lived and continued in the habit of transcribing to extreme old age. But a man of *his* genius would not submit to the drudgery of mere transcription; his invention and judgment would always be at work; new abuses, and therefore new objects of satire, would emerge from time to time: and as a new language began to be spoken, he might, though unwillingly, be induced to adopt its modernisms, in order to render his work intelligible to a second or third generation of readers. In this last respect, however, it is not improbable that his transcribers might use some freedoms; for while we deny them invention to add, we may at least allow them skill to translate.
[The point is then demonstrated with a parallel printing of a passage from the three MSS and the same in one of Crowley's 1550 prints.]

As the æra of these Visions is now ascertained to have preceded the great work of Chaucer by twenty years, the author must be considered as the first English poet; for that he was a poet, and a great poet, will be denied by few, who have taken pains to understand him. He was also, with Bishop Hall's permission, the first English satirist.[157] In this character it is the duty of an impartial editor to state his excellencies and his defects.

The writer of these Visions had the first, though not perhaps the most splendid, qualification of a moral poet, an acute moral sense, with a vehement

---

[157] 'I first adventure, follow me who list, / And be the second English satirist'. Joseph Hall, *Virgidemiarum: Satires in Six Books* (Oxford, 1753), prologue. – W.

indignation against the abuses of public and the vices of private life; to this was added a keen sarcastic humour, and a faculty of depicting the manners of low life with an exactness and felicity, which have never been surpassed, but by the great satirist of the present day.[158] His conscience appears to have held the torch to his understanding, rather than the reverse. He judges of actions by feelings, more than by induction. His casuistry is sometimes miserably perplexed, and his illustrations very unhappy. The first of these defects is to be ascribed to his acquaintance with the schoolmen, the second to his ignorance of classical antiquity: in his views of morality an understanding naturally perspicuous was clouded by the one, while in his powers of adorning a subject, a taste perhaps naturally coarse was left wholly unpolished by the other. He often sinks into imbecility, and not unfrequently spins out his thread of allegory into mere tenuity. But, on other occasions, when aroused by the subject, he has a wildness of imagination, which might have deserved to be illustrated by the pencil of Fuseli, and a sublimity (more especially when inspired by the great mysteries of revelation) which has not been surpassed by Cowper.

He had a smattering of French, but no Italian. I have endeavoured in vain to discover in these Visions any imitations of Dante, whose Inferno and Purgatorio, in some respects, resemble them. But the boldness of those works, which the familiarity of the Italians with the vices of their Popes rendered tolerable, and even popular, beyond the Alps, would have appalled the courage of a tramontane satirist, and shocked the feelings of his readers, in the fourteenth century.

To the author of these Visions has been ascribed by some Protestant writers an higher inspiration than that of the muse, and his famous prediction of the fall of the religious houses has invested him with the more sacred character of a prophet. — Hickes in particular has not scrupled to declare, that in this instance he was 'divino numine afflatus'.[159] Let it however be inquired, whether, after all, there is any thing in this prediction to exalt it above one of those lucky conjectures, which are certainly not out of the reach of natural sagacity, or casual accomplishment.

That the writer was a man of quick discernment and foresight, almost every page of the work will prove. He understood the natural tendency of

---

[158] The Rev. Dr George Crabbe (1754-1832), a didactic poet.

[159] 'Ac þer shal come a kyng and confesse yow religiouses, / And bete yow, as þe Bible telleþ, for brekynge of youre rule, / And amende monyals, monkes and chanons, / And puten hem to hir penaunce [...]' *Piers Plowman* B X, 316-19. The passage was much celebrated in the sixteenth century as a prediction of the dissolution of the monasteries and reform of the English church. Quotation from Hickes untraced; he refers to the 'prediction', *Thesaurus*, I, 107.

enormous evils to redress themselves: and from what he had seen of the conduct of a spirited and vigorous Monarch, in pillaging the religious houses at pleasure, he would naturally be directed to a King as the probable instrument of their destruction. The evil would increase, correctives would lose their effect, and extermination would naturally follow. Meanwhile the prediction was couched in general and guarded terms: but genuine prophecy dares to be particular. Thus, for example, had it been foretold, several centuries before, that a King should destroy the altar of Bethel, this, though from the singleness of the event, and the circumstance of place, it would have approached much nearer to the character of prophecy, might yet have been considered merely as a bold and happy conjecture verified by a casual accomplishment. But when we read that a King,[160] *Josiah by name*, should do this, and when, at the distance of about three hundred years, we find a Sovereign of that name, who actually did destroy the altar of Bethel, the authenticity of such a prediction being proved, it is impossible to refuse to it the attribute of inspiration.

[...]

The erudition of Langland, if such were really the author's name, besides his Saxon literature, consisted in a very familiar knowledge of the Vulgate, and the schoolmen: the first of which appears to quote from memory, as he frequently deviates from the letter of that version; and I have no reason to suppose that the old Italian translation was then in use. His citations from the schoolmen I am unable to trace; my own knowledge of those forgotten writers, the great lights of their own and the following ages, scarcely extending beyond a small portion of Aquinas; and though not unacquainted with scholars, I should be at a loss to apply to any one, in the hope that he would be able to point out to me a reference to Scotus or Peter Lombard.

With these deficiencies, and many more, the present work is delivered to its readers: of whom, however, none but the most candid, and the most attentive, as well as intelligent, will be aware of the difficulties which have attended it. The Visions concerning Peirs Plouhman are, beyond comparison, the most obscure work in the English tongue; for when the phraseology of other ancient poets is illustrated, and their allusions to ancient facts and usages, often of a public and permanent nature, are explained, the labour is at an end; but here, in addition to a language infinitely more antiquated than that of any of them, other, and almost insuperable, difficulties remained; first, to disentangle the whole plan of the visions, which had never been attempted before; secondly, to lay open the obscurities, and to reconcile the apparent inconsistencies of the allegory; afterwards, to clear the connection of the

---

[160] Kings xiii. 2. – W.

author's ideas and the transitions from one argument to another; and, lastly, to trace innumerable allusions, of which, from their fugitive and temporary nature, at the distance of more than four centuries, many must, after all, be abandoned as hopeless.

[...]

He [the editor] wishes to conciliate no favour to the work, by lamenting that it was undertaken in the languor of bad health, or that it was only prosecuted in the intervals of leisure which an active and occupied life allowed: both the facts, indeed, are true; but these, if likely to have injured the work in any material degree, were reasons why it ought not to have been begun; if otherwise, they will not contribute to lessen its actual defects. In short, he is ready to confess that, for the space of two years, it has received from him attention sufficient to have rescued it from very gross imperfections, and consequently, that its faults of this degree, whether more or fewer in number, are to be ascribed to a cause more humiliating than the indolence or carelessness of the Editor.

Such as it is, however, he may be permitted to hope that, even in the present appetite of mankind for easy and dissipating objects of literary pursuit, there are some readers who will be happy in an opportunity of being introduced to the spirited and vigorous Father of English Poetry, if not divested of all his difficulties and still clad in the formidable array of black letter, yet more familiar and accessible than in the rugged and repulsive garb in which he was left by the former editor.

Readers of a more serious cast will contemplate, some with philosophical curiosity, and others with pious satisfaction, the successful struggles of a powerful mind, which, in an age when evangelical truth had well nigh been suffocated under a load of ceremonies and traditions, and when virtue, public and private, had declined in the same proportion, by a comparison of the prevailing corruptions, both in faith and practice, with the word of God, though not wholly purged from every remnant of error and superstition, had yet been led, in an uniform progress of investigation and discovery, to the purifying fountain of living waters in the example, the merits, and the intercession of the Redeemer.

9. Edward Vernon Utterson (1776?-1856)

Edward Vernon Utterson, FSA, was a lawyer of Lincoln's Inn and a founder member of the Roxburghe Club. In 1835, he retired to the Isle of Wight and set up the Beldornie Press. Most of his works were privately printed or published through the Roxburghe Club; the extracts here are from an edition of the romances of *Sir Triamour, Sir Isumbras, Sir Degaré, Sir Gowther* along with some short poems from manuscripts and black-letter prints. The work was produced through a commercial mainstream publisher and is more scholarly than Utterson's other work.

E. V. U[tterson], ed. *Select Pieces of Early Popular Poetry: Re-Published Principally from Early Printed Copies, in the Black Letter*, 2 vols (London: Longman, Hurst, Rees, Orme and Brown, 1817).

From: Preface (I, v-xviii).

At a period when the attention of the public has been so much attracted to objects of antiquarian lore, an apology need hardly be offered for requesting its patronage in favour of the little work now submitted to its acceptance. The subject of our national antiquities has within the last thirty years been an object of particular investigation and research, and it has fortunately met with enquirers whose ability and persevering industry have thrown much light on various particulars relating to our manners and history during the middle ages. Still, however, new topics present themselves, fresh subjects for enquiry are started, and if in the occasional republication of portions of our early literature few additional illustrations of received opinions are now to be discovered, yet the revival affords corroboration of former conjectures, which is thus strengthened into conviction; it affords materials for the philologist wherewith to analyse the structure of our language, or suggests to the poet interesting images of ancient manners, which, chosen by taste, and remodelled by genius, tend to enliven the narrative, and increase its interest. [...] When we witness the favour which has deservedly been shewn to the works of one of the most popular of our living poets, we may fairly presume that some portion at least of the success which he has achieved is to be attributed to the subjects which have been selected by his judgment, and embellished by his taste: he has wooed the poetic muse to familiarise his readers with our ancestral customs:—she has answered the invitation; and, waving over us her magic wand, we find ourselves at one time inmates of the gothic hall, witnessing the rude splendor of its chieftain in his hours of festivity; at another time, accompanying the challenger to the listed field, we are made partakers of, or witnesses to, the gallant deeds of feudal chivalry.[161]

It is no small praise to the productions of the early minstrels, that the subjects of the simple poems, which in the middle ages were recited from castle to castle, should, in the present enlightened state of society, again rise into notice and consideration, interest us by their simplicity, and charm us by the naïveté of their representations. When the unlettered warrior of that distant period sought for amusement in the intervals of action, he was compelled to rely on the talents of others, instead of drawing on his own stock of materials: no classic attainments gratified his rudely-gifted mind; no scientific pursuit afforded subject for experiment, or sources of reflexion. It was therefore only in the recitation of the minstrel that the upper classes of society in the middle centuries sought for intellectual enjoyment, or at least that species of it which results from the united charms of poesy and music. It was principally in the love ditty, or the romance,[162] that the minstrel found a source of profit to himself, and of delight to his hearers.

In the rude attempt of these early poets we are not to expect rich or highly-finished colouring; where a life of idleness presented itself in the occupation of a minstrel, we ought not to wonder if many assumed the Tabart and the Badge who were deficient in every qualification for the profession. Even those who were sufficiently gifted by nature to produce a poem, which should possess merit sufficient to excite attention in the auditory, or to invite repetition, appear to have had little power beyond that of making a vigorous sketch of the subject, without attempting to give body and colouring to the meagre outline. 'It is to be observed', says Ritson, in his observations on minstrels, 'that all the minstrel songs which have found their way to us are merely narrative; nothing of passion, sentiment, or even description, being to be discovered among them'.[163] Simplicity was their principal recommendation, accompanied, it is believed, by great accuracy of representation in those parts of the narrative which referred to the dress and habits of the personages introduced.

To account, therefore, for the renewed popularity which has attended this subject, we must principally look to the little sketches of manners carelessly introduced, which, as illustrating the ruder ages, and pourtraying the progress

---

[161] Scott's *Minstrelsy of the Scottish Border* was in its fifth edition by this time; *The Lay of the Last Minstrel* was in its fifteenth.

[162] The word *romance* is here used in its most usual acceptation, that of a lengthened work of fiction. – U.

[163] [Joseph Ritson, ed.] *Ancient Songs* (London, 1790), p. xvi.

of society, are become interesting subjects of research to the antiquary, the historian, and the poet.

The best modern imitations of the romance poems have been necessarily more gorgeously adorned. They have been clothed in attractive language, enjoying the pomp of verse, and embued with the delicacy of sentiment; added to which, all the powers of description have been brought into action to give perfection to the tale. The enlightened taste of the present day required these adjuncts; but we must still feel a pleasure, of no trifling extent, in tracing the rude outline which has led to such results, in examining the germ which has flowered so luxuriantly.

In indulging at the present period in enquiries which must necessarily partake of much conjecture relative to the literary amusements of our remoter ancestors, it may fairly be supposed that these amusements would be varied at different periods, according to the immediate occupations and pursuits in which they were engaged, and would likewise take their tone of colouring from the situation and rank in life of the respective parties. Thus the romance of chivalry seems principally to have been composed for the gratification of knights and nobles, as the poem frequently commences with an invitation to the '*Lords*' to listen and attend; whilst, on the other hand, it is probable that those in the lower class of life were amused with recitations of a nature more readily addressed to their feelings and occupations, and which were occasionally satirical, and generally ludicrous. Still, however, this classification, if not altogether fanciful, must have been sometimes liable to exception.

Previous to a military incursion, when the feudal tenants were summoned to the castle of their lord, the subordinate partisans must have listened to the romantic achievements, which, chaunted by the gothic Tyrtæus, excited the valour of their chief: and probably the baron himself would sometimes incline from the 'hye deyse', on which he was seated at his repast, to attend to the humorous lay, which formed the more appropriate amusement of his humble dependents.

The former description of poems, however, seem to have been attended with a better fate than their lowly competitors, since the class of romances still preserved even in English is very numerous, and most of which bear internal evidence of their remote antiquity; whilst, on the other hand, comparatively few lengthened poems of a ludicrous, satirical, or miscellaneous nature of very early date are now extant, although that there was formerly a great abundance of that description we learn from the introductory passage of the old poem 'Lay le Freine', which begins,

> We redeth ofte, and findeth y-write,
> And this clerkes wele it wite,
> Layes that ben in harping,
> Ben y-founde of ferli thing:

Sum bethe of wer, and sum of wo,
Sum of joie, and mirthe also,
And sum of trecherie, and of gile,
Of old auentours that fel while,
And sum of bourdes and ribaudy, &c.[164]

Most, however, of our old romantic poems are translated from the French,
a circumstance nevertheless which does not in the least degree tend to
invalidate their interest, or lessen their authority, as throwing light on the early
dress, usages, and habits of the English; since, owing to the intimate
connection of the two countries during the early reigns of the Plantagenet
dynasty, there was little discrepancy between them in the above-mentioned
particulars; and in fact, the natural ties which so long united this island with its
nearest continental neighbours, were not dissolved, until the long wars of
Edward 3d. excited an irritation which severed the two nations more
completely, and eventually produced an almost total alienation. But even if
this were not so, there are solid grounds for believing that a very large portion
of the romances, existing in the language from which they are thus
emphatically *entitled*, were written or composed in this country at a period
when that language formed the principal vehicle of poetry as well as of
courtly conversation.

With respect, however, to the lighter early English poems, their originality
must, it is believed, be still more apocryphal, since several of them at least are
obviously translations from, or imitations of, ancient French fabliaux.

[...]

In the arrangement adopted by the editor in the publication of these
volumes he has divided the romances of chivalry from the more humorous
poems, considering them not only as being specimens of distinct classes, but
as being the productions of two different æras. The first volume is confined to
romances, which, although (with the exception of one) taken from printed
copies, nevertheless contain strong internal evidence of their being composed
at a period long anterior to the invention of printing, even if such antiquity
were not proved in many instances by their being found in early MSS.
Notwithstanding three of the romances contained in the first volume had
already been analysed by Mr. George Ellis, the editor conceived that the
publication of them in their complete state would not be the less welcome to
the antiquary and philologist. Every one must admire the elegant work of that
gentleman, and desirable to a large proportion of readers as his epitome must

---

[164] Cf. *Lay le Freine*, ll. 1-9, in Thomas C. Rumble, *The Breton Lays in Middle English*
(Detroit: Wayne State University Press, 1965), p. 81.

ever be, it was imagined that a limited reprint of the entire poems would be acceptable to those who would wish to see the story in its rude simplicity, clothed in the very garb which rendered it acceptable to our unlettered forefathers. The untutored Polynesian is much more an object of interest and curiosity, with no other clothing than his war-mat and feathered helmet, than if fully equipped in the costume of European society.

The second volume is confined entirely to humorous and satirical pieces of a later but still distant period, since most, if not all of them, are only now to be found printed in the black letter, and can hardly in their present shape and language be carried farther back than the middle of the 16th century. It may be considered as some recommendation of this latter volume, that most of the pieces contained in it were the subjects of panegyric by that accurate and intelligent antiquary Ritson, in compliance with whose suggestion this work originated.

The rigid moralist of the present day may perhaps feel inclined to censure the phraseology of some of these latter poems as occasionally swerving from the language of decency: such accusation might be well founded if the ideas of the poet were to be measured by the standard of modern correctness: but decency is the child of refinement, and every one, at all acquainted with the manners and mode of living of mankind during the middle ages, must be fully aware, that although there was less of delicacy in the language, and perhaps in the habits of society, yet that in the strictness of moral principle our ancestors hardly yielded to their more polished descendants.

10. Robert Southey (1774-1843)

Robert Southey, the one-time radical poet, was a confirmed conservative by the time his name appeared on this new edition of Malory's works. The edition was originally undertaken by Walter Scott and Southey's work is confined principally to the preface. This is very diligent, but, like many such prefaces and introductions, Southey's says little about the actual text it is introducing, and focuses instead on learned discussion of sources. He makes several negative judgements, on moral grounds, of sections of the Arthurian prose cycle (objecting, for example, to the explicit adulteries of Lancelot and Tristram), but does not have parallel remarks to make about Malory. Such remarks as he does make about Malory are reprinted here.

The recent *Robert Southey: A Life* by Mark Storey (Oxford: Oxford University Press, 1997) has almost nothing to say about the Malory edition.

Robert Southey, ed. *The Byrth, Lyf, and Actes of Kyng Arthur*, 2 vols. (London: Longman, Hurst, Rees, Orme, and Brown, 1817).

From: Preface (I, i-ii, xxxi-xxxii).

Rich as the English is in every other branch of literature, it is peculiarly deficient in prose romances of chivalry, a species of composition in which the Portugueze and the French have excelled all other nations. The cause of this deficiency may perhaps be found in our history. At a time when the feelings and fashion of the age tended to produce and encourage such works, and when the master-pieces in this kind were composed, our language had not found its way among the higher classes, and our prose-style in consequence was wholly unformed. We had metrical romances in abundance, because they were in the proper sense of the word popular; they were designed for recital, and all who had ears to hear were fit audience. But for long compositions in prose readers were required, and in those ages reading was a rare accomplishment even in the highest ranks: this is one reason, among others, why poetry has in all countries preceded prose; and in this country French was at that time the language of those for whom books were written. Just as the English tongue acquired a decided prevalence, and had been stampt for immortality by Chaucer, the civil wars began, and the men, without whose patronage literature could make no progress, were engaged in a fierce struggle, not merely for power, but for life. When the long contest between the houses of York and Lancaster was terminated, and the government assumed a settled form under the Tudors, the glory of chivalry was on the wane. The character of war had been changed by the general use of gunpowder; this produced, though somewhat more slowly, a change in its costume; and the intellectual activity of the age was at the same time excited and almost engrossed by the momentous struggle for religious liberty.

For the same reasons that during the golden age of chivalry no original compositions of this description were produced among us, no translations were made from the numerous works which had appeared in French. To this circumstance the Morte Arthur is owing: it is a compilation from some of the most esteemed romances of the Round Table. Had the volumes from which it is compiled existed in English, Sir Thomas Malory would not have thought of extracting parts from them, and blending them into one work. This was done at the best possible time: a generation earlier, the language would have retained too much of its Teutonic form; a generation later, and the task of translation would have devolved into the hands of men who performed it as a trade, and equally debased the work which they interpreted, and the language in which they wrote.

[...]

Nothing can be more inartificial in structure than the Romances of the Round Table. Adventure produces adventure in infinite series; not like a tree, whose boughs and branches bearing a necessary relation and due proportion to each other, combine into one beautiful form, but resembling such plants as the prickly pear, where one joint grows upon another, all equal in size and alike in shape, and the whole making a formless and misshapen mass. Even this clumsy mode of transition is often disregarded, and the author passes from adventure to adventure without the slightest connection, introducing you without prologue or prelude of any kind to a new scene, and bringing forward a new set of personages. [...]

These folios [principally, the French romances, but by implication Malory's work as well] were the only books of recreation when they were composed and printed; and in those ages large volumes were not regarded with that fear which is now felt by the busy, and affected by the superficial and the vain. A folio romance was the stock of amusement for weeks or months, a dozen or a score of pages sufficed for the evening's reading; and perhaps more satisfaction was gained than lost by travelling thus deliberately through the story: it became an habitual pleasure. The rapidity of modern narrative is less readily understood, and produces fainter effect; these tales were slowly received, and made a profound impression, as slow showers penetrate the deepest; and hence it was that they so strongly affected the manners and morals of the age. As the manners have become obsolete, the fashion for such works has passed away; and now for the full enjoyment of them a certain aptitude is required, as it is for poetry and music: where that aptitude exists, perhaps no works of imagination produce so much delight. It is something like that pleasure which the poet and the painter partake from forest scenery, or in following the course of a mountain stream.

11. James Heywood Markland (1788-1864)

James Heywood Markland was, like E. V. Utterson, a London lawyer and an early member of the Roxburghe Club. The work represented here is a relatively rare example for the time of interest in drama, and also more scholarly than is usual for Roxburghe Club editions.

James Heywood Markland, *Chester Mysteries: De Deluvio Noe; De Occisione Innocentium* (London: Roxburghe Club, 1818).

From: Introduction (pp. i-ii).

It was the editor's intention to have prefixed to these Plays a concise history of the origin and progress of religious dramas in Europe, with a view to ascertain, if possible, the precise period of their introduction into this country; and also to have furnished some account of the several series of Mysteries acted at York, Coventry, and other places. In the prosecution of this interesting inquiry, he had collected a considerable mass of materials, but each day's research tended to convince him that a still larger portion remained unexplored, and that the subject had hitherto received far less attention than it deserved. Sensible therefore of the impossibility of affording it common justice, within any fixed period, or of rendering his observations at all worthy of the perusal of that body for which they were immediately designed, he has been reluctantly compelled to abridge his plan, and to content himself with giving some particulars of the collection from which the present specimens are selected, with a few incidental remarks on others of a similar class.

The series of Mysteries performed at Chester, usually attributed to Randle or Ralph Higden, a Benedictine of St. Werburg's Abbey in that city, although not the most numerous, has been considered, by a competent judge, as the most ancient, as well as the most complete collection of the kind now in existence. The date usually assigned to their composition is the year 1327-8; the accuracy of which has been questioned solely by Mr. Roscoe, who not only conceives that these plays have been antedated by nearly two centuries, but that it is scarcely possible 'to adduce a dramatic composition in the English language than can indisputably be placed before the year 1500, previous to which time they were common in Italy'.[165]

---

[165] William Roscoe, *The Life of Lorenzo de' Medici*, [3rd edn.], 4 vols (Basel, 1799), I, 307 n.b. – M. [Dating the original production of the mystery plays is difficult. The long-accepted date for the Chester cycle Markland offers here is now questioned and a late fourteenth-century date offered instead, which makes impossible the authorship of Higden.]

[...]

In the second Mystery of 'The Murder of the Innocents', the Child of Herod is stated to be destroyed in the general massacre; and this, like the domestic quarrel of Noah and his Wife, is another instance of circumstances being admitted into religious Plays 'not warranted by any writt' of Scripture.

[...]

The *Murder of the Innocents* was undoubtedly a very favourite plot in the age when these performances prevailed. It occurs amongst the religious plays of York and Coventry, and in the Townley MS. A play with a similar title was acted at Constance, as noted in a preceding page, in the year 1417; and in Hawkins's Collection of Plays we have a Mystery, entitled, '*Candlemas Day, or the Killing of the Children of Israel*'. The editor informs us that it was written 'by one *Ihan Parfre* in 1512', and refers his readers to the original, (Cod. MSS. Kenelmi Digby, 1734, 133) should any doubt arise as to the authenticity of this date.[166] Warton seems to regard it as the identical play performed at Constance. If this notion be well founded, Parfre must have been merely the translator or transcriber, or he might have compiled a new play from older materials, as the representation at Constance took place nearly a century prior to the date given by Hawkins. It bears a close resemblance both in language and incident to the Chester Mystery; but as the comparison can be so readily instituted, it is unnecessary to supply extracts. The comic character of Watkin the 'Messanger', a boaster and a coward, and who may be regarded as the Sir Kay of Herod's court, appears to have been substituted for Sir Lancelot and Sir Grimbald, who figure in the latter. The introduction of these knights of romance at the court of Judaea, and the defiance which they breathe against a King of Scotland, are amusing instances of that total disregard of all chronological accuracy apparent in these homely compositions. We find that Herod upon many occasions appeals to Mahound or Mahomet as the object of his adoration. This was an effectual mode of increasing the indignation of the audience against his atrocious massacre, 'from the generous contempt in which our ancestors held infidels of every description'.[167] In the Townley Mystery there is a boast of Herod's near relationship to the Prophet, being styled 'Cousyn to Mahowne'; and in the play of Candlemas-day the King, at the point of death, thus commends himself to the impostor:

---

[166] Thomas Hawkins, *The Origin of the English Drama*, 3 vols (Oxford: Clarendon Press, 1773), I, vi. – M.

[167] William Stewart Rose, *Partenopex de Blois* (London: Longman, Hurst, Rees, and Orme, 1807), p. 145 – M.

'My Lord *Mahound*, I pray the with hert enteer,
Take my soule in to thy holy hande;
For I fele by my hert, I shal dey evyn heer,
For my leggs falter, I may no lenger stande.[168]

When the legendary stories of the Saracens were fashionable (says Warton) Mahound or Mahomet was a formidable character on our stage: thus Skelton,

Like *Mahound* in a play,
No man dare him withsaye.[169]

If we regard the state of literature, religion, and manners, during the period when these performances prevailed, we cannot wonder that they should be promoted by the Church, or that their popularity amongst the laity should have been so extensive and lasting. Ecclesiastics perceiving with jealousy the avidity with which the lays of the Minstrels were received, determined by similar arts to engage the exclusive attention of the people, even in their amusements. The following lines seem to confirm this supposition, as they prove that on the festival of *Corpus Christi*, celebrated by the performance of Plays at Coventry, York, and other places, the fictions of the Minstrels were at one period resorted to for recreation.

Ones y me ordayned, as y have ofte doon,
With frendes, and felawes, frendemen, and other;
And caught me in a company on *Corpus Christi* even,
Six, other seven myle, oute of Suthampton,
To take melodye, and mirthes, among my makes;
With redyng of Romaunces, and revelyng among,
The dym of the derknesse drowe into the west,
And began for to spryng in the grey day.[170]

---

[168] *The Killing of the Children*, ll. 354-57, in *The Late Medieval Religious Plays of Bodleian MSS Digby 133 and E Museo 160*, ed. by Donald C. Baker, John L. Murphy, and Louis B. Hall (London: EETS, 1982), p. 109.
[169] Cf 'Why Come Ye Nat to Courte?', ll. 597-8, in *John Skelton: The Complete English Poems*, ed. by John Scattergood (Harmondsworth: Penguin, 1983), p. 294.
[170] Thomas Percy, *Reliques of Ancient English Poetry*, 4th edn (London: Dodsley, 1794), II, 285. A few mis-readings have been corrected by Mr. Douce, from the MS. in his possession, being the one referred to by Dr. Percy. – M. [The poem is 'The Crowned King: On the Art of Governing'; see Rossell Hope Robbins, ed. *Historical Poems of the XIVth and XVth Centuries* (New York: Columbia University Press, 1959), pp. 228-29.]

The popular fictions of romance certainly offered much richer materials, but the Clergy could only with propriety be engaged in dramatic representations of a *religious* character; and thus the Bible, and the legendary histories of Saints and Martyrs, were resorted to, from absolute necessity. Excluded from society and from secular concerns, the Monks would not unwillingly promote a species of amusement, which relieved the tedium of monastic life, and afforded them occasional opportunities of mixing with the world. It has often been urged, that Mysteries and Moralities taught little except licentiousness and impiety. The coarse language, the irreverent use of sacred names, and the familiar exhibition of the most awful events, must now be acknowledged extremely offensive; but we must be cautious not to judge of the simplicity of those times by the sensitive delicacy of our own. They at least conveyed *some* scriptural knowledge, and diverted the mind from an exclusive devotion to war and warlike sports. In those days, when 'darkness covered the earth, and gross darkness the people', the Bible was to the multitude a sealed book, and religion was impressed upon their minds by the gorgeous ceremonies of the Church, or by its terrible anathemas, rather than by the pure and simple precepts of its divine Founder. But the insight even thus afforded into the most striking narratives of Holy Writ, by sensible representations of awful facts, where the punishment of vice, and the reward of virtue, were unfolded, could have taught nothing hurtful; and in this view these religious dramas rest upon much less questionable principles of morality than many of the popular productions of more civilized ages. Might not these plays also excite the desire of examining the *source* whence they were derived, and thus conduce, in a partial degree, to a general knowledge of the Scriptures, an investigation of the errors of the existing creed, and eventually to the overthrow of the papal power? In a later age the stage was successfully resorted to, as an auxiliary to the pulpit. Both the Roman Catholics and Protestants rendered religious plays the vehicles of opinion, where truths were frequently elicited, though too often sullied by expressions of the bitterest censure and intolerance. Amongst the Reformers, Bale stood foremost in seizing this weapon, and, whilst dramatizing in his 'Comedies' various parts of the Scriptures, he powerfully exposed the abuses of the Romish Church, and inculcated the principles he had espoused.[171] Edward VI. was induced to employ his pen in the same cause, and doubtless thought himself better employed than in 'scribbling controversial ribaldry', when he furnished, what one of his eulogists terms, a most elegant comedy, called the 'Whore of Babylon'.

---

[171] More famous today as a bibliographer, John Bale (1495-1563) wrote several plays drawing on scripture with the purpose of promoting the ideas of the reformed church.

'It is of all things (says Burke) the most instructive, to see not only the reflections of manners and characters at several periods, but the modes of making their reflection, and the manner of adapting it at those periods to the taste and disposition of mankind. The stage indeed may be considered as the republic of active Literature, and its history as the history of that state'. It is under these impressions that the Editor has presented, as it were anew, these singular productions: in the hope also, that no apologies are requisite for giving a limited circulation to compositions so curious, and, in many respects, so interesting; although they may appear offensive to the taste of the present age. He offers them as relics of the literature and amusements of our ancestors; and when we regard the spirit in which they were written, and the reverence with which they were viewed, suspicion of *intentional* profaneness or indelicacy cannot attach to the pen from which they proceeded. — 'Such spectacles', says an elegant and lamented writer, 'indicate the simplicity, rather than the libertinism, of the age in which they were exhibited. — The distinction between modesty of thought and decency, which resides in the expression, is a modern refinement; a compromise between chastity and seduction, which stipulates not the exclusion, but only the disguise of licentiousness; and may, perhaps, be a proof of a purer taste, but is no evidence of a very severe and rigid morality'.[172]

---

[172] George Ellis, 'Preface', *Fabliaux or Tales, Abridged from French Manuscripts of the XIIth and XIIIth Centuries*, new edn corrected, by G. L. Way, 3 vols (London, 1815), I, xxxvi-xxxvii – M.

12. David Laing (1793-1878)

The Edinburgh antiquary David Laing was less demonstrative and visible a figure than such peers as Scott or Frederic Madden but his influence was considerable. Though educated at Edinburgh University, he was neither a writer nor a professional scholar in any capacity, but a partner in his father's bookselling business. He became a Fellow of the Society of Antiquaries of Scotland in 1827 and in 1831 was able to sell the business and devote himself entirely to his principal interest, ballads and romances, especially those of Scotland. From its inception, Laing was the secretary of the Bannatyne Club and the real organiser of its activities. He was involved, at least in part, in the editing of 27 of its publications. He was also the main force in the Abbotsford Club towards the end of its life, editing texts for this club as well. As the owner of a bookselling business, he was well placed to publish his own editions privately, as represented by the edition excerpted here.

Like Scott claiming *Sir Tristrem* for Scotland, Laing too was inclined to drag some English productions across the Tweed, which is why he discusses Middle English verse here as if it were Scottish. Laing included many Scottish ballads in his *Select Remains*, but much of what he printed is Middle English: *The Taill of Rauf Coilyear*, *The Awntyrs of Arthur*, *Sir Orfeo*, *Thomas of Ersyldoune*, and *The Pistel of Swete Susan*.

[David Laing], ed. *Select Remains of the Ancient Popular Poetry of Scotland* (Edinburgh: Privately printed, 1822).

From: The Advertisement (unpaginated).

Little or no apology, it is conceived, will be now looked for, on submitting to the Publick a Collection, such as this is, of our ANCIENT POPULAR POETRY: neither is it necessary to detain the reader with any general reflection which the nature of its contents might be supposed to suggest. The remains of the Early Poetical Literature of our Country, and indeed, of most Nations, are allowed to possess a value, sanctioned by Time, of which neither prejudice, nor fashion can deprive them, and this may be thought sufficient to justify any attempt that is made for their preservation. They are valuable, no less in enabling us to trace the history and progress of our language, than in assisting us to illustrate ancient manners and amusements, of which they often contain the liveliest representations.

Laing on *The Awntyrs of Arthur*

THE History of the Romance-Poetry of our country, owing to the peculiar circumstances attending its transmission to modern times, is unfortunately involved in great obscurity. Although the more ancient of these remains occasionally bear internal evidence of having proceeded from the celebrated

Makars of the *North Countreye*, we remain in ignorance respecting the individuals who contributed so much to the amusement of our ancestors in these remote times, and even possess little or no positive evidence that might help us to distinguish the productions of Scotish writers from those of the English Minstrels. This may indeed be esteemed a matter of extreme unimportance, since the most valuable specimens of romantick fiction that are extant, have, in one shape or other, been made publick. The '*Sir Tristrem*', by our venerable poet, *Thomas of Ersyldoune*, who flourished about the middle part of the 13th Century, has received every possible advantage in the illustrations of its distinguished Editor: — the *Geste of King Horn*, perhaps the next in point of antiquity, has been faithfully printed by *Ritson*: and the *Lyf of Alexander*, (erroneously assigned to an English poet in the age of Edward II.) is given with no less accuracy by Weber, in his excellent Collection of Metrical Romances.[173]

The Romance which follows bears such a close resemblance in subject, style, and manner to the *Knightly tale of Golagros and Gawane*, (which should also have found a place in this Collection, had not its appearance, in a correct and authentick form, in a different publication, been speedily looked for,) that both have generally been attributed to one and the same author.[174] The antiquity of these tales is unquestionably considerable; and but for our knowledge of other similar alliterative poems, of which the dates are ascertained, and go far to rival these in point of obscurity, we might be justified in carrying them back to a very remote period. The only conjecture that can be offered respecting their author, is founded on the slight allusion in Dunbar's 'Lament for the Death of the Makers', where he says,

> Clerk of Tranent eik he hes tane
> That made the aventers of Sir Gawane.[175]

As different poems of the Adventures of Sir Gawane are known, we are prevented from ascribing one or other of them to *Clerk*, with any degree of certainty; besides, we have the authority of *Wyntoun* for assigning them to *Hucheon*, another of our early Poets, (by whom the reader will find a

---

[173] Comments on these romances by each of the editors mentioned can be found in the relevant sections.

[174] The poem of *Golagrus and Gawain* was first edited by Pinkerton in his *Scotish Poems, Reprinted from Scarce Editions* (London, 1792); Laing himself brought out a limited edition reprint of the original print of this poem in 1827. There was no other edition before Frederic Madden included the poem in *Syr Gawayne* (Edinburgh: Bannatyne Club, 1839).

[175] Cf William Dunbar, 'The Lament for the Makaris', ll. 65-66, in *William Dunbar: Selected Poems*, ed. by Priscilla Bawcutt (London: Longman, 1996), p. 109.

specimen, in the same alliterative style, in the present volume,) who says,

> He made the gret Gest of Arthure,
> And the Awntyre of Gawane.[176]

The Author of these Romances, whoever he may have been, has certainly added something new to the Poetry of his Country. In them there is both originality of incident and manner: — for although they doubtless were founded on popular tradition, the Author surely would not have chosen such an intricate and cumbrous mode of versification, had they been mere translations, or had he profited by the example of the numerous productions of English Romance-Poetry, during its best period, namely, from the middle of the fourteenth to the early part of the fifteenth century.

---

[176] Cf *The Original Chronicle of Andrew of Wyntoun*, ed. by F. J. Amours, 6 vols, STS 50, 53, 54, 56, 57, 63 (Edinburgh: Blackwood, 1903-14), IV (1906), 22, ll. 4332-34.

13. Sir Frederic Madden (1801-73)

The great figure in Middle English editing before Skeat, Sir Frederic Madden, was the Keeper of Manuscripts in the British Museum through the middle third of the nineteenth century, a position which placed him at the heart of British antiquarian scholarly life. Madden had little academic training, and he was in no sense a literary critic. But his editions of romances and Laȝamon's *Brut* were widely influential and he was a revered (and feared) figure by the time the younger scholars of the 1860s established the Early English Text Society. The *Havelok* edition launched Madden's career in Middle English. Amongst other things, Madden here takes a position on the editing of Middle English texts, in a statement which predates the better known credo offered in 1839 in *Syr Gawayne*.[177]

On Madden, see further Robert W. Ackerman and Gretchen Ackerman, *Sir Frederic Madden: A Biographical Sketch and Bibliography* (New York: Garland, 1979); on his scholarly impact see Hans Aarsleff, *The Study of Language in England, 1780-1860* (London: Athlone; Minneapolis: University of Minnesota Press, 1983), pp. 199-201; on his editing see A. S. G. Edwards, 'Observations on the History of Middle English Editing', in *Manuscripts and Texts: Editorial Problems in Later Middle English Literature*, ed. by Derek Pearsall (Cambridge: Brewer, 1987), pp. 34-48 and *MME*, ch. 5.

Frederic Madden, ed. *The Ancient English Romance of Havelok the Dane; Accompanied by the French Text: With an Introduction, Notes, and a Glossary* (London: Roxburghe Club, 1828).

From: Introduction (pp. iii-lv).

The ancient English Metrical Romance of HAVELOK, which is now for the first time submitted to the press, was discovered by accident in a volume preserved among the Laudian Mss. in the Bodleian Library. Of its value, not only in a Glossographical point of view, or as an accurate picture of the manners and customs of former times, but also as serving in a singular manner to illustrate the history and progress of our early poetry, there can be but one opinion, and on each and all of these accounts, it must certainly be considered as a highly interesting addition to the specimens we already possess of ancient English metrical composition.

---

[177] Sir Frederic Madden, ed. *Syr Gawayne: A Collection of Ancient Romance-Poems, by Scotish and English Authors, Relating to that Celebrated Knight of the Round Table* ([Edinburgh.]: Bannatyne Club, 1839), p. xlv.

Among our modern writers on the subject, Tyrwhitt appears to have been the first to lament the loss of the 'RIME' concerning Gryme the Fisher, the founder of Grymesby; Hanelok the Dane, and his wife Goldeburgh, daughter to a King Athelwold, 'who all now', adds the same ingenious author, 'together with their bard,   — illacrymabiles

Urgentur ignotique longâ
Nocte —[178]

These words are re-echoed by Ritson in his Dissertation on Romance and Minstrelsy [*AEMR*, I], p. lxxxviii. but with his accustomed research and accuracy, he points out several of the early historians who notice the Story, particularly Gaimar, Knyghton, Warner, and Camden, all of whom will hereafter separately be considered. He concludes however: 'whether this poem were originally composed in English, or were no more than a translation from the French, cannot be now ascertained, *as it seems to be utterly destroyed'*.—It forms the greatest satisfaction of the present Editor, to have been the humble means of retrieving from oblivion a poem so long supposed to have perished, and by its publication to throw some few rays of light on the obscurity deplored by the preceding writers, as well as on the conjectures advanced by them. To effect this, it is proposed to divide the present Introductory Memoir into three heads, stating I. The Historical and Traditional evidence on which the story is founded; II. Remarks on the originality and style of the English Poem, compared with the French text, and on the period of its compositon; III. Account of the Mss. from which both the English and French Texts are now published.

I.

[Madden opens with a consideration of the Anglo-Norman *Lai d'Haveloc* and goes on to a highly detailed discussion with many passages from the manuscripts to which he refers printed in full. He examines the Anglo-Norman versions of romance, then turns to Robert Mannyng's mentions of the tale, other mentions of the story, and local Grimsby traditions about Grim and Havelok.]

Such is the evidence to authenticate the Story of Havelok the Dane. The Editor conceives it wholly unnecessary for him to bestow a moment on the task of confirming or controverting the opinions already advanced. The demarcations of Fiction and History, now so rigorously observed, were at that early period unknown or neglected. The rhyming Chronicler, and the monkish Historian who wrote in prose the events of ancient times, received with the same degree of credence every circumstance handed down to them

---

[178] *CTC*, IV, 54 n.51.

by document or tradition, and not possessing the means or the judgement to discern between truth and falsehood, admitted into the sober page of History legends founded on the wildest efforts of imagination. Hence it is, to use the language of Percy, that the historical narratives of the North so naturally assume the form of a regular Romance. To this cause must we ascribe the romantic traditions preserved concerning Ragnar Lodbrog and the huntsman Bruno Brocard, in all its variations; the singular legends respecting Guy and Colbrand, and Bevis of Southampton; the no less curious Histories of King Attla, and of King Alefleck, and of his travels to India and Tartary; (all of which, with several more in existence, might form a Dano-Saxon cycle of Romance highly worthy the attention of the poetical antiquary), to which we may add the interesting romance of Moris and Constance, inserted by Nicolas Trivet in his Chronicle, and the curious gest of Dan Waryn, mentioned by R. de Brunne, and partly still preserved in the story of Fulco Fitz Warin, quoted by Leland, and exstant in a Ms. of the Royal Library. In all these may probably be traced some real historical personages and events, mingled with a mass of fable and invention. In the Romance before us, in like manner, the names of real personages seem to have been adopted, without any regard to the time of their existence, and some slight circumstance actually occurring in History, might have been esteemed a sufficient basis for the superstructure subsequently raised by imagination. Thus, for instance, Æthelwolf, Æthelbright, and Guthrum, might be transported into the Athelwold, Athelbright, and Gunter of the Romance, whilst the marriage of Ethered's daughter to Gormo, as asserted by the Danish Historians, might be converted into the fiction of Goldeburgh's marriage with Havelok. The local traditions of Lincoln and Grimsby, most certainly, lend a certain degree of support to the story, and must have been founded on transactions which we cannot wholly reject as fabulous. At all events, whether we regard the tale at present as a web of mingled truth and fiction, or as a pure creation of fancy, we must admit that for ages it was chronicled and read, and in the immediate province to which it so particularly refers, was considered quite as much intitled to belief, as any other portion of our National Annals.

II. The preceding extracts have extended to such a length, as to preclude us from offering many remarks on the Poem itself. We have already admitted the superior antiquity of the French text. This, in itself, may be considered nearly as great a curiosity as the English Romance, both from its being the most ancient French Romance (properly authenticated) existing on a subject not sacred, and also from its being the *first* ever published in this country. Without at present entering too deeply into the question of French or English originality of invention, we are willing to allow, the composer of the English story had probably read, and might also have copied, in some passages (which are pointed out in the Notes) the legend as it existed in the Norman language. But from the variations in the tale, the complete change of time and action, the dissimilarity of the names, and the variety of circumstances and amusing details introduced so graphically by the English poet, and not exstant in the French, there is quite as much claim to originality as in the Romance of Sir Tristrem, which was unquestionably preceded by a French prototype.[179]

The opinion, however, of Tyrwhitt, repeated by Ritson, Warton, Ellis, and Sir W. Scott, that no English Romance existed prior to the days of Chaucer, which is not a translation of some earlier French one, must be received with considerable modification. The ancient Romance of Kyng Horn is decidedly of English growth, and this opinion, first advanced by Percy, is confirmed by the superior judgment of Conybeare.[180] But it may justly be asked, why should nearly all the writers on the subject of English Poetry, have united to deprive our countrymen of the merit of invention or original composition, and so constantly have referred us to a foreign source for the patterns they imitated for nearly 200 years? Is it not far more consonant to propriety and reason, to believe, that the Romances founded on English history and tradition, the scene of which is laid in Britain, such as Merlin, Morte Arthur, Sir Tristrem, Lancelot, Kyng Horn, Havelok, Guy of Warwick, &c. should be the production of English authors writing in French, rather than of Norman poets, who (as Sir W. Scott observes) can scarcely be supposed, without absurdity, to have visited the remote corners of the kingdom merely to collect or celebrate the obscure traditions of their inhabitants. Tyrwhitt is the only writer who has ventured to make this suggestion [...][181]

---

[179] Scott's claim for the priority of the 'Scottish' *Sir Tristrem* (see the Scott extract) over the continental versions had been quickly demolished. It was the only major point from his original argument that he conceded. Madden here reflects the preoccupation of English scholars with finding a romance that could be said to be originally English, as opposed to a translation from French. *Havelok* does not appear to be directly based on Gaimar's *Histoire des Engleis* or the AN *Lai d'Haveloc*; on this difficult question, see G. V. Smithers, ed. *Havelok* (Oxford: Clarendon Press, 1987), pp. liv-lv.

[180] John Josias Conybeare, *Illustrations of Anglo-Saxon Poetry*, ed. by William Daniel Conybeare (London, 1826), p. 237 n.; see also [Richard Price, ed.] *The History of English Poetry [...] by Thomas Warton*, rev. edn, 4 vols (London: 1824), I, 46 n.u.

[181] *CTC*, IV, 69 n.55. We had ourselves formed this opinion long previous to our knowledge of Tyrwhitt's sentiments [...]. – M. [The study of 'Anglo-Norman' antiquities had been on the rise in the second half of the eighteenth century, with the study of architecture, represented in the work of Andrew Coltée Ducarel, particularly prominent. The notion of 'Anglo-Norman' literature was slower to come into general usage. By the early nineteenth century it was becoming established, particularly under the influence of the antiquarian of Normandy, Abbé Gervais de la Rue (1751-1835). His opinions, eventually summarised in his *Essais Historiques sur les Bardes, les Jongleurs et les Trouvères Normands et Anglo-Normands*, 3 vols (Caen: Mancel, 1834), had general currency much earlier (amongst such figures as George Ellis and Scott) thanks to de la Rue's six years' exile in England in the 1790s, when he carried out extensive researches among English manuscripts and was a member of the Society

[Madden argues this point further.]

It is sufficient therefore on these grounds to conjecture, that the French text of Havelok might also have been composed by a native of Britain.

The writer of the English text was undoubtedly a native of the district formerly comprised under the name of Mercia. We can even advance one step further, and assert him to have been an inhabitant of Lincolnshire, as appears not only from the phraseology, founded upon what Dr. Whitaker calls the Mercno-Saxon,[182] but also from the evidence of the writer, in which he says of Lincoln:

> And hwan he came unto the borw,
> Shamelike ben led ther thoru,
> Bi southe the borw, unto a grene,
> That thare is yet, als I whene.—v. 2826.[183]

The age of the poem is the next consideration, and we think it will be admitted, without difficulty, to rank among the earliest specimens of our Romance-Poetry, and to possess equal claims to antiquity with Kyng Horn or Sir Tristrem. The great names of Hickes and Warton have unfortunately been the cause of so many errors in forming an opinion of the relative age of our early poetry, that we must still deplore the want of a work on the subject, supported by the authority of Mss. and founded on a sober and patient investigation of the progress of the English language. The notices by which we are enabled to trace the rise of our national poetry from the Saxon period to the end of the 12th century, are few and scanty. We may, indeed, comprise them all in the Song of Canute recorded by the monk of Ely,[184] (who wrote after 1166.) the words put in to the mouth of Aldred, Archbishop of York, who died in 1069.[185] the verses ascribed to St. Godric, the hermit of Finchale, who died in 1170.[186] the few lines preserved by Lambarde and Camden, attributed to the same period,[187] and the prophecy said to have been set up at

---

of Antiquaries.]

[182] See Thomas Dunham Whitaker, ed. *Visio Willī de Petro Plouhman* (London: Murray, 1813), p. vi; also in the Whitaker extract.

[183] Cf Smithers, ed. ll. 2827-30.

[184] A few words in Middle English in the *Historia Ecclesiae Eliensis*, lib. II, ch. 22, in *Historiae Anglicanae Scriptores quinque ex vetustis codicibus MSS [...]*, ed. by Thomas Gale, 2 vols (Oxford: Sheldonian Theatre, 1691-87), I (1691), 505.

[185] A curse in the vernacular attributed to Ealdred, bishop of Worcester (from 1044); cf *Willelmi Malmesbiriensis Monachi De Gestis Pontificum Anglorum*, ed. by N. E. S. A. Hamilton, RS 52 (London: Longman, 1870), p. 253.

[186] Joseph Ritson, *Bibliographia Poetica* (London: Nicol, 1802), pp. 1-4. – M.

[187] [Joseph Ritson, ed.], *Ancient Songs* (London, 1790), p. xxviii. – M.

here, in the year 1189, as recorded by Benedict Abbas, Roger Hoveden, and the Chronicle of Lanercost.[188] To the same reign of Hen.II. are to be assigned the metrical compositions of Layamon and Orm, and also the legends of St. Katherine, St. Margaret, and St. Julian,[189] with some few others, from which men may learn with tolerable accuracy the state of the language at that time, and its gradual formation from the Saxon to the shape it subsequently assumed. From this period to the middle of the next century, nothing occurs to which we can affix any certain date, but we shall probably not err in ascribing to that interval the poems ascribed to John de Guldevorde,[190] the Biblical History,[191] and poetical Paraphrase of the Psalms,[192] quoted by Warton, and the Moral Ode published by Hickes.[193] Between the years 1244. and 1258. we know, was written the versification of part of a meditation of St. Augustine, as proved by the age of the Prior who gave the Ms. to the Durham library. Soon after this time also were composed the earliest songs in Ritson and Percy, (1264) with a few more pieces it is unnecessary to particularise. This will bring us to the close of Henry III. reign, and beginning of his successor's, the period assigned by our poetical antiquaries to the Romances of Sir Tristrem, Kyng Horn, and Kyng Alisaunder, and which we think Havelok, on very fair grounds, is intitled to claim. But as the language could not perceptibly change within twenty or thirty years, we should have no objection to fix its composition between the years 1270-1290. and there are some circumstances in the poem (explained in the Notes) which would strengthen this probability.[194]

[...]

The popularity of the Romance of Havelok must have been considerable,

---

[188] Joseph Ritson, ed. *Ancient Engleish Metrical Romanceës*, 3 vols (London, Nicol, 1802), I, lxxiii-lxxiv n. – M.

[189] Bodl MS 1883 (Bodl 34). – M. [Madden refers to the legends of St. Katherine of Alexandria, St. Margaret of Antioch, and St. Juliana of Cumae.]

[190] i.e. *The Owl and the Nightingale*, sometimes attributed to a 'John of Guildford'; MSS Cotton Caligula A IX, Jesus Oxford 29.

[191] Which biblical history Madden refers to is unclear; his reference is 'Ms. Bennet, Cant. R. 11'.

[192] i.e. the *Surtees Psalter*, MS Cotton Vespasian D VII, MS Bodl 3027 (921).

[193] Mss. Digb. 4 Jes. Coll. Oxon. 29. – M. [i.e. the so-called *Poema Morale* found with *The Owl and the Nightingale* in Jesus College Oxford 29; see Hickes, *Thesaurus*, I, p. 222-24.]

[194] This is roughly what current thinking is on the date of *Havelok*; see *MEL*, p. 459. Smithers, *Havelok*, argues for a later limit of 1310 (pp. lxiv-lxv). Madden is generally accurate in this respect (or at least in accord with contemporary opinion).

since we not only find it quoted by several of the early Chroniclers (as we have before shewn), but also by the anonymous translator of Colonna,[195] ranked together with the most famous Romances of antiquity [...] This Romance, in all probability, was addressed to the same class of people for whom Robert of Brunne wrote his Chronicle, and composed also by one not conversant with the Court; for, as Sir W. Scott has remarked, the English language when first adapted to the purposes of poetry, was abandoned to the peasants, whilst the nobles listened to the Lais, Romances, and Fabliaux of Norman(?) trouveurs. Hence we may understand why Robert of Brunne speaks of it as written by 'lowed men'. It constitutes, perhaps, its greatest singularity and value, that it presents the only instance exstant of a Romance written for the 'comonalty', exhibiting faithfully, in the vernacular dialect, the language, habits, and manners of the period. In this respect it is of infinitely greater importance to the Glossographist, than either Sir Tristrem or Kyng Horn, and also infinitely more amusing, and in either view will prove no small addition to our present stock of ancient English literature. In point of style, the Romance will bear comparison with any other composition of that age, and is, in many respects, superior to every specimen we possess prior to the time of Langland and Chaucer. The minuteness of detail is not such as to weary, while the attention is continually kept up by the change of person or scene.

[...]

III. [...] In copying from these Mss. [i.e., the French texts as well as the English *Havelok*] the Editor has scrupulously adhered to the orthography of each, and has only assumed the liberty, authorised by every one who has preceded him in the task, of introducing marks of punctuation, of dividing or uniting words improperly connected or disjoined by the scribe, or occasionally correcting the errors occasioned by a letter manifestly false, as, in the English Romance, *th* (þ) for þ, *y* for *th* (þ), and *vice versa*, and of substituting Capital letters for smaller ones, when required. The Saxon forms also of ẏ, ꝑ, and þ have been replaced by the more modern equivalents of *y*, *w*, and *th*, as tending to render the English poem more intelligible, and less difficult to read. With these exceptions, the transcripts will be found to correspond literally with their respective originals.

A few words are necessary on the mode of compilation adopted in the Glossary, in which it has been the Editor's object to follow, as far as possible, the examples of Tyrwhitt and Chalmers, and to produce what might be

---

[195] The opening of the Laud Troy Book mentions Havelok among many other romance heroes; cf *The Laud Troy Book*, ed. by J. Ernst Wülfing, 2 vols, EETS os 121, 122 (London: EETS, 1902-03), I, 1, l. 21.

considered an additional contribution towards that great desideratum A DICTIONARY OF THE OLD ENGLISH LANGUAGE.[196] With the above writers, Etymology has been considered as a pursuit exceeding the bounds prescribed to a Glossarist, unless fixed on some firm and certain basis, and on that account it has been deemed sufficient simply to indicate the root, (except in doubtful or rare cases of its use), and in instances where the derivation is uncertain, it has been left to the researches of future Glossographers. The use of a Glossary formed on a grammatical basis, and illustrated by examples, has long been known to the writer, but the difficulties of composing it must be obvious to all who have ever made the attempt, and on that account some indulgence is craved for the present performance. A few terms still remain, the sense of which is unexplained. Some of these are doubtless to be attributed to the blunders of the scribe, but there are others, which, until our knowledge of the ancient English language becomes more extended, must still be reserved for the discoveries of future laborers in the same path with ourselves.

---

[196] Tyrwhitt's glossary to his *CTC* appeared in a fifth volume to that work in 1778; George Chalmers (1742-1825), the Scottish antiquary, edited the poems of David Lyndsay with a glossary in 1806.

14. Henry Hallam (1777-1859)

Henry Hallam was a graduate of Christ Church, Oxford, a lawyer, and gentleman historian; his *Introduction to the Literature of Europe* was one of his three principal works, the others being *View of the State of Europe during the Middle Ages* (1818) and *The Constitutional History of England* (1827). These works were pitched at a popular level and all went through many editions and translations in the course of the nineteenth century. He was the father of a better remembered Hallam, Arthur Henry, the subject of Tennyson's *In Memoriam*.

See François Mignet, *Notice Historique sur la vie et les travaux de M. Hallam* (Paris, 1861).

Henry Hallam, *Introduction to the Literature of Europe, in the Fifteenth, Sixteenth, and Seventeenth Centuries*, 4 vols (London: Murray, 1837-39).

From: Chapter 1, 'On the General State of Literature in the Middle Ages to the End of the Fourteenth Century' (I, 57-62).

Nothing can be more difficult, except by an arbitrary line, than to determine the commencement of the English language; not so much, as in those of the continent, because we are in want of materials, but rather from an opposite reason, the possibility of tracing a very gradual succession of verbal changes that ended in a change of denomination. We should probably experience a similar difficulty, if we knew equally well the current idiom of France or Italy in the seventh and eighth centuries. For when we compare the earliest English of the thirteenth century with the Anglo-Saxon of the twelfth, it seems hard to pronounce, why it should pass for a separate language, rather than a modification or simplification of the former. We must conform, however, to usage, and say that the Anglo-Saxon was converted into English: 1. by contracting or otherwise modifying the pronunciation and orthography of words; 2. by omitting many inflections, especially of the noun, and consequently making more use of articles and auxiliaries; 3. by the introduction of French derivatives; 4. by using less inversion and ellipsis, especially in poetry. Of these the second alone, I think, can be considered as sufficient to describe a new form of language; and this was brought about so gradually, that we are not relieved from much of our difficulty, whether some compositions shall pass for the latest offspring of the mother, or the earliest fruits of the daughter's fertility.[197]

The Anglo-Norman language is a phrase not quite so unobjectionable as the Anglo-Norman constitution; and as it is sure to deceive, we might better lay it aside altogether.[198] In the one instance, there was a real fusion of laws and government, to which we can find but a remote analogy, or rather none at all, in the other. It is probable, indeed, that the converse of foreigners might have something to do with those simplifications of the Anglo-Saxon grammar, which appear about the reign of Henry II., more than a century after the Conquest; though it is also true, that languages of a very artificial structure, like that of England before that revolution, often became less complex in their forms, without any such violent process as an amalgamation of two different races. What is commonly called the Saxon Chronicle is continued to the death of Stephen, in 1154, and in the same language, though with some loss of its purity. Besides the neglect of several grammatical rules, French words now and then obtrude themselves, but not very frequently, in the latter pages of this Chronicle. Peterborough, however, was quite an English monastery; its endowments, its abbots, were Saxon; and the political spirit the Chronicle breathes, in some passages, is that of the indignant subjects, *servi ancor frementi*, of the Norman usurpers. If its last compilers, therefore, gave way to some innovations of language, we may presume that these prevailed more extensively in places less secluded, and especially in London.

We find evidence of a greater change in Layamon, a translator of Wace's romance of Brut from the French. Layamon's age is uncertain; it must have been after 1155, when the original poem was completed, and can hardly be placed below 1200. His language is accounted rather Anglo-Saxon than English; it retains most of the distinguishing inflections of the mother-tongue, yet evidently differs considerably from that older than the Conquest by the introduction, or at least more frequent employment of some new auxiliary forms, and displays very little of the characteristics of the ancient poetry, its periphrases, its ellipses, or its inversions. But though translation was the means by which words of French origin were afterwards most copiously introduced, very few occur in the extracts of Layamon hitherto published; for we have not yet the expected edition of the entire work.[199] He is not a mere translator, but

---

[197] It is a proof of this difficulty, that the best masters of our ancient language have lately introduced the word semi-Saxon, which is to cover every thing from 1150 to 1250. See [Benjamin.] Thorpe's preface to Analecta Anglo-Saxonica [London: Arch, 1834.], and many other recent books. – H.

[198] 'Anglo-Norman' literature was still a relatively new notion (see Madden extract, note 181) whereas the Anglo-Norman constitution was an eighteenth-century invention, familiar from George Lyttelton's *History of the Life of King Henry the Second*, 4 vols (1767-71).

[199] Frederic Madden had been commissioned to edit the *Brut* in 1831, as part of the

improves much on Wace. The adoption of the plain and almost creeping style of the metrical French romance, instead of the impetuous dithyrambics of Saxon song, gives Layamon at first sight a greater affinity to the new English language than in mere grammatical structure he appears to bear.

Layamon wrote in a monastery on the Severn; and it is agreeable to experience, that an obsolete structure of language should be retained in a distant province, while it has undergone some change among the less rugged inhabitants of a capital. The disuse of Saxon names crept on by degrees; some metrical lives of saints, apparently written not far from the year 1250, may be deemed English;[200] but the first specimen of it that bears a precise date is a proclamation of Henry III., addressed to the people of Huntingdonshire in 1258, but doubtless circular throughout England. A triumphant song, composed probably in London, on the victory obtained at Lewes, by the confederate barons in 1264, and the capture of Richard Earl of Cornwall, is rather less obsolete in its style than this proclamation, as might naturally be expected. It could not have been written later than that year, because in the next the tables were turned on those who now exulted, by the complete discomfiture of their party in the battle of Evesham. Several pieces of poetry, uncertain as to their precise date, must be referred to the latter part of this century. Robert of Gloucester, after the year 1297, since he alludes to the canonisation of St. Louis, turned the chronicle of Geoffrey of Monmouth into English verse; and on comparing him with Layamon, a native of the same county, and a writer on the same subject, it will appear that a great quantity of French had flowed into the language since the loss of Normandy. The Anglo-Saxon inflections, terminations, and orthography, had also undergone a very considerable change. That the intermixture of French words was very slightly owing to the Norman conquest will appear probable, by observing at least as frequent an use of them in the earliest specimens of the Scottish dialect, especially a song on the death of Alexander III. in 1285. There is a good deal of French in this, not borrowed, probably, from England, but directly from the original sources of imitation.

The fourteenth century was not unproductive of men, both English and Scots, gifted with the powers of poetry. Laurence Minot, an author unknown to Warton, but whose poems on the wars of Edward III. are referred by their publisher Ritson to 1352, is perhaps the first original poet in our language

---

program of the Society of Antiquaries to print 'Anglo-Saxon' literature ahead of the Danish initiative in this area proposed by N. F. S. Grundtvig. Madden's edition of both versions of the text did not appear until 1847 and some detractors thought it had taken too long.

[200] Hallam is referring to Bodl MS 2567 (Bodley 779), which contains many saints' lives and is dated to c. 1400.

that has survived;[201] since such of his predecessors as are now known appear to have been merely translators, or at best amplifiers of a French or Latin original. The earliest historical or epic narrative is due to John Barbour, archdeacon of Aberdeen, whose long poem in the Scots dialect, The Bruce, commemorating the deliverance of his country, seems to have been completed in 1373.[202] But our greatest poet of the middle ages, beyond comparison, was Geoffrey Chaucer; and I do not know that any other country, except Italy, produced one of equal variety in invention, acuteness in observation, or felicity of expression. A vast interval must be made between Chaucer and any other English poet; yet Gower, his contemporary, though not, like him, a poet of nature's growth, had some effect in rendering the language less rude, and exciting a taste for verse; if he never rises, he never sinks low; he is always sensible, polished, perspicuous, and not prosaic in the worst sense of the word. Longlands, the supposed author of Piers Plowman's Vision, with far more imaginative vigour, has a more obsolete and unrefined diction.

From: Chapter 2, 'On the Literature of Europe from 1400 to 1440' (pp. 170-71).

On the early fifteenth century

The English language was slowly refining itself, and growing into general use. That which we sometimes call pedantry and innovation, the forced introduction of French words by Chaucer, though hardly more by him than by all his predecessors who translated our neighbours' poetry, and the harsh latinisms that began to appear soon afterwards, has given English a copiousness and variety which perhaps no other language possesses. But as yet there was neither thought nor knowledge sufficient to bring out its capacities. After the death of Chaucer, in 1400, a dreary blank of long duration occurs in our annals. The poetry of Hoccleve is wretchedly bad, abounding with pedantry, and destitute of all grace or spirit. Lydgate, the monk of Bury, nearly of the same age, prefers doubtless a higher claim to respect. An easy versifier, he served to make poetry familiar to the many, and may sometimes please the few. Gray, no light authority, speaks more favourably of Lydgate than either Warton or Ellis, or than the general complexion of his poetry would induce most readers to do.[203] But great poets

---

[201] Hallam is incorrect about Warton, who discussed Minot and was the first to print part of his poetry in 1781: *HEP*, III, 103-4 n. z; III, 146-51. The poet's work was discovered by Thomas Tyrwhitt, who mentioned it in *CTC*, IV (1775), 67 n.54.

[202] It is now dated to 1377.

[203] Thomas James Mathias, ed. *The Works of Thomas Gray* (London: Shakspeare Press, 1814), II, 55-80. – H.

have often the taste to discern, and the candour to acknowledge, those beauties which are latent amidst the tedious dullness of their humbler brethren. Lydgate, though probably a man of inferior powers of mind to Gower, has more of the minor qualities of a poet; his lines have sometimes more spirit, more humour, and he describes with more graphic minuteness. But his diffuseness becomes generally feeble and tedious; the attention fails in the school-boy stories of Thebes and Troy; and he had not the judgment to select and compress the prose narratives from which he commonly derived his subject. It seems highly probable, that Lydgate would have been a better poet in satire upon his own times, or delineation of their manners; themes which would have gratified us much more than the fate of princes.

15. James Orchard Halliwell (1820-89)

The precocious and prolific James Orchard Halliwell (later Halliwell-Phillipps) was a fellow of both the Society of Antiquaries and the Royal Society before he was nineteen years old. He had already published several works, including *The Voiage and Travaile of Sir John Maundevile* (1839), which was based on an eighteenth-century edition. Halliwell was an associate of Thomas Wright; together they published *Reliquiae Antiquae: Scraps from Ancient Manuscripts Illustrating Chiefly early English Literature and the English Language* in two volumes (London, 1841-43). Halliwell edited several Middle English texts in the 1830s and 1840s, many for the Camden Society, founded in 1838, and the Percy Society (1840), but later he took to issuing private printings of expensively produced limited editions. He was an indefatigable collector of early dramatic records, now probably better remembered for his editions and biography of Shakespeare than work in Middle English. But through weight of numbers if not his scholarly influence, he deserves to be remembered as a key figure in mid-nineteenth-century Middle English.

See further Philippa Levine, *The Amateur and the Professional: Antiquarians, Historians and Archaeologists in Victorian England, 1838-1886* (Cambridge: Cambridge University Press, 1986), pp. 10, 19, 21. On Halliwell and drama, see further Theresa Coletti, 'Reading REED: History and the Records of Early English Drama', in *Literary Practice and Social Change in Britain*, ed. by Lee Patterson (Berkeley: University of California Press, 1990), pp. 248-84.

James Orchard Halliwell, ed. *The Harrowing of Hell, A Miracle-Play Written in the Reign of Edward the Second* (London: Smith, 1840).[204]

From: Introduction (pp. 3-7).

Those who take a real interest in the theatrical representations of our country, will willingly be at the pains to peruse the earliest existing dramatic composition in the English language. Such is the 'Harrowing of Hell', set forth in the following pages, — a most singular specimen of the difference between the taste of our ancestors of the fourteenth century and our own. What the readers of modern comedy will say to the miserable doggerel of the

---

[204] The play is in MS Harl 2253 and edited by W. H. Hulme, *The Middle-English Harrowing of Hell and Gospel of Nicodemus*, EETS, es 100 (London: EETS, 1908).

contest between Jesus and Satan, I know not; but its extreme curiosity and intrinsic historical value ought to place the consideration of its poetical beauties entirely out of the scale; and I venture to hope that the modern version which accompanies this most interesting relic of our forefathers, will contribute its mite to render the history of the stage interesting, at least, to performers themselves, if not to the public at large.

It is unnecessary to enter here at length into the history of this species of dramatic poetry, and the more especially as the wide circulation of Mr. Collier's admirable work on the subject has left nothing to be wished for, save the discovery of fresh documents.[205] Suffice it to mention, that different portions of the Old and New Testament, and of the apocryphal writings, were made the subject of popular dramatic exhibition, in more ancient times by the priests themselves, and afterwards by trading laymen. The sacred nature of the subject was, in itself, an attraction for the ignorant spectators in times of intellectual slavery; and the ridiculous poetry which graces or disgraces the several scripture characters in all these early dramas, is one proof among many of the lamentable state of mind among the large majority of the people of those days. Let us take, for instance, the following dialogue between Noah and his wife, when he is trying to persuade her to enter into the ark, which occurs in the series of miracle plays formerly acted at Chester:—[206]
[Halliwell then gives, in modernised form, the dialogue.]

Can anything more grotesque or absurd be imagined? And yet this is a genuine specimen of what were the leading and grand tragedies of the time, — spectacles that served to impart to the populace some idea of those divine histories, from the perusal of which they were precluded owing to their ignorance of the Latin language.
[A summary of the play's action follows.]

James Orchard Halliwell, ed. *Morte Arthure. The Alliterative Romance of the Death of King Arthur. Now First Printed from a Manuscript in Lincoln Cathedral* (Brixton Hill: Privately printed, 1847).

From: Preface (pp. ix-xx).

The concluding scenes of the eventful life of that hero-king, whose romantic and chivalric exploits, fabled though they be, were cherished for centuries as records of the mighty valour of our ancestors, are nowhere related

---

[205] John Payne Collier, *The History of English Dramatic Poetry to the Time of Shakespeare and Annals of the Stage to the Restoration*, 3 vols (London: Murray, 1831).
[206] MS. Harl. 2013. – H.

with so much detail as in the remarkable poem printed in the following pages; and it is singular that it differs in some respects from all other romances on the subject hitherto discovered. Following in the main the account given us in the History of Geoffrey of Monmouth, it nevertheless furnishes curious variations in minute particulars, and the whole narrative is amplified with even more than the licence usually taken by the old romancers. The exaggeration of circumstances, and the prolixity with which the most trifling occurrences are treated, may be, perhaps, in some measure considered two of the leading characteristics of early alliterative poetry; but they are here carried to excess, and present us with one of the most striking examples of that peculiar style, written in a language offering a valuable series of archaisms for philological consideration.

Arthur, having conquered France and several of the principal kingdoms of Europe, holds a feast of the Round Table with extraordinary splendour at Carleon [...]
[Halliwell summarises the plot.]

It will be seen from this brief analysis that the conduct of the story in our alliterative romance does not differ very materially from that related by Geoffrey of Monmouth; but in comparing the two narratives, the terseness of the one and the amusing amplification of the former will be readily perceived. In fact, we have already detailed the entire plot of the romance, if plot it can be called; and yet, notwithstanding the sterility of his materials, our author has certainly accomplished the arduous task of maintaining a considerable degree of interest as he proceeds with his tale, without the aid of artistic contrivance. Nor can his poetical talents be passed without commendation. Compare this poem with other productions of the same period, and we shall find it far above mediocrity. It would have furnished Warton materials for a most interesting chapter, but the historian of English poetry had never had an opportunity of perusing it. Concealed far away at a time such treasures were not appreciated, it has been left for this late period to witness its appearance in the modern world of letters.

16. John Robson (fl. 1840s)

Like his more illustrious predecessor Thomas Percy, John Robson was inspired to this publication by his discovery of a manuscript (MS Ireland Blackburne) containing the three poems *The Awntyrs of Arthur, Sir Amadace* and *The Avowing of Arthur*, rather than because of any particular training in medieval literature. Robson brought his discovery to the attention of Sir Frederic Madden, who secured the interest of the Camden Society. The editing work was probably heavily supervised by Madden; Robson's prefatory remarks are his own however, and indicate the extent to which ideas about the minstrels and minstrel production of romances in the Percy-Scott tradition persisted into the nineteenth century. This edition appears to have been Robson's sole work in Early English Studies.

John Robson, ed. *Three Early English Metrical Romances* (London: Camden Society, 1842).

From: Introduction (pp. vii-x).

The ancient minstrels, as a body, were editors and publishers, rather than original composers. They had to perform duties which, in these days, are divided amongst various caterers for the public in matters of taste. The office of minstrel was neither that of poet, editor, actor, nor musician, but a compound of all. To him it was indifferent where, or how, he acquired the tales, which it was his business to enact or recite, and upon which his popularity and living depended; generally speaking, we may imagine that it was a safer game to repeat well-known and popular stories, than to try a doubtful hazard with something new, or original. At the same time, it would be most desirable to give to the old tales an air of novelty, by introducing appropriate variations, and that he should, as far as possible, accommodate to his hearers, what had, perhaps, been composed for their fathers or grandfathers. We may see how this has been done in the two ballads of Chevy Chace;—and through how many phases must the tale of Amys and Amelion have passed before it assumed the form of Alexander and Lodowicke!

But the minstrels were also representatives of publishers, and from a very picturesque passage in one of Petrarch's letters to Boccaccio we find a more intimate connection between them and the great lights of that age, than we might otherwise have supposed.

[Robson then gives a long quotation from a letter by Petrarch to Boccaccio, in which the minstrel profession is apparently referred to. It begins: 'You know the vulgar and banal breed that makes a living on words not its own; they have spread among us to the point of nausea. They are men of no great talent, but great memory and great drive and even greater effrontery, who frequent the palaces of rulers and powerful men, devoid of anything of their own, yet dressed in others' verses. Whatever someone has neatly said, especially in the vernacular, they declaim with inordinate emphasis, seeking the nobility's favour, money, clothing, and gifts'.[207]]

How far this description may apply to the minstrels of the north, it would be, perhaps, presumptuous to say; the internal evidence of some of the Metrical Romances goes far to prove that they were composed in the Cloister, and, like the poems which Petrarch gave to his friends the Troubadours, must have been given to the minstrel to publish, *aut prece aut pretio.*[208]

The three poems now printed [*The Awntyrs of Arthur, Sir Amadace*, and *The Avowing of Arthur*] very probably formed part of the stock of some individual of this by-gone profession. They have apparently been written from recitation, and are remarkable for the complete contrast of matter, style, and diction. The first two or three pages have evidently been taken down by one who was not intimate with the form of the stanza; some lines are divided, and some run into each other, just as we might suppose would be the case till the writer had made himself acquainted with the intricacies of the versification. A professed minstrel, or even a person who had read the poem through, would have avoided such irregularities.

It may be too, that the recitation of these and similar productions, was accompanied by something of dramatic action, as the 'he sayd', and 'ho sayd', are very frequently additions which the metre itself will not allow.

---

[207] Petrarch, *Rerum Senilium*, lib. v, ep. 2; see Francis Petrarch, *Letters of Old Age: Rerum Senilium libri I-XVIII*, trans. by Aldo S. Bernardo, Saul Levin, and Reta A. Bernardo, 2 vols (Baltimore: Johns Hopkins University Press, 1992), I, 157.

[208] Petrarch in fact writes that the performers he describes 'are rude, wheedling pests' to him in their attempts to obtain his original material; neither this nor his words quoted above suggest that the 'minstrels' (not a word he actually uses) were his friends, or licensed to 'publish' works by performance, nor that they had anything in common with the exalted figure, derived from Percy, that Robson has in mind.

17. Francisque-Xavier Michel (1809-87)

Francisque-Xavier Michel was a French philologist and professor of literature in Bordeaux from 1831, who in 1835 worked in English libraries on official business. At this time he transcribed the Oxford manuscript of the *Chanson de Roland* and published the first edition of this text in 1837. He became acquainted with Sir Frederic Madden, Thomas Wright, and other English antiquaries on his travels, and his works show their influence although his interventions in Middle English are rare. The very thorough *Horn et Rimenhild* is similar to Madden's *Syr Gawayne*, also produced for the Bannatyne Club, in that although it is an edition of a single important text it includes other texts in a genre-based anthology. So the Middle English *Geste of Kyng Horn*, as Michel called it, appears here as a supplement to the edition of the French version of the tale. In his introduction, Michel comments on issues which had arisen with Walter Scott's edition of *Sir Tristrem*.

Francisque Michel, ed. *Horn et Rimenhild: Recueil de ce qui reste des poëmes relatifs à leurs aventures, composés en François, en Anglois et en Écossois, dans les treizième, quatorzième, quinzième et seizième siècles* [...] **Paris: Bannatyne Club, 1845.**

From: Preface (pp. xlix-liii).

C'est sans aucun doute à ce pays [Great Britain], et non pas au nôtre, qu'appartient l'auteur du Roman de Horn, qui est peut-être également celui de l'histoire d'Aelof; plusieurs passages du poëme que nous publions semblent l'indiquer d'une façon décisive. Si l'on m'objecte que par les mots *as noz, li nos, li nostre,* qu'emploie Thomas, le trouvère a pu tout aussi bien faire allusion à sa qualité de chrétien qu'à sa patrie, je répondrai qu'il indique clairement son pays par le choix de son sujet, par le dialecte qu'il emploie, par les connoissances dont il fait preuve, et par une foule d'autres circonstances dont le détail seroit fastidieux. Non content de croire, comme je le fais, que Thomas naquit dans la Grande-Bretagne, ou du moins y séjourna quelque temps, Sir Walter Scott voudroit qu'il fût Écossois, et penche à l'identifier avec le fameux Thomas d'Erceldoune, ou le Rimeur, pour la réputation duquel il a tant fait. Il est vrai que ce n'est point le roman françois qu'il lui attribue, mais bien la rédaction angloise, à laquelle, bien entendu, il donne la priorité.[209] Cette opinion sur *mestre Thomas*, qui n'est appuyée

---

[209] Michel refers the reader to Scott's *Sir Tristrem*, 4th edn (Edinburgh: Constable, 1819),

d'aucun document, d'aucune preuve concluante, est restée propre à son auteur, qui, un peu plus versé dans la lecture des poëmes françois des XIIe et XIIIe siècles, n'eût pas manqué de reconnoître que les trouvères, quand ils se nommoient, ne le faisoient qu'en parlant d'eux à la troisième personne. En somme, il est à regretter que l'homme éminent dont nous parlons n'ait pas imité la réserve d'un de ses compatriotes, le docteur Leyden, qui, ayant à écrire une note sur un roman populaire en Écosse en 1548,[210] se borne à rapporter la conjecture d'un savant antiquaire auquel ce roman sembloit être le même que celui de *Horn-child*.[211]

Mais si le Thomas auquel nous devons le roman françois de Horn n'est point Thomas d'Erceldoune, quel est-il donc? Est-ce Thomas de Kent, auteur du *Roman de toute chevalerie*? Est-ce *Thomas von Britanie*, dont Gotfried de Strasbourg traduisit en allemand le Roman de Tristan dans le XIIIe siècle, ou le Thomas nommé dans le second fragment du manuscrit Douce et dans le second fragment du manuscrit du Rév. M. W. Sneyd? Est-ce l'auteur d'un poëme anglo-norman sur la mort de la Sainte-Vierge et sur son enterrement dans la vallée de Josaphat? Comme nous l'avons déjà dit ailleurs, nous n'avons aucun moyen de résoudre ces questions. Cependant, s'il nous falloit choisir entre ces écrivains, nous procéderions par voie d'exclusion de la manière suivante: nous commencerions par écarter Thomas de Kent, par la raison que son Roman de toute chevalerie est en tout point tellement inférieur à celui de Horn, que, pour nous, il accuse une main différente; nous en agirions de même à l'égard du dernier des Thomas que nous avons énumérés, non pas parce qu'il étoit prêtre, mais par le motif que le trouvère qui porte ce nom dans le manuscrit Harléien 5234, paroît ne le devoir qu'à une erreur de copiste, et s'être réellement appelé *Hermans*. Il ne nous resteroit alors que *Thomas von Britanie*, et le Thomas dont les manuscrits Douce et Sneyd nous ont conservé des fragments: ces deux-là et celui auquel on doit le Roman de Horn pourroient bien n'être qu'un seul et même personnage, supposition à laquelle le passage que nous avons cité plus haut du prologue du Roman du roi Atla prête quelque vraisemblance;[212] toutefois, il faut admettre que, sous le titre d'histoire d'*Aelof*, l'auteur entendoit parler non seulement du Roman

---

pp. lix-lxi; see also the Scott extract.

[210] *The Thail quhou the kyng of Estmureland mareit the kyngis dochtir of Vestmureland.* Voyez *The Complaynt of Scotland* (Edinburgh: Constable, 1801), p. 98. – M. [John Leyden (1775-1811) had assisted Scott with the transcription of *Sir Tristrem*.]

[211] Le savant antiquaire dont veut parler l'éditeur de cet ouvrage n'est autre que Ritson. Voyez le tome III de ses *Ancient Engleish metrical Romanceës* (London, 1802), p. 266. – M. [The sagacious antiquary to whom the editor of this work refers is none other than Ritson. See Volume III of his *Ancient Engleish metrical Romanceës* (London, 1802), p. 266.]

[212] Omitted.

d'Allof, mais encore de celui de Horn, qui n'en est qu'une branche, et qu'il a
cité cette histoire en même temps que le Roman de Tristan, parce que ces
deux ouvrages provenoient de la même main.

Quoiqu'il en soit, il faut se résigner à ne voir dans le Roman de Horn
qu'une traduction, ou plutôt un *rifacimento*, en attendant que le hasard fasse
découvrir quelque document qui jette un jour nouveau sur la question et
permette de la reprendre en sous-œuvre.

Quant à l'auteur du poëme anglois, il seroit assez intéressant de savoir
jusqu'à quel point il est original, c'est-à-dire s'il a inventé tous les détails
dont se compose son sujet, ou s'il les a puisés, soit dans un ouvrage plus
ancien, soit dans la tradition populaire. Malheureusement les monuments
historiques de l'Heptarchie sont trop peu nombreux pour qu'on puisse y
trouver tout ce qu'on désireroit, et dans ceux qui nous restent, il n'y a rien
qui se rapporte à Horn, à Rimenhild et aux autres héros de cette *geste*. Sans
doute on ne peut nier que les aventures de *Kyng Horn* n'aient été populaires
dans le *Border*, sur la frontière de l'Angleterre et de l'Écosse, et même plus
au nord: les ballades que nous réimprimons en font foi, sans compter qu'il y
a dans le comté de Fife, sur le Forth, une paroisse qui porte le nom de
Kynghorn; mais rien ne nous prove que cette popularité ne soit pas
postérieure à la composition du poëme anglois, et que l'auteur de cet ouvrage
n'ait pas mis en œuvre des fables apportées du Nord par les conquérants
saxons ou danois.

Horn and Rimenhild: A Collection of the extant poems relating to their adventures, composed in French, English and Scots in the thirteenth, fourteenth, fifteenth and sixteenth centuries.

The author of the Romance of Horn, who is perhaps also the author of the
story of Aalof, belongs without doubt to that country [Britain] rather than to
ours [France]; several passages in the poem we publish here seem to indicate it
decisively. If it is objected that through the expressions Thomas uses — *as
noz, li nos, li nostre* — the troubadour was just as likely to be referring to his
belonging to Christendom as to his homeland, I would respond that he clearly
indicates his country through his choice of subject, through the dialect he
employs, through the things he shows he knows, and through a host of other
circumstances, the details of which are not worth giving. Not content to
believe, as I do, that Thomas was born in Great Britain or at least stayed there
some time, Sir Walter Scott would have liked him to have been Scottish, and
inclines towards identifying him as the famous Thomas of Erceldoune, or the
Rhymer, for the reputation of whom he has done so much. It is true that it is
not the French romance which he attributes to him, but the English redaction,
to which, of course, he gives priority over the French version.

This opinion on 'mestre Thomas', which is not attested in any document
or by any conclusive proof, has remained peculiar to his author who, had he

been a little better versed in the reading of French poems of the twelfth and thirteenth centuries, would not have failed to note that the troubadours, when they name themselves, do it only by speaking of themselves in the third person. In all, it is to be regretted that the eminent man of whom we are speaking did not imitate the restraint of one of his compatriots, Dr Leyden, who, having to write a note on a romance popular in Scotland in 1548, confines himself to reporting the conjecture of a sagacious antiquary to whom the romance seemed to be the same as that of *Horn Child*.

But if the Thomas to whom we owe the French romance of Horn is not Thomas of Erceldoune, who then is he? Is he Thomas of Kent, author of the *Roman de toute chevalerie*? Is he Thomas of Britain, whose *Tristan* Gottfried von Strassburg translated into German in the thirteenth century, or the Thomas named in the second Douce fragment and the second manuscript fragment of Rev. M. W. Sneyd?[213] Is he the author of an Anglo-Norman poem on the death of the Blessed Virgin and her interment in the valley of Josaphat? As we have already said elsewhere,[214] we have no means of resolving these questions. However, if we had to choose between these writers, we would proceed by a route of exclusion in the following manner: we would commence by eliminating Thomas of Kent, because his *Roman de toute chevalerie* is in every way so inferior to *Horn* that to us it suggests a different hand; we would use the same argument in respect of the last of the Thomases we have enumerated, not because he was a priest, but for the reason that the *trouvère* who bears this name in the Harleian manuscript 5234 appears to owe it only to a scribal error and to be really called *Hermans*. There would then remain to us only Thomas of Britain and the Thomas of which the Douce and Sneyd manuscripts have preserved fragments; these two, and the person to whom we owe the romance of Horn, could well be one and the same person, a supposition to which the passage from the prologue of the romance of King Atla we have cited above lends some credibility; at the same time it must be admitted that, under the title of the story of Aalof, the author intended to speak not only of the romance of Aalof, but also of that of Horn, which is but a branch of it, and that he has cited this story at the same time as the romance of Tristan, because the two works derived from the same hand.

Whatever the truth is, we must resign ourselves to seeing in the *Roman de Horn* only a translation, or rather a 'rifacimento', in the hope that chance might uncover some document which will one day throw some new light on

---

[213] Michel had edited these fragments and the remaining *Tristan* materials as *The Poetical Romances of Tristan*, 3 vols (London: Pickering, 1835-39); the 'Thomas' references are at II (1835), 41, l. 862, III (1839), 81, l. 682.
[214] Michel, ed. *Tristan*, I, lxi.

the question, and allow us to reconsider it as a secondary work.

As to the author of the English poem, it would be rather interesting to know how far he is original, that is to say, whether he has invented all the details which make up his subject, or whether he has drawn them either from an older work or from popular tradition. Unfortunately the historical monuments of the Heptarchy are far too few to allow one to find everything there one would wish, and, in those that remain to us, there is nothing relating to Horn, Rimenhild and the other heroes of this *geste*. Without doubt it is undeniable that the adventures of King Horn were popular in the Border region between England and Scotland, and even further north; the ballads we reprint prove it, without even considering that there is in the county of Fife on the Forth a parish which bears the name of Kynghorn. But nothing proves to us that this popularity was not posterior to the composition of the English poem, and that the author of this work had not put into his work stories imported from the North by Saxon or Danish conquerors.

18. Thomas Wright (1810-77)

Thomas Wright came from a poor background but was able to study at Trinity College, Cambridge, through the generosity of a family friend. He settled in London in 1836, joined the Society of Antiquaries in 1837 and became perhaps the most prolific medievalist antiquarian of the nineteenth century. He anticipated the more famous Skeat by editing both *Piers Plowman* (1842) and the *Canterbury Tales* (1847-51); he edited Malory's *Morte d'Arthur* in 1858, Hoccleve's *Regement of Princes* for the Roxburghe Club in 1860, and numerous smaller texts. He worked fast — his income depended on his labours, which were sometimes commissioned — and he was consequently not careful or accurate. Neither was he highly learned. Partly for this reason he has sunk into relative obscurity, but there are also political and personal elements evident in a lofty disdain for Wright on the part of fellow antiquarians: as the close friend of James Orchard Halliwell, he was implicated in the alleged theft by Halliwell of some manuscripts from Trinity; in addition 'Wright's economic and thus social ambivalence may well have contributed in large measure to his cold reception from the well-heeled and socially assured establishment of the Society of Antiquaries' (Levine, p. 22). None of this should obscure the fact that Wright's impact on medieval studies in his time must have been immense, both because of the sheer volume of output and the fact that much of what he did, even before the advent of the EETS, was relatively widely accessible. A few of his works, such as his *Political Songs*, remain useful today.

Wright's literary scholarship does not involve much evaluation or criticism, and he is given to a great deal of plot summary. Reprinted below are some remarks on Robin Hood, and some introductory reflections on political ballads.

On Wright's Chaucer edition see Thomas W. Ross, 'Thomas Wright', in *Editing Chaucer: The Great Tradition*, ed. by Paul G. Ruggiers (Norman, Okla.: Pilgrim Books, 1984), pp. 145-56; on his Langland edition see Charlotte Brewer, *Editing 'Piers Plowman': The Evolution of the Text* (Cambridge: Cambridge University Press, 1996), pp. 50-62. See also Philippa Levine, *The Amateur and the Professional: Antiquarians, Historians and Archaeologists in Victorian England, 1838-1886* (Cambridge: Cambridge University Press, 1986).

Thomas Wright, *Essays on Subjects Connected with Literature, Popular Superstitions, and History of England in the Middle Ages*, 2 vols. (London: Smith, 1846).

From: 'On the Popular Cycle of the Robin Hood Ballads' (II, 188-211).

[...] We come now to that singular production, the 'Lytell Geste of Robyn

Hode', which was first printed by Wynkyn de Worde, at the latter end of the fifteenth century, and which would seem to be an attempt to string together some of the ballads that were then popular, into something like a consistent story.[215] It is, in fact, an epic poem, and it is, as such, both perfect and beautiful.

One, perhaps, of the ballads which contributed to the formation of this poem, may have been simply the adventure of Robin Hood and the Knight, which here occupies the first and second 'fyttes', and is made to run more or less through the whole.

[Wright summarises the story of Robin Hood and Sir Richard of the Lee.]

The next ballad which seems to have been used in the compilation of this 'geste', was the same story, a little varied in its details, with that of Robin and the potter [...]

[Summary follows.]

The third ballad used in the formation of this 'geste', was one of Robin Hood and the monk. Little John, with Much and Scathelock, go up to the Sayles and Watling-street, and in Barnisdale meet with two black monks and their attendants. The latter were defeated, and one of the monks was brought to dine in the outlaw's 'lodge'.

[Summary follows.]

Perhaps the only other ballad used by the compiler of the 'geste' was that which furnished the last two fits, the meeting of Robin and the king; and it would seem that he had used the 'explicit' of the ballad itself, or that he had it in his mind, when he wrote at the end — 'Explycit kynge Edwarde and Robyn Hode and Lytell Johan'. The mention of king *Edward*, the first instance of the name of a king which occurs in these ballads, is itself curious. Does it show that the ballad which the writer of the 'geste' used, was written in the reign of one of the Edwards, and that in the cycle sung at the Robin Hood festivals, when the king was introduced, they gave him the name of the king at the time reigning, as we have seen was the case in a collateral cycle.

[Summary follows.]

We have now given an abstract of all the remains of the cycle of Robin Hood, in its older form. We have seen that it consisted of the common popular stories of outlaw warfare in the green wood, as they were sung at the festivals and rejoicings of the peasantry, with whom, at the time the songs were made, such tales must naturally have been favourites. As far as we can judge, the

---

[215] *Here begynneth a lytell geste of Robyn hode* (de Worde, 1506?, *STC* 13689; facsimile: Amsterdam, Theatrum Orbis Terrarum; New York: Da Capo, 1970). On the structure and composition of the *Gest* see Stephen Knight, *Robin Hood: A Complete Study of the English Outlaw* (Oxford: Blackwell, 1994), pp. 70-81.

different incidents of the cycle were not numerous, and it is probable that the compiler of the 'geste' introduced into it all that he knew. This poem, indeed, seems at the period of its publication to have been the grand representative of the cycle, and to have contained at least most of that which was commonly sung about the roads and streets.

[...]

When ballads began to be printed, and were spread over the country in the shape of broadsides, the few which had existed when their chief repository was the memory of the peasantry, was found to be insufficient. The more easily it was gratified, the more greedy became the desire after novelty. But the ballad-writers of after-times were not endowed with very inventive minds; and it was, therefore, much more usual to change a little the circumstances and persons of the older stories, and to publish them to the world as new, than to write originals. It would not be difficult to point out examples of this among the modern ballads. That originals, however, were written, there can be no doubt. It was now, indeed, that outward causes began to affect the cycle, for the romances of the Normans had become degraded, and had taken popular forms, and even their stories have found a place among those of Robin Hood and Little John.

The foregoing slight review of the material of the cycle, and of the nature of the stories which formed it, brings us at once to conclude that the character and popular history of Robin Hood was formed upon the ballads, and not the ballads upon the person. There arises, however, thereupon, an interesting question — who was the person that in these ballads bears the name or title of Robin Hood? — a question at the same time which certainly does not admit of a very easy solution.

The notion that he was a person living in the time of our first Richard or third Henry, seems to rest entirely on the passage in the history of Fordun, which passage, as we have already said, was written perhaps not earlier than the middle of the fifteenth century,[216] and of which the only foundation was one of the ballads in which the name of a king Henry occurred, probably proving only that the ballad was written in the reign of a king of that name. Wyntown, also, who places Robin Hood at the date 1283, by his mention of Inglewood and Barnesdale, had evidently the ballads in his mind.

> Lytil Jhon and Robyn Hude
> Wayth-men were commendyd gud:

---

[216] The passage about Robin Hood in Fordun's *Scotichronicon* does as Wright says belong to the mid-fifteenth-century continuation (by Walter Bower). See Thomas Hearne, ed. *Johannis de Fordun Scotichronicon [...]* 5 vols (Oxford: Sheldonian Theatre, 1722), III, 774 n.

> In Yngilwode and Barnysdale,
> Thai oysyd all this tyme thare trawale.[217]

The life, by Ritson, prefixed to his edition of the Robin Hood ballads, with the pedantic notes which illustrate it, is the barren production of a poor mind. The 'accurate' *mister* Ritson, who condemned with such asperity the slightest wanderings of the imaginations of others, has therein exhibited some truly pleasant vagaries of his own. He gives us an essay upon the *private character* of the outlaw! His mode of accounting for the silence with which the chroniclers and historians of those times have passed over the name of Robin Hood, is itself curious: — 'The principal if not sole reason why our hero is never once mentioned by Matthew Paris, Benedictus Abbas, or any other ancient English historian, was most probably his avowed enmity to churchmen; and history, in former times, was written by none but monks. They were unwilling to praise the actions which they durst neither misrepresent nor deny. Fordun and Major [who, by the way, only retailed Fordun in this matter] being foreigners, have not been deterred by this *professional spirit* from rendering homage to his virtues'!![218] Where Ritson learnt that it was the habit of early historians to omit mention of those who had an 'avowed enmity to churchmen', or what influence the fact of their being foreigners could have on their *professional* spirit, does not appear to be a thing easy to be discovered. The circumstance that no one ever heard of such a place is not sufficient to justify even a suspicion in his mind that there ever existed such a town as Locksley, in Nottinghamshire, where the latter ballads place Robin's birth. Lastly, after all that Ritson might have thought proper to advance to the contrary, we are inclined to join with Mr. Parkin, whom he quotes with a sneer, in thinking the pedigree of Robin Hood, which was given by Dr. Stukeley, to be 'quite jocose'.[219]

Mr. Barry, in his 'Thèse de Littérature', has advanced an ingenious and much more plausible theory.[220] He, as we have already observed, supposes that

---

[217] Cf *The Original Chronicle of Andrew of Wyntoun*, ed. by F. J. Amours, 6 vols, STS 50, 53, 54, 56, 57, 63 (Edinburgh: Blackwood, 1903-14), v (1907), 137, ll. 3525-28.

[218] [Joseph Ritson, ed.] *Robin Hood: A Collection of all the Ancient Poems, Songs, and Ballads, now Extant, Relative to that Celebrated English Outlaw*, 2 vols (London, 1795), I, xv; the bracketed interpolation is Wright's.

[219] Against Percy, Ritson had espoused the tradition that held Robin Hood to be a displaced aristocrat and he printed a genealogy of Robin as earl of Huntingdon (*Robin Hood*, I, xxi). This was derived from William Stukeley's *Palæographia Britannica*, 3 parts (London, Stamford, 1743-52), II (1746), 115; Charles Parkin's objection, quoted by both Ritson and Wright, is in *A Reply to the [...] Objections Brought by Dr Stukeley [...]* (Norwich, 1748), pp. 27, 32.

[220] Constant-Étienne-Alfred-Edward Barry, *Thèse de Littérature sur les Vicissitudes et les*

Robin Hood was one of the outlaws who had resisted the first intrusions of the Normans, and compares him with Hereward, who returned from foreign lands to avenge the injury done to his family by William, by the death of the Norman who had had the temerity to intrude upon his heritage, and who gathered his friends and supporters and retired to the fastness of the isle of Ely, where he long bade defiance to the Conqueror.

[...]

Mr. Barry supposes that songs, such as those which Ingulf mentions as having been sung in the public ways in honour of the popular hero Hereward, were the original form of the Robin Hood ballads.[221]

We think, however, that Mr. Barry has gone too far. There is no other ground but bare conjecture for supposing the personage named Robin Hood to have been actually one of the Saxons outlawed by their opposition to the Normans, and there are many reasons for adopting a contrary opinion. Yet it is very possible that, when the sudden change from Saxon to Norman rule was no longer felt, and when the deeds of these Saxon heroes began to be forgotten, the Robin Hood cycle, let it have originated where it may, gradually succeeded to, and took the place of, the ballads which celebrated Hereward and Waltheof.

Still, however, supposing the Robin Hood cycle to have succeeded the ballads which celebrated the last Saxon heroes, we have made no progress towards a discovery of the original personage who had become its hero. Was he the representative of some northern chieftain whose actions had gained a place among the national myths, and who had become an object of popular superstition? Many circumstances join in making this supposition at the least extremely probable.

We know that the ballads of this cycle were intimately connected with the popular festival held at the beginning of May. Indeed, either express mention of it, or a vivid description of the season, in the older ballads, shows that the feats of the hero were generally performed during this month. Unfortunately, we cannot distinctly trace back further than the fifteenth century the history of these games, and their connexion with the name of Robin Hood. [...]

Ritson [...] asserts that the May festival owed its origin to meetings for the purpose of practising with the bow. There can be little doubt, however, that Ritson was wrong, that the archery was an addition to the festival, and that the latter was, in its earlier form among our Pagan forefathers, a religious

---

Transformations du Cycle Populaire de Robin Hood (Paris: Rignoux, 1832), pp. 6-8.

[221] Ingulf, abbot of Croyland in the late eleventh century, was credited with a chronicle which recorded the deeds of the semi-legendary Saxon hero, Hereward. The chronicle is however a late-medieval forgery.

celebration, though, like such festivals in general, it possessed a double character, that of a religious ceremony and of an opportunity for the performance of warlike games.

[...]

We are, however, not opposed to the conjecture which has been made, that the name Robin Hood is but a corruption of Robin of the Wood, because we find analogies in other languages. The name of Witikind, the famous opponent of Charlemagne, who always fled before his sight, concealed himself in the forests, and returned again in his absence, is no more than *witu chint*, in old High Dutch, and signifies the *son of the wood*, an appellation which he could never have received at his birth, since it denotes an exile or outlaw. Indeed, the name Witikind, though such a person seems to have existed, appears to be the representative of all the defenders of his country against the invaders. The old Norse expressions *skoggangr* and *skogarmadr*, which denote an outlaw, are literally *one who goes in the woods*, *a man of the woods*, as is *urdar-madr*, *one who hides himself among the rocks*. They correspond to the Anglo-Saxon *weald-genga*.

[...]

One of the strongest proofs, perhaps, of the mythic character of Robin Hood, is the connexion of his name with mounds and stones, such as our peasantry always attributed to the fairies of their popular superstition. A tumulus was generally the habitation of the underground people, a well or a ruin was the chosen place of their gambols, and a spot which exhibits marks of some violent natural convulsion was testimony of their vengeance. These were the dwarfs of the northern mythology; but the giants of the same creed left also marks of their presence in the loose masess [*sic*] of stone which, in their anger or in their playfulness, they had thrown to immense distances, and in others, more regularly placed, which had once served to mark the length of their steps.

[...]

At other times Robin Hood figures as one of the giants. Blackstone Edge in Lancashire, as we learn from Roby's *Lancashire Legends*, is called Robin Hood's bed or Robin Hood's chair.[222] On a black moor called Monstone Edge, is a huge moor-stone or outlier, which, though part of it has been broken off and removed, still retains the name of Monstone; it is said to have been quoited thither by Robin Hood from his bed on the top of Blackstone Edge, about six miles off. [...]

The legends of the peasantry are the shadows of a very remote antiquity,

---

[222] *Traditions of Lancashire* by John Roby (1793-1850) appeared in 1829 and in many subsequent editions.

and in them we may place our trust with much confidence on a subject like the present. They enable us to place our Robin Hood with tolerable certainty among the personages of the early mythology of the Teutonic peoples.

From: 'On Old English Political Songs' (II, 256-90).

No class of literary antiquities has progressed more rapidly with us during the last twenty years than the study of early English poetry. Until the time of Warton, it was hardly supposed that the history of English poetry could be traced back beyond the days of Chaucer; and Warton's history is very incomplete, and abounds with inaccuracies. Percy, by the popular character of his *Reliques*, called a little more of public attention to the subject. Ritson was certainly the first who carried any true zeal to his researches among early English poetical manuscripts, and who edited the texts with conscientiousness; but his vain pedantry and acrimony of temper, and his entire want of judgment, detract much from the utility of his labours. After Ritson's time, this class of literature dwindled again into little more than a plaything for bibliographers. In more recent times it has been taking its stand on a better footing; and more accurate philological notions have been brought to the study of our language in its earlier and middle stages. That these notions, however, are but yet in their infancy, is proved by the fact that so worthless a text as that of Tyrwhitt's Chaucer has been suffered to be reprinted more than once within the last two or three years.[223]

The supremacy of the Anglo-Norman language has created rather a wide gap between the disappearance of the pure Anglo-Saxon poetry and the commencement of the early English; for, during the long period between the conquest and the middle of the thirteenth century, we find only two poems of any magnitude, the chronicle of Layamon and the Gospel Harmony of Orm, and one or two short pieces, such as the proverbs of Alfred, a Bestiary, a fragment on the popular subject of the body and the soul,[224] and the poem of the Owl and the Nightingale.[225] The language of most of these is in a state of rapid transition, which has commonly received the title of Semi-Saxon. A large portion of them partake of the older Saxon form of alliteration, mixed with rhyme. The English language appears to have regained its position of supremacy after the great baronial struggle under Simon de Montfort; and

---

[223] This slight reflects the fact that Wright would have been engaged at this time on his own *Canterbury Tales* edition, the first part of which appeared the following year. It was the first since Tyrwhitt's in which the editor consulted manuscripts in any extensive fashion, but it is still highly indebted to Tyrwhitt.

[224] i.e., 'The Grave'.

[225] Edited by Wright for the Percy Society in 1843.

from this period to the war of the Roses it has been sometimes denominated, by those who follow the nomenclature of Dr. Grimm, Middle-English. During the latter part of the thirteenth century and the beginning of the fourteenth, the English poetry appears with the forms and much of the spirit of the French and Anglo-Norman poetry, of which it was taking the place.

The longer poems — especially the religious poetry — of the first half of the fourteenth century, are dull and heavy. But, under Edward III, the old alliterative poetry, which had probably continued to exist orally, suddenly reappeared in the spirited and extremely popular political allegory of the 'Visions of Piers Ploughman'. Immediately after this work came the real father of modern English poetry, Geoffrey Chaucer. The production of those high cultivations of poetry represented by Chaucer appears to have been the result of a long age of intellectual movement, which, after his death, gave place to an age of more than ordinary intellectual darkness, when English poetry becomes, it is true, very abundant, but when it possesses very little merit. John Lydgate is the type of the poetical literature of this age.

In general, during the whole of the period of which we are speaking, we find the greatest share of poetic spirit in the popular songs and ballads. The English lyric poetry of the reign of Edward I is, from the form of the language, somewhat obscure, but it is often very elegant. We have much good lyric poetry in the fourteenth century, and a few charming specimens even in the fifteenth. The political songs barely partake of this character, and they always present at least that vivacity which is the necessary consequence of popular excitement.

[The remainder of the chapter summarises and excerpts political songs, many of which Wright had published in *Political Songs of England* (1839) — see *Thomas Wright's Political Songs of England*, intro. by Peter Coss (Cambridge: Cambridge University Press, 1996) — and, with James Orchard Halliwell, in *Reliquiae Antiquae*, 2 vols (London, 1841-43).]

19. Walter William Skeat (1835-1911)

Having trained as a mathematician and retired from his country curacy on grounds of illness while still young, W. W. Skeat returned to Christ's College, Cambridge, eventually occupying the Elrington and Bosworth chair of Anglo-Saxon in 1878 as its first incumbent. In Middle English, he became perhaps the foremost editor of his time, responsible for editions of all three versions of *Piers Plowman*, for the compendious Clarendon Chaucer, and many other texts.

Much of his work has been highly influential on twentieth-century editing; a great deal of his writing is still easily obtained. The extract that follows is from a lecture entitled 'The Language of Chaucer' in the Skeat archive at King's College, London (Skeat Papers 3/5). It was delivered in 1874 or 1875; the occasion for it is not recorded, but it shows Skeat in informal, proselytising mode, obviously speaking to a lay audience which he is trying to persuade of the value of reading Chaucer. Perhaps the London Working Men's College, co-founded by Skeat's friend and colleague Frederick Furnivall, might have provided the occasion for the lecture. One or two deleted passages suggest that Furnivall was in the audience.

The lecture is written on the backs of old exam answers on Shakespeare, and appears to be the actual text Skeat used. It has two kinds of revision. Some words and lines are crossed out, apparently as the lecture was being written, in ink. More sparing alterations made in pencil perhaps reflect a later revision, and possible re-use of the piece. In this transcription, I have restored some deletions (in diamond brackets) where their interest seemed to warrant it, and have occasionally and silently adjusted the paragraphing. The text has been reproduced with the permission of King's College, London.

For biography and a detailed account of his Langland editions, see Charlotte Brewer, *Editing 'Piers Plowman': The Evolution of the Text* (Cambridge: Cambridge University Press, 1996), esp. pp. 91-113; on his Chaucer editing see A. S. G. Edwards, 'Walter Skeat', in *Editing Chaucer: The Great Tradition*, ed. by Paul G. Ruggiers (Norman, Okla.: Pilgrim Books, 1984), pp. 171-89, and Eleanor Hammond, *Chaucer: A Bibliographical Manual* (New York: Macmillan, 1908), pp. 144-47.

Walter William Skeat, *The Language of Chaucer.*

I have chosen for the subject of my lecture the language of Chaucer. Now this subject is one so important and interesting in itself, and so closely connected with that larger and still more important one, the history of the English language, that it is hardly possible, in the compass of one brief lecture, to deal with it adequately, in a regular and systematic manner. I shall therefore, with your permission, merely draw attention to some of the more remarkable points and results, with the hope of arousing an interest in it, and of pointing out what is the present state of our knowledge of it, as ascertained by those who have taken especial pains to study it. And perhaps these two objects, of awakening interest and of stating results, are more easily attained by indulging in desultory and general remarks than by adopting the more regular form of a set essay.

Those who are most interested in the matter are aware that the whole subject of the study of English, both as regards the language and the literature, after suffering much undeserved neglect, is now beginning to receive an amount of attention more in accordance with its merits. This is particularly the case as regards the study of the language, and has been the natural result of the growing conviction, that it is impossible to attempt to understand our language, as it exists at present, without careful and particular study of it in the forms in which it *used* to exist in previous times. And it is only just to mention here that the greatest impulse to the study has been given mainly by one man, whose name is pretty well known to most students, and whose course of usefulness is, I hope, still far from having reached its close, and that man is Frederick John Furnivall.[226] Mr. Furnivall's ardour in the cause has been extraordinary; sometimes perhaps <his zeal has almost passed the bounds of discretion, and> he has adopted opinions which we are not all inclined to endorse; but still, <some of his expressions are such as many would not endorse. Still,> there stands the fact, that he seems to possess a born genius for the getting up and conducting of literary Societies, and an astonishing aptitude for calling attention to interesting points of discussion, and setting students thinking about them. He has been for many years, and is still, the Secretary of the London Philological Society.[227] In 1864 he started the Early English Text Society, of which he is the Director; in 1868 he started the Chaucer Society, for which he has been the principal and almost the sole worker; and, in the same year, the Ballad Society. And, as if this was not enough, he last year set on foot the New Shakespeare Society, which has already begun to do good work, having issued, only a few weeks ago, accurate reprints of the first and second quartos of the play of Romeo and Juliet. It is hardly too much to say, that the publications of the Early English Text Society, amounting in the course of ten years, to no less than seventy-five volumes or parts of volumes, have almost completely revolutionised the study of Early English literature. Formerly, old texts were so scarce that writers were able to make, and sometimes did make, the most astonishing assertions about the meanings and usages of old words, and no one was able to contradict them

---

[226] Furnivall's middle name was in fact James.

[227] Furnivall became a co-secretary of the London Philological Society in 1853 and sole secretary from 1862.

or to expose their absurdities, for lack of trustworthy material, especially of such material as could be expected to be found in the hands of the many. But now it is very different; for, although some writers still talk about what they do not understand, and place upon paper the most extraordinary statements, as many readers of our weekly periodical literature are probably aware, we possess one great advantage in this, that we have the means of exposing their mistakes whenever it happens to be necessary to do so. Any one who quotes an old English word can now be brought to book; he can be cross-questioned about his references, and will not command attention if he fails to give them; and if he makes a mistake, it can be readily exposed. All this is a very great gain; it makes all the difference between seeing our way straight before us and being compelled to grope along in the dark.

All these books have naturally aided the study of Chaucer. The publications of the Chaucer Society, in particular, furnish us with a great amount of new and trustworthy material. Fortunately, our knowledge of Chaucer has for some time been tolerably accurate, especially from a literary point of view, owing to the admirable edition of his works published exactly a hundred years ago, in 1775, by Thomas Tyrwhitt; and I feel bound to say that, when I look at Tyrwhitt's edition as a whole, when I find in it a tolerable text, a sufficient glossary, and a splendid collection of learned and scholarly notes, I am ready to admit at once that Tyrwhitt's edition is the best complete one, and I even think it will be sometime before it is surpassed; and I much doubt if it will ever be quite superseded.[228] Still, as might be expected in the course of a century, a great number of new points of enquiry have come up, and have been ably dealt with by various writers. In particular, the question of the *scansion of Chaucer's lines* has found an able expositor in the person of Professor John Child, of Harvard College, Cambridge, Mass. The *pronunciation* of English in the times of Chaucer and of Shakespeare — a problem of peculiar difficulty — has been, to a great extent, solved by the perseverance and phonetic knowledge of Mr. A. J. Ellis; whilst Dr. Morris has cleared up nearly all the important details with respect to that peculiar dialect of English in which Chaucer wrote, and the characteristics of that dialect as

---

[228] Tyrwhitt edited a celebrated edition of the *Canterbury Tales* but never a complete Chaucer. Yet Skeat makes this mistake here and a few lines further on. The reason is probably that he had never seen the original Tyrwhitt edition but possessed only *The Poetical Works of Geoffrey Chaucer* printed by the publisher Edward Moxon in 1843, incorporating Tyrwhitt's *Canterbury Tales* and featuring a misleading title page which suggests Tyrwhitt was the editor of all the texts. Skeat was later highly critical of this title page; on this see Joseph A. Dane, *Who Is Buried in Chaucer's Tomb?: Studies in the Reception of Chaucer's Book* (East Lansing: Michigan State University Press, 1998), p. 176.

exhibited in its various grammatical inflections.[229] At the same time, the researches of Mr. Ellis on pronunciation have cleared up a great deal of the mystery of the old spelling; so that, to sum up all, it must be obvious that, to have gained new light upon the scansion, the pronunciation, the spelling, the dialect, and the grammar, is to have gained a great deal, and places us in a very favourable position. Young students may now learn, with due care, in the course of a few weeks, many mysteries with which Tyrwhitt, the editor of the best complete edition of the poet's works, was at no time acquainted.

Some advance has also been made in the solution of the highly important question — what *is* Chaucer, i.e. which of the works attributed to him are genuine. Tyrwhitt began it, by decidedly rejecting some of the works attributed to him in the old black-letter editions, as, e.g. the Plowman's Tale. Various later researches enable us to reject a great deal more. Two tests, in particular, have been applied. The one external, which is obtained by observing what works are really attributed to Chaucer in early MSS., upon sufficient authority; and the other internal, founded upon the observation of certain peculiarities of rime that are found in his genuine poems but are absent in the spurious ones. These two tests, as might have been expected, give results that, to a certain extent, agree together; and enable us to reject, with confidence, such pieces as the Court of Love, the Flower and the Leaf, the Complaint of the Black Knight (now known to have been written by Lydgate), and the poem which bears the impudent title of Chaucer's Dream, first printed in 1597. <and which is no more Chaucer's than it is mine.>[230]

These preliminary remarks, though I fear they are a little dull, are necessary in order to enable me to express myself more forcibly in what follows. To some amongst you, the substance of them is, I hope, familiar; whilst others, perhaps, will have been enabled by them to see that nearly all the points of interest as regards Chaucer's language, viz. his use of words, his scansion, his pronunciation, the spelling adopted by the scribes whom he

---

[229] Alexander Ellis, *On Early English Pronunciation with Especial Reference to Shakspere and Chaucer*, 5 parts (London: simultaneously for the Philological Society, the EETS, and the Chaucer Society, 1869-89); F. J. Child, 'Observations on the Language of Chaucer and Gower', *Memoirs of the American Academy* ns 8 (1862), pp. 445-502; 9 (1866), pp. 265-314 (presented in rearranged and summarised form in Ellis, cited above part I, 342-397); Richard Morris, *Historical Outlines of English Accidence* (London: Macmillan, 1872).

[230] 'Chaucer's Dream' was in fact first printed in 1598, in Thomas Speght's Chaucer edition; Speght gave the title (which was sometimes used to refer to the *Book of the Duchess*) to a poem now known as 'The Isle of Ladies'. These poems were accepted as genuine until the 1870s; all had appeared in the Aldine Edition of the British Poets in Richard Morris's *The Poetical Works of Geoffrey Chaucer*, 6 vols (London: Bell and Daldy, 1866), and reappeared in the 1870 revision of what was in its time the standard Chaucer.

employed, his dialect, his grammar, his rhythm and the rimes employed by him, have been well and carefully considered, and may be looked upon as ascertained with sufficient accuracy to enable us to use his works as a standard example of the Middle-English period. Most of the mists have been cleared away, and the study is now free to all who choose to undertake it. It is, moreover, of great interest, and throws a flood of light upon the history of the words which we employ at present; concerning which many are content to remain, during their whole lives, in a state of ignorance which will, I hope, in a few years become comparatively rare, and perhaps, in another fifty years, may come to be reckoned as disgraceful. I know of only one serious objection that *can* be made to the reading of Chaucer's Canterbury Tales (for it scarcely applies to the rest of his works), and that is one which can be fairly and truly made; viz. that some of his stories are expressed in such free and licentious language as is not acceptable to the taste of the nineteenth century. This objection I admit to be a fair one; but I feel, at the same time, very much inclined to retort upon objectors, that I do not think the literature of the nineteenth century is always better, or always gains by comparison. For though the general tone of our literature is certainly good, and though some of our modern novels are unsurpassed for the excellence of their moral effects, nevertheless, for some mysterious reason, it is precisely amongst the very class of books which are written for the amusement of our wives and daughters, it is precisely amongst the class of the so-called fashionable novels, that some of the most outrageous assaults upon good morals have been made; and that too in the worst possible manner, not broadly or openly, but insidiously and by insinuation. Very often, too, when such novels are perfectly free from all such taint, they are written in such a sickly, morbid, enervating style that they produce a very bad mental effect; so much so that, in my opinion, many would do far better even if they were to take to the Canterbury Tales, and read it all through, every word of it. But, happily, I can meet the objection in a far more efficient way, by removing it altogether. The two volumes of selections from the Canterbury Tales, published by the Oxford Clarendon Press, the one edited by Dr. Morris and the other by myself, contain quite enough to begin upon.[231] In them you have 7000 lines of Chaucer's best work, printed from the earliest and best MSS., and rendered suitable for the use of boys and girls in our schools. Not only is there enough there to begin upon, but there is enough to go a long way upon; for any

---

[231] Richard Morris, ed. *The Prologue, the Knightes Tale, the Nonne Prestes Tale, from the Canterbury Tales* (Oxford: Clarendon Press, 1867); Walter Skeat, ed. *The Prioresses Tale: Sire Thopas: the Monkes Tale, the Clerkes Tale, the Squieres Tale, from the Canterbury Tales* (Oxford: Clarendon Press, 1874).

reader who masters the contents of those two small volumes will come to know a great deal, not only about Chaucer, but about English grammar and English etymology, two subjects which nearly everybody thinks ought to be learnt, and which very few know how to teach. I have long been persuaded that the chief reason why English is so seldom practically taught in schools is simply because the masters are, in many cases, wholly incompetent to teach it, from a want of acquaintance with Early English. Not that it is their fault either, for most of the best books on the subject are of very recent date.

And here I wish at once to dash into the middle of the subject, and to put the question to you — what do you imagine Chaucer to be like? Now if such of you as have never read a line of his writings will frankly admit that you do not know, I should take that to be an extremely satisfactory answer, and one free from prejudice. For the most extraordinary part of the matter is just this, that I have frequently put this question, and find the most extraordinary and unfounded notions respecting our grand old poet to be most deeply rooted in the public mind. One common answer to the question — 'what is Chaucer like?' is — 'oh, horribly difficult, you know; all in old English; written with such bad spelling; and with such extraordinary grammar. What's the good of it?' That, I say, is a common popular opinion; and how it came about, it is very hard to say. It contains just a few grains of truth, but, on the whole, is not only false, but shamefully false. It has often amused me to ask such a question, and to receive such an answer; my method of dealing with it is always the same, and has often been successful. I simply go and fetch Dr. Morris's book, and put it into my friend's hands. Then comes the beating about the bush; it generally takes five minutes to induce my friend even to *look* at it, interrupted at intervals with the remark — 'Oh, but I know I can't read it'. It is rather illogical, of course, to be sure that you *know* all about a book you may never have seen before; but the point is better left unargued, and a little persuasion may very well be used instead. Well, my friend reads a little; stumbles a bit, and is near breaking down with it. I interpose, and offer to read a little myself; then we get as far as — 'Oh, yes, I can understand it when you read it'; and there is one point gained. Not to be tedious, I will merely record my experiences, viz. that, after some help and advice, the final result has nearly always been the admission on the part of the convert, that he or she 'didn't know that Chaucer was at all like *that*'; that 'it is very interesting'; and that it is sufficiently easy. Which may fairly be reckoned as a triumph.

Let me deal more directly with some of the prevalent false notions concerning Chaucer.

And first, as to the notion that it is difficult.

Of course there is a sprinkling here and there of words that are entirely obsolete, and a much larger sprinkling of words that are obsolescent, i.e. that is, which occur with tolerable frequency in English literature, but are disused at the present day. But the difficulty has been greatly exaggerated; and when people have an idea that Old English is to them an unknown tongue, they forget that there is a good deal of the same in a book which they often at any rate hear read to them, viz. in the Authorised Version of the Bible. We are all expected to know *something* about it, if we are to understand the commonest texts. For example, the word *quick* means living in the Apostles' Creed, and it has the same meaning in other places, as when, for example, we say that 'the word of the Lord is *quick* and powerful', i.e. living and powerful; or that Korah, Dathan, and Abiram 'went down *quick* (i.e. alive) into the pit'. And if we know what *quick* means in one place of old English, we know what it means in another, and we can have no difficulty in understanding what Chaucer says about Palamon and Arcite, where he describes them as lying severely wounded and half-dead upon the plain before Thebes —

'Nat fully *quike*, ne fully deede they were';[232]

Again, it is not difficult to remember that *harness* used to mean body-armour as worn by men, because it is clearly so used in I Kings, xx.11; 'Let not him that girdeth on his *harness* boast himself as he that putteth it off'. This helps to explain what is meant in the account of the death of Ahab, where we read that 'a certain man drew a bow at a venture, and smote the king of Israel between the joints of the *harness*', i.e. as we should now say, between the joints of his armour. And if we know this, we shall find little difficulty in understanding what Chaucer means when he speaks of the spoilers who sought the battle-field in order to strip the *harness* from the bodies of the slain. The word occurs in the same sense again in a well-known line in Shakespeare, where Macbeth expresses his final resolution in the phrase —

'Blow, wind! come, wrack!
At least we'll die with *harness* on our back!'[233]

And it would be very easy to shew, in a similar manner, that a considerable number of the obsolescent words found in Chaucer are merely such words as ought to be familiar to everybody who is capable of understanding the authorised version of the Bible and the plays of Shakespeare. Indeed, I am disposed to think that, if a comparison be fairly instituted between the language of Chaucer and that of Shakespeare, the one will be found almost as full of difficulties as the other, especially as Chaucer's text is free from such

---

[232] *CT*, I, 1015.
[233] *Macbeth*, v. 5. 50-51.

defects as abound in Shakespeare, owing to the extraordinary misprints that are to be found in the celebrated First Folio edition. Those who really find Chaucer too difficult will never make good scholars of Shakespeare; whilst those who are really familiar with Shakespeare's language, and can tell readily what all the more unusual words mean, will not find very much in Chaucer that is absolutely new to them. The truth is that there is a good deal of false pretence <and humbug> in the matter of reading English literature. For some mysterious reason, readers have a strange dread of opening a copy of Chaucer, from a false fright with regard to the supposed intricacy and complexity of it, and it is a sort of fashion to agree that one need not know much about it. On the other hand, it is a fashion to pretend to an intimacy with the writings of Shakespeare even on the part of such as have never read him; so much so, indeed, that persons who have not even so much as read all the plays of Shakespeare once through, and who have no practical acquaintance with all his manifold peculiarities, are only too ready to rush into print with all sorts of conjectural emendations and wild guesses, as if there was some sort of glory to be obtained by the invention of suppositions which have only to be printed in order for their absurdity to become obvious to all men except their originator. If Shakespeare were only to be really read and studied about half as much as his text is talked about and maltreated, he would be far better understood than he is at present, and Chaucer at the same time would be less neglected also. The two authors go together a good deal more than might be supposed; there are sufficient indications that Shakespeare, at any rate, was fairly well acquainted with the older poet's writings; whilst Chaucer, in his sketch of the various characters who undertook a pilgrimage to St. Thomas's shrine at Canterbury, gives abundant evidence of possessing that fine dramatic power which is so well-developed by the later artist. To which considerations we may add that which has been already urged, viz. a fair amount of similarity in the words which they have employed.

I should like to take just one example of the manner in which the vocabularies of English poets resemble each other; especially as it is rather a striking one. Suppose we compare the language of Chaucer, a poet of the fourteenth century who used a Midland dialect tinged with Southern peculiarities, with that of Burns, a poet of the eighteenth century who employed, in some of his poems and to a certain extent, his native dialect of Ayrshire. Do we find much resemblance between them? The answer is, that their writings occasionally illustrate each other by the most exact correspondences. It is many years ago since I first drew up a rough list of words common to both these authors; and though it was done very hastily and imperfectly, merely as an amusement of an odd half-hour, it is much too long a list to be reproduced here; so that I shall content myself by adducing a few examples.

The word *bete* in Chaucer, formed from the same root as the word *better*, signifies to make better, to improve; and is applied, in particular, to the improving or bettering of a fire by adding fresh fuel to it, so as to make it burn more brightly. This occurs in the Knightes Tale, where Palamon is represented as sacrificing to Venus, and promising the goddess that, if she will deign to hear his prayer, he will always do sacrifice on her altar, and keep the fires thereon always brightly burning.

> And on thin auter, where I ryde or go,
> I wol don sacrifice, and fyres *beete*.[234]

Now turn to Burns's epistle to Davie, a brother poet, and see what Burns says about his sweeheart, his darling Jean.

> It warms me, it charms me,
>   To mention but her name;
> It heats me, it *beets* me,
>   And sets me a' on flame! [235]

[Skeat notes many other such examples.]

These instances are quite sufficient to shew how much these authors have in common, as regards their vocabulary. Let us pause for a moment to draw from this fact the just inference. It certainly does not shew that Chaucer wrote in broad Scotch; but it proves simply this, that a considerable number of old English words, found in many of [the] best writers, such as Wickliffe, Langley [*sic*], Chaucer, Spenser, Shakespeare, in the Authorised Version of the Bible, and even so late as in Milton, have gradually dropped out of the language, as now written and spoken in England. At the same time, many of them are still preserved in the various provincial dialects; and, amongst those dialects, the Lowland-Scotch has been especially fortunate in preserving a large number. Besides which, most of these words are by no means confined, even at this day, to Scotland, but are almost equally well-known in the North of England. *Ferly*, a wonder, *gar*, to cause, *keek*, to peep, *thole*, to suffer, *wood*, mad, not to trouble about the rest of the set, may all be found duly recorded in the North-of-England Glossary compiled by Mr. Brockett, of Newcastle-upon-Tyne.[236]

To pass on to another point. I can fully believe that, if any popular notions are afloat as to the grammar of Chaucer, they are probably to his disadvantage rather than otherwise. Nothing could be more unjust. Owing to

---

[234] *CT*, I, 2252-53.
[235] 'Epistle to Davie, A Brother Poet', ll. 109-12.
[236] John Trotter Brockett, *A Glossary of North Country Words, in use*, corr. and enl. by W. E. Brockett, 2 vols. (Newcastle upon Tyne: Charnley, 1846).

his regular and constant use of numerous inflections which in modern times
are almost wholly ignored, his grammar is of a distinct, regular, and systematic
character; and to understand it is, in my opinion, the best clue to the grammar
of modern English that can very well be devised, especially if there be
superadded to it the knowledge of a few of the most elementary constructions
in what is commonly called Anglo-Saxon. The fault of nearly all English
grammars (except some of the most recent ones) has commonly been, the
ignoring of old English; although, in the end, the desire to avoid supposed
archaisms is sure to lead to uncertainty and blundering, and is a most
egregious mistake. All this will soon become abundantly evident to any who
will be at the pains to read over the grammatical remarks contained in the
Introduction to Dr. Morris's edition of Chaucer's Prologue; for which reason
I forbear to pursue the subject further.

Next, I will consider the question of old English spelling. Concerning this,
popular opinion, being, as is often the case, in a small degree right and in a
very large degree utterly wrong, is certainly fairly unanimous. The prevalent
notion is, that the spelling is very bad, wholly without law or order, and at any
rate of no great consequence. It is the old story of taking up opinions at
second-hand, in preference to taking the trouble of investigating for oneself.
Error lives by laziness, and only honest hard work can finally slay it. In this
case, however, the error is the more pardonable, because it is only very
recently that a clue has been obtained to that irregularity of spelling in old
MSS. which turns out to be far more apparent than real. Only six years ago,
the spelling remained unexplained; and it was to be expected that such recent
information should travel slowly, and that the latest discoveries should not yet
be generally known. The researches of Mr. Ellis with regard to Old English
pronunciation presented but a dim and hopeless appearance at their first
beginning. It was not till after he had struggled some time with but indifferent
success that a ray of light at last came, to use his own expression, 'from a
corner which had hitherto been very dark'. It is a fact that we owe the
beginning of our knowledge of the subject to a treatise written in Welsh.
Salesbury's Welsh and English Dictionary, published in 1547, contains a
short, but most important essay upon English pronunciation, written in quaint
old Welsh.[237] It is the boast of that language that its system of spelling is
remarkably good, and that it suits its symbols to its sounds with remarkable
accuracy. Here, then, was a beginning; and when once some sort of a grasp of
the subject was obtained, the subsequent dealing with it became much easier.
Carefully feeling his way from point to point, advancing very slowly but still
surely, Mr. Ellis, after an immense amount of labour such as would have

---

[237] William Salesbury, *A Dictionary in Englyshe and Welshe* (London, 1547).

daunted a good many men, at last succeeded in demonstrating, with sufficient clearness and force to satisfy most minds, that a clue existed both to our old pronunciation and to our old spelling, and that to solve the mystery of the one was to solve the mystery of the other, since the two things are intimately connected with each other, and have been so from the earliest times.

The researches of Mr. Ellis, though not even yet completed, have established a principle which has already thrown much light upon both our old and present language, and will help us to gain a closer knowledge of it than a few years ago seemed possible. It is, in fact, a remarkable discovery, the full force of which has not yet been at all generally perceived; and it affords me the greater pleasure to announce this, because I confess myself to be one of those who, at the first outset, had but little faith in Mr. Ellis's labours, and had no expectation at all that his success would be so great and so brilliant. What, then, does his discovery amount to? It amounts to this, that we now know the old spelling to have been anything but lawless, anything but senseless, anything but contemptible. There was indeed a period of bad spelling, say from about the time of Henry the sixth to the time of queen Mary, where what is technically called Middle-English was being broken up and reduced to the Tudor-English, a period when scribes, from old associations, were in the habit of writing a final *e* at the end of many words where it was by no means pronounced; but when we go a little further back, when we come to the time of Chaucer, or to any period preceding him, we see our way clearly enough, and can tell why words were spelt as they were. The oldest and best scribes had one intelligible principle to guide them, and were fairly successful in obeying it. In one word, their spelling was *phonetic*; they were not guided by the *eye*, as is now the case (for the modern rule is to spell words as we *see* them spelt in books), but they were guided by the *ear*. They spelt words as they pronounced them, and they pronounced words as they spelt them, according to the only sensible principle that can possibly be thought of. It is the great rule in nearly all languages, and it is very fairly carried out in a great number of modern languages, such as Welsh, and German, Italian and Spanish. There is no language in which the spelling differs as widely from the pronunciation as our modern English, as is most notorious; but that defect is not to be charged upon our ancestors. The reason of the modern divergence between sounds and symbols is a strange one, and is contrary to what we might have expected. Mr. Ellis has proved that we commonly lay the blame in the wrong place. Most of us have probably at some time formed the notion that, if we spell not as we pronounce, it is mainly the fault of the spelling. That supposition is now shewn to be no longer tenable, for the truth is the other way; it is mainly the fault of our pronunciation. Our pronunciation has been refined again and again till it is no longer the same thing that it was five hundred years ago. The spelling has changed a little, but the pronunciation has altered much. It has altered more quickly and more widely than that of any other European language; and in this fact we have the real key to all the modern differences between the sound and its symbol or sign. In Chaucer's time, the pronunciation of English resembled that of the continental languages; there was no great difference, accordingly, between the vowel-sounds in English and the vowel-sounds in French, and that is one reason why, in the thirteenth and fourteenth centuries, French words passed into English with such ease and in such great abundance, whereas it is very seldom that we borrowed French words at a later time. Some old pronunciations are still preserved, in a fossil state, in our modern spelling, as, for example, the old guttural sound indicated by *gh*, as it occurs in *night, light, ought*, &c. Now that we know all this, we find the spelling adopted by the best scribes of the Chaucer MSS. (for the handwriting is never that of the author, but of some professional scrivener) — we find the spelling, I say, of the best scribes to be remarkably good. In particular, the spelling of the Ellesmere MS. is excellent. We have only to study it a little carefully, and we can understand it perfectly; we can follow every sound of every syllable, and have only to sound the syllables according to what the spelling was meant to represent, and we can pronounce the words as Chaucer would himself have pronounced them, though that is in such a manner as only a trained ear can follow, and is an achievement hardly to be learnt in a day, though it might perhaps be learnt in two or three days.

My position, then, with regard to Chaucer is this; that I believe most of the popular opinions regarding him to be fallacies; instead of allowing his language to be obsolete and difficult, I maintain that it is only so in a very limited degree; that the difficulties are upon the surface, and vanish the moment that we boldly face them; that many of the words which he uses are such as we all ought to know very well, if we really read, instead of only pretending to read, our Bible, our Shakespeare, our Burns, our Spenser. I maintain that the grammar is of peculiar clearness and precision, and on that account most valuable as a guide to the grammar of modern English. I maintain that, in the best MSS. (I do not say in the worst), the spelling is intelligible, distinct, correct, and truly phonetic, representing the sound of the word with quite sufficient accuracy in every instance; and not only does it explain to us the spelling of Chaucer's time, but it explains to us a great many modern spellings, as is admirably exemplified in the latest, and (with the exception of Mr. Ellis's) the only work of value upon the subject, viz. the History of English Sounds, by Mr. Sweet, published only last month at the joint expense of the Philological Society and the English Dialect Society.[238]

---

[238] Henry Sweet, *A History of English Sounds* (London: English Dialect Society, 1874); see extract in Part I.

Granting Shakespeare to be our first poet, I claim for Chaucer that he is the second; or if he has any equal, there is none to equal him but Milton; he certainly surpasses Spenser and surpasses Dryden, both of whom attempted to imitate him with very indifferent success.

Walter W. Skeat, *Questions for Examination in English Literature: Chiefly Selected from College-Papers Set in Cambridge, With an Introduction on the Study of English*, **2nd rev. edn (London: Bell, 1887).**

Examination questions on the *General Prologue* to the *Canterbury Tales* set by Skeat for Christ's College, Cambridge in 1866.

1. Give some account of the Teutonic branch of the Indo-European family of languages. What connection has English with Swedish, and with Dutch?

2. Decline the personal pronouns used in Anglo-Saxon; and explain the difference between *strong* and *weak* verbs. Distinguish clearly between *wit, wot, wist, wisse,* and *y-wis.*

3. What was the Saxon *gerund*? In the phrases 'I may teach', 'that is to say', why is *to* inserted in the one case and not in the other? Is the phrase — 'this house to let' — ungrammatical?

4. Give some account of the writings of Cædmon and Layamon, and of the language in which they were written.

5. Discuss the versification of Chaucer; and explain under what circumstances the final *e* ought to be pronounced.

6. Enumerate the personages described in the Prologue. What characters does Chaucer assign to the Frere, the Sompnour, and the Pardonere?

7. Explain the following words and phrases, with notes on the words italicized, and give, where you can, the etymology of these words:

    (*a*) To *ferne halwes, kouthe* in sondry londes (14).

    (*b*) Of fustyan he wered a *gepoun*
          Al bysmotered with his *habergeoun* (75).

    (*c*) He yaf nat of that text a pulled hen (177).

    (*d*) I saugh his sleeves *purfiled* atte hond With *grys* (193).

    (*e*) Of yeddinges he bar utterly the prys (237).

    (*f*) His purchas was wel better than his rente (256).

    (*g*) *Sownynge* alway thencres of his wynnynge (275).

    (*h*) An *anlas* and a *gipser* al of silk (357).

    (*i*) His *herbergh* and his mone, his *lodemenage* (403).

    (*k*) To seeken him a *chaunterie* for soules (510).

    (*l*) He was a *jangler*, and a *golyardeys* (560).

    (*m*) And yit this *maunciple* sette here *aller* cappe (586).

8. Discuss the meanings and derivations of the following words; Cristofre – pricasour – chevysaunce – courtepy – vavaser – wymplid – bawdrik –

fetysly – motteleye – mormal – rouncy – nose-thrules – acate – vernicle.

Explain the phrase – 'for the none'.

9. What was a *lymytour*? what were the 'ordres foure'? Give some account of the poem called 'Piers Plowman's *Crede*'.

10. Parse the words italicised in the phrases – Or if men *smot* it – As Austyn *byt* – For *him* was *lever have* at his beddes heede – to drynke us *leste* – *herkneth* what I seye (149, 187, 293, 750, 855).

Examination questions on *General Prologue*, the *Clerk's Tale*, and the *Squire's Tale* set at Trinity Hall, Cambridge.

1. What were the chief political and religious movements in England in Chaucer's time? In what way was he connected with any of them? Are any traces of his own leanings observable in his writings?

2. Enumerate the personages in the party of pilgrims to Canterbury. Where did they first halt? Relate the incidents of the journey. At what period does the poem break off?

3. Give an account of the position occupied or the calling followed by a Franklin, a Frere, a Sompnour, a Manciple, a Pardoner, a Reeve, and a Sergeant-at-Law in Chaucer's time.

4. Sketch out a description of the Squire and of the Clerk of Oxenford as vividly as you can, keeping true to Chaucer's conception.

Examination questions on the *Knight's Tale* set by Skeat specifically for female students.

About the year 1871, arrangements were made for instructing ladies by correspondence. The scheme proved perfectly practicable, and in a great measure successful; and by way of giving some idea of the method of its working, I have included this paper, as being a specimen of those actually set, and — what is more to the purpose — actually answered by ladies, and answered very well too. In fact, it is one very great advantage of such an excellent subject as the English Language and Literature that, with a little supervision and management, it can easily be adapted for female students, who, at least in some cases within my own experience, take a keen and intelligent interest in it, and reap much benefit therefrom.

1. Whence did Chaucer derive materials for his Knightes Tale? Give a *brief* account of the writings of Boccaccio.

2. In what play of Shakespeare is Theseus introduced, and how? What do you know about 'King Capaneus' (l. 74), 'Creon' (l. 80), and 'Thebes' as referred to in the Knightes Tale?

3. Explain the scansion of the following lines: – 117, 176, 248, 267, 513, 688, 785.

Give three instances in which 'Arcite' is accented on the *first* syllable.

4. Write out, in modern English prose, the passages 147-166; also 298-

310; also 663-681; with a *few* notes on expressions that seem remarkable.

5. Give from memory, in your own words, a good description of the temple and statue of Mars.

6. In lines 1282-1319, explain the words — cote-armure, harnays, for-blak, alauntz, mosel, torettz, fyled, dyapred, cowched, bret-ful, cytryn, freknes, yspreynd, ymeynd, deduyt. Give, if you can, the derivations of *dyapred, cowched, bret-ful, ymeynd*, and *deduyt*.

7. In ll. 417-432, make a list of all the purely *English* words, *not* of French origin. Give the German words answering to them, as well as you can, where cognate German words can be found.

8. Beginning at l. 320, explain why the final *e* should be pronounced in *foughte, kyte, wrothe, leeve, moote, tweye, hadde* (330), *highte*.

9. Explain fully the phrases —

    (*a*) for to deyen in the peyne (275).

    (*b*) Wel hath fortune ytorned thee the dys (380).

    (*c*) We witen nat, &c. — mows (402, 403).

    (*d*) And writen — graunte (447, 448).

    (*e*) I noot which hath the wofullere myster (482).

    (*f*) his selle fantastyk (518).

    (*g*) Ne sette I nought (712).

    (*h*) his thonkes (768).

10. Explain and derive the words *dereyne*, or *darrayne*; *purveans, breeme, waymenting, felonye, schode, qualme, outhees* (1154)

Select Bibliography

Bibliographical references for commonly cited texts can also be found in Abbreviations, pages ix-x.

Aarsleff, Hans. *The Study of Language in England, 1780-1860.* London: Athlone; Minneapolis: University of Minnesota Press, 1983.

Ackerman, Robert W., and Gretchen Ackerman. *Sir Frederic Madden: A Biographical Sketch and Bibliography.* New York: Garland, 1979.

Bate, Walter Jackson. 'Percy's Use of his Folio-Manuscript', *Journal of English and Germanic Philology* 43 (1944), 337-48.

Berkhout, Carl T., and Milton McC. Gatch. *Anglo-Saxon Scholarship: The First Three Centuries.* Boston: Hall, 1982.

Brewer, Charlotte. *Editing 'Piers Plowman': The Evolution of the Text.* Cambridge: Cambridge University Press, 1996.

Bronson, Bertrand H. *Joseph Ritson: Scholar-at-Arms*, 2 vols. Berkeley: University of California Press, 1938.

Busby, Keith, and Terry Nixon, Alison Stones, and Lori Walters, eds. *Les Manuscrits de Chrètien de Troyes: The Manuscripts of Chrètien de Troyes*, 2 vols. Amsterdam and Atlanta: Rodopi, 1993.

Cameron, Angus F. 'Middle English in Old English Manuscripts', pp. 218-29 in Beryl Rowland, ed. *Chaucer and Middle English Studies in Honour of Rossell Hope Robbins.* London: Allen & Unwin, 1974.

Chandler, Alice. *A Dream of Order: The Medieval Ideal in Nineteenth-Century English Literature.* London: Routledge & Kegan Paul, 1971.

Clunies Ross, Margaret. *The Norse Muse in Britain, 1750-1820.* Trieste: Edizioni Parnaso, 1998.

Coletti, Theresa. 'Reading REED: History and the Records of Early English Drama', pp. 248-84 in Lee Patterson, ed. *Literary Practice and Social Change in Britain.* Berkeley: University of California Press, 1990.

Dane, Joseph A. *Who Is Buried in Chaucer's Tomb?: Studies in the Reception of*

Chaucer's Book. East Lansing: Michigan State University Press, 1998.

Davies, R. T. *Medieval English Lyrics*. London: Faber, 1963.

Davis, Bertram H. *Thomas Percy: A Scholar-Cleric in the Age of Johnson*. Philadelphia: University of Pennsylvania Press, 1989.

Dickins, Bruce, and R. M. Wilson, eds. *Early Middle English Texts*. London: Bowes & Bowes, 1951.

Donatelli, Joseph M.P. 'The Medieval Fictions of Thomas Warton and Thomas Percy', *University of Toronto Quarterly* 60 (1991), 435-51.

Donatelli, Joseph M.P. 'Old Barons in New Robes: Percy's Use of the Metrical Romances in the Reliques of Ancient English Poetry', pp. 225-35 in Patrick J. Gallacher and Helen Damico, eds. *Hermeneutics and Medieval Culture*. Albany: SUNY Press, 1989.

Douglas, David C. *English Scholars 1660-1730*. 2nd rev. edn London: Eyre & Spottiswoode, 1951.

Edwards, A.S.G. 'Observations on the History of Middle English Editing', pp. 34-48 in Derek Pearsall, ed. *Manuscripts and Texts: Editorial Problems in Later Middle English Literature*. Cambridge: Brewer, 1987.

Edwards, A.S.G. 'Walter Skeat', pp. 171-89 in Ruggiers, ed. *Editing Chaucer*.

Fairer, David. 'The Origin of Warton's History of English Poetry', *Review of English Studies* 32 (1981), 37-63.

Frantzen, Allen J. *Desire for Origins: New Language, Old English, and Teaching the Tradition*. New Brunswick: Rutgers University Press, 1990.

Friedman, Albert B. *The Ballad Revival: Studies in the Influence of Popular on Sophisticated Poetry*. Chicago: University of Chicago Press, 1961.

Gamerschlag, Kurt. 'Henry Weber: Medieval Scholar, Poet, and Secretary to Walter Scott', *Studies in Scottish Literature* 25 (1990), 202-17.

Girouard, Mark. *The Return to Camelot: Chivalry and the English Gentleman*. New Haven: Yale University Press, 1981.

Grierson, H. J. C., ed. *The Letters of Sir Walter Scott*, 12 vols. London: Constable, 1932-37.

Groom, Nick, ed. and intro. *Reliques of Ancient English Poetry*. Facsimile of 1st edn London: Routledge/Thoemmes Press, 1996.

Hamer, Richard. *A Manuscript Index to the Index of Middle English Verse*. London: British Library, 1995.

Hammond, Eleanor. *Chaucer: A Bibliographical Manual*. New York: Macmillan, 1908.

Harris, Richard L. *A Chorus of Grammars: The Correspondence of George Hickes and his Collaborators on the 'Thesaurus linguarum septentrionalium'*. Toronto: Pontifical Institute of Mediaeval Studies, 1992.

Harris, Richard L. 'George Hickes', in *MSBS2*, pp. 19-32

Hudson, Anne. 'Middle English', pp. 34-57 in A. G. Rigg, ed. *Editing Medieval Texts: English, French and Latin Written in England*. New York and London: Garland Publishing, 1977.

Hudson, Anne. 'Robert of Gloucester and the Antiquaries', *Notes and Queries* 214 (1969), 322-33.

Hughes, Shaun F.D. 'The Anglo-Saxon Grammars of George Hickes and Elizabeth

Elstob', pp. 119-147 in Berkhout and Gatch, eds. *Anglo-Saxon Scholarship*. Boston: Hall, 1982.

Johnson, Lesley. 'Tracking Laȝamon's Brut', *Leeds Studies in English* 22 (1991), 139-65.

Kane, George. *Piers Plowman: The Evidence for Authorship*. London: Athlone, 1965.

Ker, N. R. *Catalogue of Manuscripts Containing Anglo-Saxon*. Oxford: Clarendon Press, 1957.

Knight, Stephen. *Robin Hood: A Complete Study of the English Outlaw*. Oxford: Blackwell, 1994.

Lerer, Seth. *Chaucer and His Readers: Imagining the Author in Late-Medieval England*. Princeton: Princeton University Press, 1993.

Levine, Philippa. *The Amateur and the Professional: Antiquarians, Historians and Archaeologists in Victorian England, 1838-1886*. Cambridge: Cambridge University Press, 1986.

Lipking, Lawrence. *The Ordering of the Arts in Eighteenth-Century England*. Princeton: Princeton University Press, 1970.

Lowenthal, David. *George Perkins Marsh: Versatile Vermonter*. New York: Columbia University Press, 1958.

Machan, Tim William. *Textual Criticism and Middle English Texts*. Charlottesville: University Press of Virginia, 1994.

Mignet, François. *Notice Historique sur la vie et les travaux de M. Hallam*. Paris, 1861.

Murray, K. M. Elisabeth. *Caught in the Web of Words: James A. H. Murray and the 'Oxford English Dictionary'*. New Haven: Yale University Press, 1977.

Pearsall, Derek. *The Life of Geoffrey Chaucer: A Critical Biography*. Oxford: Blackwell, 1992.

Pickford, Cedric E. 'Sir Tristrem, Sir Walter Scott and Thomas', pp. 219-28 in W. Rothwell, W.R.J Barron, David Blamires and Lewis Thorpe, eds. *Studies in Medieval Literature and Languages in Memory of Frederick Whitehead*. Manchester: Manchester University Press, 1973.

Rinaker, Clarissa. *Thomas Warton: A Biographical and Critical Study*. Urbana: University of Illinois, 1916.

Robinson, Fred C. *The Tomb of Beowulf and other Essays on Old English*. Oxford: Blackwell, 1993.

Ross, Thomas W. 'Thomas Wright', pp. 145-56 in Ruggiers, ed. *Editing Chaucer*.

Ruggiers, Paul G. ed. *Editing Chaucer: The Great Tradition*. Norman, Okla.: Pilgrim Books, 1984.

Rumble, Thomas C. *The Breton Lays in Middle English*. Detroit: Wayne State University Press, 1965.

Storey, Mark. *Robert Southey: A Life*. Oxford: Oxford University Press, 1997.

Sutherland, John. *The Life of Walter Scott: A Critical Biography*. Oxford: Blackwell, 1995.

Vance, John A. *Joseph and Thomas Warton*. Boston: Twayne, 1983.